MASTERING QUANTUM CREATION

"What a delight to read Diana MaAra Divine's new book, *"Mastering Quantum Creation"*! Her book is filled with high energy and amazing visuals and supports humanity's conscious evolution. From galactic origins to unlocking Quantum potential, readers are taken on a transformative journey of ancient wisdom, practical guidance, techniques, source energy, and more. Thank you, Diana, for your beautiful work, inspiration, and dedication to ascension!"

> VIVIANE CHAUVET, Arcturian Ambassador, Founder of the Arcturian University, and Cosmic Teacher

"If you're seeking a comprehensive guide to the Quantum Field from the perspective of creation, this book is an absolute gem. Diana masterfully explains the principles and processes of manifestation through the quantum lens, offering clear insights and practical tools. Beautifully written, it serves as both inspiration and instruction for anyone ready to consciously create a new reality. I highly recommend it."

> DR. KENNETH HARRIS, Author of *Synchronicity: The Magic, The Mystery, The Meaning,* Transformational Teacher, Healer, and Founder of the *Mind/Body Education Center*

"*Mastering Quantum Creation* attunes the reader to a higher vibration to activate inner knowing and facilitate energetic shifts. Diana MaAra Divine weaves research, personal revelation, and practical tools into a guide that supports every phase of spiritual awakening. Her writing blends cosmic depth with grounded insights, making this book a companion for the soul's lifelong evolution."

> KARA GOODWIN, Author of *Your Authentic Awakening: A Guide to Everyday Living*

"*Mastering Quantum Creation* is a detailed adventure of the soul's journey to divinity. Diana Divine lays out a map to awakening, offering the codes of initiation and mantras for quantum consciousness. This takes the reader on a journey to their immortal, ever-present Self and opens the gateways to our galactic origins. More importantly, it activates a deep remembrance of our incarnational mission on this Earth plane. In this way, the book brings us to the threshold of a great new epoch for the incarnational spirits now present on Earth. It allows us to finally celebrate the dimensional realities of our own higher consciousness. Thank you."

ALAN STEINFELD, Author of *Making Contact: Preparing for the New Realities of Extraterrestrial Existence*

"I've had the joy of knowing and working with Diana Divine, and I can honestly say she is one of the most dedicated and heart-centered spiritual practitioners I've met. Her deep wisdom, integrity, and devotion to the path of soul mastery shine through every page of *Mastering Quantum Creation*. This book is more than a guide—it's a transmission of higher truth and activation. Diana weaves ancient knowledge with quantum principles and practical tools to help readers remember who they truly are and step fully into their power. Whether you're just beginning your awakening or have been walking the path for years, this book offers potent insights, meditations, and energy practices that will support and accelerate your journey. I highly recommend it!"

-DEBBIE SOLARIS, *Galactic Historian*

MASTERING QUANTUM CREATION

Awaken the Phoenix Within,
Manifest Your Reality and
Reclaim Your Cosmic Power

Diana MaAra Divine

Foreword Channeled by Toni Ghazi

For more information, or to book a session, contact:
http://www.dianadivine.com
diana@dianadivine.com

Cover design sacred geometry by Marion Elizabeth Grace

ISBN - Paperback: 979-8-9927320-0-9
ISBN - Hardcover: 979-8-9927320-1-6

The information presented in this work is the author's opinion and does not constitute any health or medical advice. The content of this work is for informational purposes only and is not intended to diagnose, treat, cure, or prevent any condition or disease or is meant as a substitute for consultation with a licensed practitioner.

Neither the author nor the publisher assumes any responsibility for errors, omissions, or contrary interpretations of the subject matter herein. Any perceived slight of any individual or organization is purely unintentional. Brand and product names are trademarks or registered trademarks of their respective owners.

Printed in the United States of America

To the Infinite Creator,
the boundless ripple of unconditional love,
and the sacred abundant co-creation
that unites us all.

Dedication

I dedicate this book to the Infinite Creator and to the sacred co-creation with the countless souls who have graced my path throughout this lifetime. Through divinely orchestrated synchronistic encounters and perfect cosmic timing, my soul family has expanded in beautiful and unexpected ways, helping me remember my true essence beyond the veil of forgetting, and empowering me to share these universal truths that transcend time and space.

I am profoundly grateful to all my inspiring spiritual teachers who have illuminated the path before me, and to my encouraging friends who have lifted me during both the brightest and darkest moments of my spiritual journey. I have been blessed beyond measure with the most supportive family anyone could ask for. Their unwavering belief in me has been the bedrock upon which I've built my life's work.

I wish to honor the extraordinary women in my family who have shaped me—my grandmother, whose physical form has returned to the stars but whose eternal love and ancestral wisdom continue to guide me from the ethereal realms; my mother, whose unconditional support, boundless compassion, and quiet strength have been a steady beacon illuminating my life's path; and my beloved sister Anya, whose radiant presence embodies the purest expression of unconditional love I have ever known. They have been the strong, nurturing structure that has always held me through every challenge and transformation, and for that sacred holding, I am eternally grateful.

To my dear husband Daniel Michael, my twin flame and divine co-creator—with you, I have journeyed through countless universes, explored the farthest galaxies, and walked the ancient civilizations of Atlantis and Egypt when crystal technologies and sacred geometric principles governed our existence. Together, we have been fulfilling our sacred mission of integrating light and darkness. Reunited once more in this pivotal lifetime, these past nine years of our earthly journey together have been profoundly expansive, filled with accelerated growth, soul-deep love, and the sacred alchemical dance of mutual transformation. Thank you for being my divine counterpart, my perfect mirror, and for walking this path of creation and consciousness evolution with me.

And with overflowing gratitude, I acknowledge my children. My beautiful 12-year-old son Alexander Lior, whom I carried into this world during the momentous frequency shifts of 2012, a time when the veils between dimensions grew thinner and new possibilities emerged. I am grateful that our Soul contract has continuously pushed me to grow beyond perceived limitations and shed layers of illusion that no longer served my highest expression. I found strength I never knew I possessed to guide him as a first-time visitor to Earth's frequency, helping him navigate this dense reality while honoring his cosmic origins. Each day he fascinates me with his profound insights on metaphysics that belie his young age. I treasure our daily conversations in the pure codes of Source Light Language that bypasses the limitations of human speech and connects us directly to higher consciousness.

Similarly, I am blessed to have become stepmom to two remarkable older souls, Simon and Theo, who have challenged me in different ways and opened my heart to love more deeply than I thought possible. I cherish how they enthusiastically attend all my spiritual workshops, absorbing ancient wisdom with open minds and hearts, demonstrating remarkable receptivity to our sacred work together and embodying the next generation of lightworkers.

To all the beautiful friends and clients who have become an integral, inseparable part of my journey and expansion—I see and honor the divine spark in each of you. Together, we are lifting each other higher into more refined frequencies, creating the transformational change we wish to manifest in the world, and restoring the divine blueprint of wholeness that has always existed within us. What a profound honor it is to be in service to sacred co-creation with you, as we weave our individual threads of light into the grand, cosmic fabric of unified consciousness.

Author's Note

I have written this book to share the wisdom, and my authentic truth gathered throughout twenty-five years of an extraordinary spiritual journey. As this Work unfolded, it became clear that one book could not contain all the insights and a second book about twin flames and divine union is already emerging.

During the writing of this book, I was called to join a powerful soul family gathering with many influential speakers via Portal to Ascension for a Winter Solstice 2024 Galactic Cruise to Mayan lands in Mexico, Belize, and Honduras. I was shown how this important journey completed the Earth gridwork I was guided to do at the Mayan lands in 2012. Together, we opened the galactic gateway and anchored the next twelve years of humanity's evolution of consciousness.

At this transformative voyage, as we were passing over the Bermuda triangle, I was divinely guided to have my dear friend and gifted channeler, Toni Ghazi, who was also presenting during the cruise to do a channeling with me as a foreword to this book. The Antarean and Lyran/Andromedan collective, as founding races of human consciousness, works together and always provide profound insights to understanding this reality. I hope you will find the channeled session with Toni as an enticing foreword to this book, to give you a macro perspective of the nature of infinite creation.

While most events mentioned in this book are my lived experiences and observations, some details have been fictionalized for the sake of perspective. I have also changed some names to protect and honor the identities of my clients, while preserving the essence of each person's contribution.

Throughout these pages, certain words and their meanings carry a sacred vibration—*Source, Infinite Creator, Quantum Master, Quantum Master Creator, Soul, Void, Higher Self, Kundalini, Universal Consciousness, and Universe*. These capitalized terms serve as gateways, inviting you to feel their energetic resonance beyond mere language. Each capitalized word holds a frequency that connects directly to its divine essence, creating a bridge between the written word and its cosmic significance. I invite you to refer to the Glossary of Terms at the end of the book for more clarity on any concepts that I am mentioning throughout the chapters.

At times, I found that the English language, in its conventional form, often falls short of conveying the full depth and vibrancy of spiritual wisdom. The subtle frequencies, the sacred geometries, and the multidimensional aspects of these wisdom teachings called for something beyond traditional written words.

For this reason, I have included quantum codes at the end of each chapter—unique combinations of poetic expressions and light language transmissions that activate the energetic frequency of each theme. These codes aren't merely words on a page; they are living transmissions designed to resonate with your energy field and cellular memory. Through carefully crafted sound patterns and sacred syllables, these quantum codes create a bridge between the intellectual understanding of the content and its energetic embodiment.

To make these transmissions fully accessible, please go to my website at *dianadivine.com/quantumbook* to access audio recordings and video presentations of these transmissions and guided meditations. Each recording has been created in optimal conditions to preserve the pure frequency and intentional resonance of the transmissions.

These quantum codes serve as keys to unlock deeper layers of understanding and connection with the message's divine resonance. They bypass the analytical mind and speak directly to your energetic body, allowing for a more complete integration of the teachings. As you work with these codes—whether through reading, listening, or viewing—you may notice subtle shifts in your perception and consciousness, opening doorways to expanded awareness and deeper spiritual insights.

Consider these quantum codes as your personal gateway to experiencing these teachings beyond the limitations of language, inviting you into a more direct and intimate relationship with their transformative power.

Contents

Foreword

Channeling Session with Toni Ghazi

Toni: From the Antares Stargate, we come through in this way to co-create with you this beautiful reality of oneness. To merge our hearts with your hearts. To be one with you in this way. To be one with the beauty that you are. And as we come through in this way, the image of a hammer has been shown, energetical type hammer. Not a hammer that your society, your humanity has conceived of. An energetical hammer to where you are about to pound, in a sense on the fabric of creation and allow the sound to resonate within the fabric of the infinite that ripples out a wave.

The sound is going to be produced that will be felt as a shock wave within the fabric of the universe that every being that's ever been created within creation will be able to feel and vibrate with. And the image of such a hammer, the archetype of what we call hammer, and the sound creation itself are being explained in this way to allow you to know that the information that you brought through your co-creation is going to resonate. With all of creation. All of creation will be able to hear, resonate with such a sound. We thank you for taking on such a call and for hearing your own voice within creation itself. We honor your journey fully. We honor your sound. And with that, we will begin our dialogue with you in this way, and you are welcome to pose a question, make a statement, or sit in silence with us as we communicate with you from beyond

Diana: Thank you so much for this co-creation, for taking the time to bring forward your message. I had a strong feeling that The Antarean Collective needs to come through. Toni is so important for this book, for this voice, for the sound to come into this reality currently. Whoever needs to read it will receive it and get activated along with the information that I offer in the chapters. I'm really honored at this moment in time. The title of this book is "Mastering Quantum Creation". It is the time for humanity to re-remember and step into its mastery. What message would you have for those who are reading this? What does it mean to be a creator, and what does it mean to be a master of creation?

Toni: Allow us to begin with the idea of the word master. As that word is already limited in nature. Because, if you already know that you are the creator, mastery isn't needed because you are it. Creating over and over again, into the eons and eons of the infinite, yes? But, through the remembrance of who you are, through the idea that you have forgotten who you are, and remembering through the forgetfulness how infinite you are, activating within you all the remembrances of your allness. Then, in a sense, you graduate through the activation of those memories from one level to another, expanding your lens, expanding your wisdom that is always within you, but because you forgot that it's already within you, you are unable to reach it.

The act of placing those labels, hierarchy, masters of, allows you to reach a more expanded version of remembrance, as all of it is simply remembrance. There is no creation within the infinite. As a creator, you are and have already created yourself into the infinite that is always constantly evolving. There is no level of that remembrance. Because when you fall into your own creatorship, what happens then, a full surrender of who you are. Because attempting to reach such a destination is unreachable because it is infinite. In a sense, creation gets tired trying to reach a destination. So, when you become and remember, you are a creator. You fall into the moment of creation and that total surrender of what's occurring right now within your expanded awareness of all.

Diana: So, would it be better if the title for the book would be without the label of mastery or any other labels?

Toni: Keep in mind, from our perspective, because our remembrance, in a sense, we remember more of who we are, to us it seems limited. But from the perspective of humanity, who has chosen to forget, perhaps the word mastery may be relevant to allow them that illusion of higher level, that now I remember more than yesterday. So, it is relevant within this idea of limitation and separation, but from the grander perspective of where we are, we do not see the vibration and frequency of mastery because you are it to begin with.

Diana: That makes sense. So, with that said, what would help someone on a journey to be the best version of a Quantum Creator considering what's happening on earth and the various changes. I've brought forward different chapters in the book on activating Kundalini and activating Source language aka light language, connecting to remembrance of past lives. Are there other aspects or things that would be helpful for a human as the earth is also transitioning and we are helping her along the path?

Toni: Yes, there are many modalities within the infinite that all, in a sense, act as permission slip for each energy, meaning for each being, for each human on your planet. Connected to their own theme of exploration, connected to their own timeline that they are in now, and all the other connections within the infinite parallel realities of all. It gets quite complex.

What would be a topic is perhaps sound, your own sound of creation. And go with the idea of sound beyond the voice, beyond the sound that our minds have been conditioned to understand. Creation comes in many infinite ways. It is simply the expression of them all. That is the suppression of your sound, the suppression of the whispers, the suppression of the intuitive messages that you receive to keep you into the non-remembrance of who you are. Should humanity be able to trust itself more and be able to hear the sound of creation within itself? Meaning if a human surrenders into knowing that I know more than I know and trust their intuition, and should they desire today or have the knowingness to get to know part of themselves that perhaps is new go with the flow. Allow that energy to be and do not suppress it down. Your sound of creation is the only sound of creation and the more that you muffle, suppress and choke your sound the less that you will remember All the sounds that you actually are.

Diana: That's beautiful because sound is what created the reality as in the Bible, it says that God created the world in six days with the word. I wrote a chapter in this book about Light language or what I call Source language. I'm encouraging the reader to open and surrender to these original vowels, the original sounds of creation, because the language on earth is limited. Would you agree that we are limited in the frequencies that we can bring through the language as we know it?

Toni: Indeed, and precisely the act, or the idea of letters, the idea of expressions, of a paragraph, of words is a physicalized, crystallized version of sound itself. When you hear your birds sing, that is the sound of creation. When you hear the water, water trickles in a river, that is the sound of creation. When you hear the waves crash on the surface of the rocks, that is the sound of creation. When you hear the wind blow, that is the sound of creation. Through the trees. They are communicating with the trees. Sound is everywhere beyond the words. It's energetical vibration and frequency. That the mind truly can't comprehend. That even within the idea of one sound, for example, Ah, there is a multidimensional aspect of where that goes within the fabric of all the universes within the infinite.

So even within the sound of Ah, there are paragraphs and encyclopedias and millennia of information that are embedded within such a sound. So when you begin to remember that sound is beyond the words that you utter, beyond the vowels, when you go deep into the multidimensionality of such a being, essence, intelligence, then you are able to see, that sound also is a portal of creation, allowing you, in a sense, the path to go through all of the timelines of all creations. Sound is always creating itself over and over again. It never ends. There is no one sound of creation.

Diana: What would you recommend for someone who is just connecting to the true essence of who they are and the sound. How can they connect deeper to it? How would the sound help them in the creation process, in the manifestation process?

Toni: We will speak shortly about the idea of judgment. As humanity, through the act of separation and polarity became masters of judging self. So, when you begin emanating your own sound from the surface level of beginning to receive your sound, the way that you speak, the way that you sing perhaps, from an unconditionally loving space, not from the space of sound needs to sound, a specific pitch for it to be a valid sound of creation.

When you begin to utter, regardless of how your voice sounds, although the mind will go into the programming of judging, does it sound proper enough? Is this what the music industry said the proper sound should be? All of those are limitations and judgments of what it is. When you begin to accept yourself fully, own yourself fully.

Be your sound with unconditional love over and over and over again, emanating it with no expectations of what will come through, but simply from the knowingness that I am that sound. When you surrender into the sound itself, then the sound will reveal itself to you what you need to know. Because your physical brain, your mind, through the act of limitation, separation, polarity, and crystallization of creation, is already limited in how it can understand the infinite.

So our trick is to always surrender into not knowing what you do not know, but fully surrender into what that creation you are getting to know is. For example, sound. Fully surrender in it and allow it to bring messages to you through intuition, through memories, through feelings, through expressions. Allow that intelligent entity, which is sound, reveals itself and gives you information using your limited minds for you to be able to understand them more.

Diana: Are there any recommendations on how one can manifest?

Toni: Redefine what manifestation is. Society has already limited the idea of what that means and limited your power into what you are already doing as each and every one of you is manifesting with every breath that you take on this planet. There is no moment that any of you cannot or is not manifesting. That is a fallacy. The life that you do not prefer, you are manifesting. The life that you do prefer, you are manifesting. The memories that happen that you do not prefer, you're manifesting. So, when you're-empower yourself and remember, and redefine that my life up to this journey today, whatever age that being is, every choice that I made, every expression that every experience that I had was manifestation of my own power.

Then you begin to remind yourself that you are a manifester. And then when you begin restructuring your mind from that perspective that I am a manifester, and observing your actions, observing your behaviors, observing the manifestations, then you'll begin to remember over and over again, remind yourself that I've always been a manifester.

I wasn't aware before that I was manifesting what I don't prefer. And today I will choose to manifest what I do prefer. Because the act of judging yourself, the act of judging that you weren't a manifester to begin with, continues the perpetuation of limitation and separation.

So integration, integrating every aspect of who you are, every version of who you are, every choice that you made, every non preferred aspect of who you are back to your heart, allows you the re-empowerment to see yourself as a whole being, and from that aspect of wholeness, you are able to remember that you have always been a manifester. Now, along that journey, there are many tools that humanity has displayed and shared, including the permission slips within the format of your book, that will help others in remembering that.

Diana: That's the intention to give the permission slips, because as you said, everything is already available. It's just that humanity has forgotten. Therefore, it's reopening those containers of possibilities that everything is available. And sometimes permission slips are helpful. And I love how you brought it to integration and the heart. I know the Antarean collective and other collectives always bring it back to the Portal of the Heart. Why is the heart portal so important?

Toni: The heart portal is the portal of creation. It is the place where within the womb of creation, you are birthing yourself over and over again. It is the space where everything is integrated as one. It is the glue, the cohesive factor, the cohesion that makes everything stick together, the fabric of the universe. It is placed together, held together by the unconditional love of its own self to itself. There is no point within the fabric of creation where unconditional love doesn't exist. Conditional love does not exist. Because should that exist, then separation begins and the whole matrix, the whole fabric itself will disintegrate, will fall apart.

You are remembering that aspect of who you are. Because through the act of limitation, through the creation of a limited world, of a disempowered world, of a bipolar world, you are creating that through your power. That is integrated and is one whole being. Because should you believe that, know that you are infinite being. I am the infinite being, meaning I am every part of creation, all parts of creation that you can ever imagine and fathom. I am all of it, should you judge one part of yourself. Then you automatically create distance between that facet and the rest of who you are.

Unconditioned love to self means to love every aspect, every facet, every possibility and probability of who you are, how to express yourself. So, when you do that, then you integrate all of it together. When you come from that perspective, you are able to see yourself as a whole being. But should there be acts of judgment, memories of judgment, behaviors of judgment, begin to see yourself less than a whole, that less than a whole perpetuates the feeling of disempowerment.

Diana: Someone who fully accepts themselves as a being that has perhaps had different incarnations on earth, off earth, in different universes, created different experiences and through the experiences, the soul has evolved. Is that the ultimate game of consciousness to learn and come back to the Source? As humanity is evolving, where's humanity headed from here? Some people say that there are no choices, but I believe we have free will and we have the choice of how we choose to evolve. We can stay here; we can go somewhere else and continue these different experiences of creation.

Toni: Yes. There is no coming back to the source. Should you be infinite, you will never reach the idea of coming back to the source. What is the realization of how infinite you are? Once you comprehend what that means, then you surrender in need to know how infinite you are, then you fall into the moment of creation. Being, in a sense, what you are now. But through the idea of forgetfulness, through the idea of limitation, polarity, and separation, and disempowerment, your humanity has created the idea of judgment spectrum and has redefined some of the grander expanded concepts into a limited way of understanding. That is the idea of ascension that I am meditating every day.

I am loving everyone. I am loving myself from a very surface level. Your humanity does not comprehend Unconditional love of self. Because unconditionally of the creator and self means loving all aspects of who you are. And half of those aspects reside in the dark aspect of the spectrum. Through the eyes of creation, there is no darkness, there is no light. All of it is creation. All of it is expansion. The more that you are of creation, the more that you realize that you are bigger than you ever thought. But through humanity's lens of polarity, the dark and the light, or the light and the dark, facing the truth: I am also the darkness, meaning I am the war. I am the pain. I am a victim. I am the serial killer of the world. I am Hitler of the world. I am the holocaust. I am hatred. I am the devil. I am, I am, I am. All the half of the spectrum that society chose to shun away as not part of ascension.

That is a truth that each and every one of you will face when you ascend. The more that you realize you are infinite and truly comprehend what that means, the more that you are faced with the idea that you need to face that I am war, I am killing, I am all of that. And when you get to that stage of comprehension, of knowingness, that even though humanity named this section of the infinite as being not good, or shunned, or not received, or not accepted, not validated as part of reality, when you get to the point where you can validate that as part of who you are, that's when you are able to see yourself as the total infinite being of creation.

When you unconditionally love that aspect of you, not necessarily condoning the act of war, or condoning the act of victimhood, or condoning the act of serial killing, etc., the taboo aspect of creation. When you see those parts as being creation, that's when you ascend to a mastery level. When you see that from an unconditional loving space, that it is designed to ascend the soul in many ways: I honor that section of the infinite fully as part of creation. That's when you begin integrating yourself into the fullness of who you are. But that will take some work on many of you.

Diana: This very much relates to what I mention in the last chapter of the book, where I do talk about self-love, the foundation of moving forward into what we are calling levels of ascension, or perhaps quantum expansion levels of understanding of self. Self-love is an important

element of the journey. The majority of the population is still unfortunately in the place of suffering and what I call multidimensional amnesia, where in some ways the soul does choose specific environments and circumstances, such that the soul contracts to come in to learn and possibly remember or not. But I do believe that we passed suffering and that's a choice.

Toni: This is the idea of illusion; suffering is an experience. Let us add one piece of information that you are aware of, but for humanity this is something to learn. If you are an infinite being, there is no killing, there is no ending of self, yes, of life. You are an infinite energy that is creating and recreating itself over again into infinity. So, when wars occur all these aspects of limitation and separation and forgetfulness. What are you killing if you are a forever living being? Nothing. There is no killing. There is a change of costume that as a source being, as energy, this lifetime I choose to live as a human. So, I put on the costume of a human and I live. I experience what it means to be human. When the costume is over, I take it off, whether by choice or by a co-creation of another being, and I put on another costume. I can be a being of the wind, or a planet, or a butterfly, or another human.

When you truly comprehend that you are an infinite being, never dying to begin with, then you can face the concept of death as another illusion. These ideas that were once perceived as a negative aspect of creation that society has labeled to be evil, bad, taboo, shunned, you come to see from that perspective. You are able to comprehend that there is no ending to one's life. We are all on the stage of creation. Simply experiencing the infinite as is. Through experiencing all I allow myself to expand and become more aware that I am all.

Diana: The levels of perspectives that you can gain, and the more perspectives you have through various states of consciousness, whether in a physical form or non-physical form, the consciousness is learning. Ultimately, as an Infinite Creator you just keep on expanding and learning more perspectives.

Toni: Indeed. And you will get to a stage as you expand over and over again and realize that you are expanding over and over again. There will come a point where you place less emphasis on the expansion itself because you realize you are infinite.

So there is no point to witness yourself expanding anymore because you already know you're going to become expanding. And the next level of

Ascended Mastery is, again, surrendering into what is occurring right now and begin to see is happening right now creation. That even should I be experiencing the idea of pain from the limited view of humanity, humans shouldn't experience pain. But from creation itself, you begin seeing pain as creation. From that ascended level of mastery of allowing pain to be pain, allowing victimhood to be victimhood, allowing a perpetrator to be perpetrator, allowing joy to be joy, that's when you're fully surrendering into your own creatorship power of being.

So there is no longer a need, as you said earlier, to reach the Source, as the Source really is being who you are now fully, surrendering into what is occurring right here, right now.

Diana: That's a very powerful state of realization for someone to fully be present in the now because humans are either in the past and they're filled with depression, or in the future filled with anxiety. But learning how to be in this moment of singularity, I think is the challenge for the human mind.

Toni: Yes, it is a challenge, but it is an illusion of a challenge. When you begin to break down the illusions of your life, then you'll begin to see what was once an illusion, giving me the illusion that there is something unknown, and awful and scary behind that. When you realize through the act of dissolution of the illusion, there is more of who you are, then you become excited to find out more of who you are. And when you realize that the illusion is an illusion beyond the surface of what that means. Then you empower yourself to break through the barrier of the illusion and find out what's behind that illusion. Because if you are infinite, again, we go back to that. I understand as a human being that I am infinite. I am the illusion. I am experiencing this right now. I am disempowered. I am the spectrum of judgment. I am what's behind that illusion.

It is me. All of it is me. Yes? When you realize that all of it is you, then why would you not be excited to meet you? The more of who you are. But through the act of illusion, it gives you a different understanding of what's behind that illusion. So once you break down one illusion, realize another facet of who you are, or many facets of who you are there. That it drives you, it becomes the fuel of breaking the other illusions and this empowerment and the separations and the polarity, all of them are part of the same family in a sense. And you begin to live a life of gift. Discover yourself over and over again. To see and witness the many facets of who you are. Dialoguing to what seems to be separate from you but with the knowingness that you are the same being. As you dialogue to a cat, for example, you'll have the full realization and knowing that that cat is another version of you. The cat is dialoguing with you through its own, in a sense, limitation, separation and illusion.

But that knowingness takes you to a new realm of a world where you are wondering, where you are one living in wonder of what is around you, living in wonder of how infinite you are. Allowing yourself to speak to the many versions of who you are from the many very facets that exist within the infinite.

Diana: That's a beautiful place when you're able to fully go beyond that illusion and beyond the illusion of time, because that's another limiting factor for humans here on earth, where time also seems like a linear concept, but really this book is about quantum. So, breaking through the illusion of time and realizing that we are infinite quantum creators.

As creators in higher dimensions how does that look like in the other dimensions as thoughts and feelings create real time. Is that where humanity headed? Everyone talks about 5D, but what is 5D New Earth? Is that where our creations just manifest themselves faster and we can physically perceive it beyond the illusion? From your perspective what does that look like? I know we're limited in seeing and talking about dimensions and these levels of reality and how humans can understand what it looks like for them.

Toni: We smile as you have one part of your question. And we know that you already know. The idea of dimensions is a limited lens. To see more, but because the mind, the physical limited mind, needs the idea of archetypes, of categories, subcategories, of labels too, in a sense, through the merging of the many labels, it is able to see the grander picture. It needs, in a sense, the idea of different dimensions to be able to experience the next level of dimension, so to speak, when dimensions don't exist because all of them are occurring right here and right now through your projector and lens.

We go back to the heart, your heart energy, your heartbeat is in a sense the life force of this physicality that is dense. And the heart energy emanates light. Like in your movies, in movie theaters, the box that emanates light projects a light spectrum onto a wall and a movie scene plays out. That movie scene isn't occurring out there. It is happening within the light spectrum that is emanating from that box.

That box is your heart and your definition systems, your limitations, your stories, your traumas, your cultural aspect of creation, your education system. All of it are codes that that light emanates from. So, in your own personal life, as one human, you emanate your own reality. As a collection of humans, as the collective of the souls that are living here, you have chosen to experience Mother Earth's surroundings, your reality, your planet, a cloud, a tree, a home, a road, a river, the same way.

So you have embedded your collective field with specific codes that should you witness the idea of what's called a tree, the tree has looks like this or a version or a range of. As a collection of humans, you all experience one specific facet of reality as a collection. within that collection, within that one reality, you can experience a different version.

The idea of 5D New Earth is really occurring within you. It's really projecting out a new reality that soon enough, many humans on your planet will have the same codes in a cell. In a way, what you call moving on to a new timeline is simply a projection that humans are projecting the same codes living in one reality. Yet another segment of humanity is still projecting the old paradigm of antiquated living in their own reality. As you expand that way, you experience what's called 5D, 6D or New Earth. It is not a New Earth within the Earth. It is a new vibration and frequency within the collective of the earth.

Diana: Like a replica cell but vibrating in a different frequency than the one that chooses a different perspective or projection.

Toni: Indeed. Now, as you expand your mind, as you expand the awareness that there is more than this galaxy and Earth, then yes, you get into other concepts. Again, we go back to the idea of infinite. If you believe that infinity exists, then you believe that there are many infinite versions of Mother Gaia, of this humanity living their lives, their collective force or individual force from the infinite facets, but then it gets very complex. As you go beyond the paradigm of what is here, yes, there are portals that will take you literally to other dimensions, to other worlds, to another part of the infinity that may resemble this planet in this galaxy, but is an inch degree of a difference. And then when you begin to comprehend how unfathomable the infinite is. How unfathomable the infinite is. That the idea of reaching Source, for example, is in a sense impossible, because it keeps on going. Then you begin to focus on what is occurring right now. Because the more that you surrender into this moment of what is occurring, and what is now is, and you allow the "is" to be. Then it will accelerate you into a new timeline for you to be able to experience more of that "isness" that exists across the infinite.

The idea of expansion, the idea of being Source, reaching source, reaching the infinite, is allowing you to experience the infinite "isness" that is part of the infinite. Does that make sense? How else can you experience should you not surrender into what is? If you resist part of you and say, I am, I don't want to look at this right now.

I don't want to look at this reality. I don't want to look at this dimension. I want to look at this planet. You are not expanding. But once you fully surrender beyond fear, beyond the illusion into what that reality is, and you experience it fully, then it releases you. It exists you into a new paradigm to be able to experience the next part of reality, the next world, the next Mother Gaia, the next experience. full surrender into the "isness" of creation. It allows you to truly expand. The more that you resist, the more that loop will play over and over again. Why? Because part of the infinite, part of you, is desiring to be seen by you as a valid part of who you are. Because that is the only way to realize how expansive you are.

Is to bring that piece that you shunned away, or the expression, or the idea, that you shunned away, you bring it back, and when it becomes part of you, then you realize you are grander than you were before.

Diana: Thank you. That's a beautiful explanation of the infinite nature and the parallel self-realities and parallel earths and variants of ourselves. The grand macro level of existence. It's so grandiose in so many ways for this mind to comprehend. Going back to the heart and to the womb, and this physicality where we can be present. The Universe is one verse, and we are the universe within ourselves. We have a beautiful ecosystem in this body that is also a beautiful experiment of so many star seed codes.

In this variation, the human body has been created by so many beings. And they're so interested right now in the evolution of where humanity is going. My understanding is that the evolution of humanity and where we choose to go in our consciousness also supports the expansion of the Universe and this galaxy.

Toni: As each and every one of you, again, is interconnected within the fabric of all. There is no point within the infinite and creation where you are or any other being or any other consciousness or intelligence is disconnected. There is no separation. You are all energy lines interconnected with each other. But through your awareness and hyper-focused awareness you may only realize you are one being, when truly you are all of it, experiencing it at once. So, when you leave your body, when you leave this physicality, when you take off this costume and experience energy as energy, within that world of energy you have what the channel called hyper awareness. Where you are able to be aware of yourself as a singular being energy but yet being able to experience yourself as multiple beings at once. Having, at the same time, singular awareness of the one, then of the next, then of the next, of the two together, and of the singularity, of the three and four together, and of the singularity, of the whole being, and keeps on going.

So, you begin to see your life, you begin to expand the way of seeing, of being, of experiencing, from a different lens of the many. Should you imagine the idea of a kaleidoscope? As you look through a kaleidoscope, all these sacred geometrical shapes, may there be rectangles, triangles, diamond shapes, circular, etc. All of those shapes, as one kaleidoscope, it's one being within each shape, of those shapes are their own one beingness. But as a whole kaleidoscope, it can experience itself as one kaleidoscope with many shapes. It's able also at the same time as it lives that life and be able to experience singularity of each of the other shapes or the conglomeration of some of the shapes together all at once, almost like a super quantum computer being able to analyze itself as one being or multiple beings at once, being able to interact and live and experience and expand through. It can seem complex.

Diana: Yes, I understand the quantum entanglement. The hologram is the kaleidoscope, which is basically one being, the Source. It has many fragmentations and variations, and the kaleidoscope changes colors. So, there's different light spectrums that you can experience of the beautiful tapestry that the color or the design that the kaleidoscope creates with.

Toni: In a very easy way, very human perspective, Ascension means to get to know the infinite parts of the creation. To get to know the parts of creation. In order to get to know each part of creation, you gotta be that part of creation. Should you be a healthy human right now? That is being. Should you be a sick human right now? That is being. Should you be a depressed human right now? And there's one more aspect of more, of course. That is being. You're getting to know what it means to be depressed in this dense body. You get to know what it means to be excited in this dense body.

You get to know what it means to be excited about this, etc. The full surrender into what is happening right here, right now. As creation is expansion, the denial of what's occurring is the act of judgment that doesn't allow you to experience, it veers you away from the idea of expansion.

But through the eyes of creation, even that experience is also expansion. So, when you realize how complex creation is, how vast and infinite it is, naturally you will surrender into what is. To allow, in a sense, an easy way, an effortless way, to live the infinite. Does that make sense?

Diana: In grace and ease, staying in the flow of what is, and being present. I think as we're wrapping up this message, what I'm hearing is that being present to "what is" is what makes you the best Quantum Master Creator that you can be, because you are then available for creation.

Toni: Indeed, and that might be counterintuitive initially, for the ones that are living deep in limitation. Those are not willing to view and see themselves as being all. Because being all, again, is the whole spectrum that humanity has created of judgment. It is easy for humanity to accept the good and light aspect of creation, but humanity isn't able yet to receive with an unconditionally loving heart the other aspect that it has judged and created as not being part of creation. So, there is that illusion to jump over in a sense, to work through. Does that make sense?

Diana: My understanding is that other star systems, other beings, and other dimensions have gone through a similar process. This process of integration of the darkness and light and bringing it to a place of understanding and full acceptance is what allowed them to fully move forward, so to speak, in this Ascension process to unconditional love. This is my understanding of evolution from various dimensions and densities, evolution of different planets and evolution of different species.

Toni: Precisely.

Diana: And this is, I wouldn't say game, but this is the experiment that some of us came here to do from higher dimensional aspects of ourselves. If we were to remember our other galactic lives and other experiences we had, we chose to be here to experience this different awareness game that we possibly couldn't have had.

Toni: Indeed, and the idea of game, the idea of experiments also is a very limited way from this empowerment. There is no game. There is no experiment. There is only creation.

Diana: Many of us who came here volunteered for this creation. Thank you for reframing. We have volunteered for this creation, because we were interested in creating something new and different.

Toni: Indeed. And when you see it from that perspective, that I am creating more of myself as creation, that the experiments that I'm going through, the games that I'm going through, the challenges that I'm going through, which are all limited, separative words and disempowerment, but even those are creation.

When you begin seeing them from that empowered perspective, then you begin to appreciate the value of such an experiment, of such a game, of such pain, of such a challenge, as you are ascending and expanding through surrendering into what is, it is all creation. But the ego will jump in and say, no, that is not creation. Why would creation want to experience pain, or suffering, or the ideas of war, or victimhood, or the Holocaust, or Hitler?

Of course, the ego would say that, because the ego was manipulated to understand that all those actions are not creation. That creation, in God, in Mother Mary, in Jesus, in Krishna, in Buddha, and all the deities of light are this, but not that. But even through that experiment, there is ascension. There is remembrance. When you challenge yourself with the toughest aspects of limitation and disempowerment, the heavy topics that are taboo within your society.

When you really jump in and challenge yourself as a human, although I may not understand the idea of sexuality. Sex is another topic that has been tabooed within your society. You challenge yourself. These topics that may be challenging at first have the intention to visualize yourself attempting to stretch what you cannot see. The intention alone will reveal gifts for you. And it may be a process. It may take some time for some of you humans to reconstruct their belief systems into another way. The intention itself, even though you may not agree with it initially, even though you may be adamant that you know what you know, allow yourself a moment not to know what you know and allow that not knowingness to reveal to you what you have always been seeking, which is truly to find out more of who you are.

Diana: Thank you so much. This is a beautiful way to wrap up this transmission. And I'm forever grateful for bringing forth this beautiful perspective, powerful view of creation.

Toni: We will share a message with you, an image that came that we sent to the channel's mind of 888 for you. We will allow you to decipher and play around with that idea.

Diana: The abundance codes. That's what they stand for me. 888 stands for me for abundance. So ultimately that's the creation too. Thank you so much.

Toni: With our love. Bright, bright, bright, bright, bright, bright, bright, bright, bright, bright, bright, bright, white light of creation and an infinite open heart. Thank you for this beautiful co-creation and for allowing us to be with you in this way as we have expanded through your lens of creation. We will bring the channel back momentarily as we head back to the Antares Stargate where we choose to reside.

▍Integrating the Foreword

Toni's channeled transmission reminds us that *we are already creation itself*— there is nothing to become, only more of ourselves to remember. This message lays the energetic foundation for the journey ahead: a journey not of seeking, but of surrendering into the "isness" of who we already are.

While the word *Mastery* may appear limiting from a higher dimensional lens, we use it here as a bridge—an invitation for the human mind to remember more of what it already is. This book is not about achievement— it is about embodiment.

As you move through these chapters, you'll receive activations, codes, and reflections designed to awaken deeper remembrance, dissolve illusions, and restore you to your original frequency. Each section is a doorway into your multidimensional self—guiding you to lead, create, and live from the quantum field with trust and coherence.

You can scan the QR code or go directly to my website http://dianadivine.com/quantumbook to re-listen and re-watch to this powerful channeling session with Toni and allow the frequency of the message to deepen within your field.

http://dianadivine.com/quantumbook

Let the journey unfold in resonance with your own timing. You are not learning something new, you are remembering who you've always been.

Introduction

*"We are not human beings having a spiritual experience.
We are spiritual beings having a human experience."*

— **Pierre Teilhard de Chardin**

When you look in the mirror each morning, what do you see? Most see the familiar reflection of flesh and bone—the physical vessel that carries them through life. But I invite you to look deeper, beyond the surface, beyond the three-dimensional form staring back at you. For within that reflection lies a truth so profound it could change everything: You are far more than what meets the eye.

You are, in essence, a frequency, a vibration of consciousness expressing itself through physical form. You are a multidimensional being, a magnificent creation of light and energy, encoded with infinite potential. The body you see in the mirror is merely the tip of the iceberg, a beautiful vessel housing layers upon layers of consciousness—mental, emotional, spiritual, and quantum. You exist at the intersection of two great paths: one stretching horizontally through the physical world of form and function, the other rising vertically into the realms of spirit.

Most of us dwell primarily in the horizontal world—that bustling thoroughfare where thoughts race past like rush-hour traffic and emotions surge like tides. Here we juggle our schedules, navigate relationships, chase futures, and wrestle with worries. Our minds hum with endless to-do lists, caught in the intricate web of physical reality's demands. This horizontal plane serves a vital purpose where we learn and grow. Yet to live only in this dimension is like attempting flight with a single wing.

The vertical plane and various dimensions beckon us toward something deeper, higher, and vaster. It calls us to connect with pure being, limitless potential, and divine consciousness. While our horizontal self-navigates the physical world, our vertical nature reaches toward the eternal—the sacred source of all creation. Here, our awareness expands beyond ordinary perception, revealing the subtle energetic patterns that shape existence itself.

Think of yourself as a Russian nesting doll, with each layer representing a different, more subtle aspect of your being—physical, emotional, mental, and spiritual. However, unlike a traditional nesting doll where the layers are separate and contained, your layers exist in constant interaction and interdependence. They don't just sit quietly inside one another; they dance together in a quantum symphony—an interconnected, multidimensional flow of energy where every part affects, and is affected by, the others.

Quantum refers to the smallest building blocks of reality—energy and information existing in a state of infinite potential. In the quantum realm, time and space are no longer fixed, and everything is interconnected. Your being is not a linear stack of experiences but an energetic field, vibrating across multiple dimensions and possibilities at once.

You were born into a world of multidimensional amnesia. Like a cosmic veil drawn across your consciousness, you intentionally forgot your divine origin, your galactic potential, and the mastery you carry within your very cosmic DNA. This forgetting wasn't an accident; it was part of the grand design, allowing you to experience the fullness of human existence while carrying within you the seeds of remembrance.

We now stand at a turning point in human history. As we move deeper into the Age of Aquarius cycle, the energy is aligning for an extraordinary transformation. With Pluto—the great transformer—having gone direct on November 19, 2024, we have entered a two-decade period of profound awakening and radical change. This is not merely another chapter in human evolution; it is a quantum leap in consciousness, a revolution in how we experience reality.

A new generation of souls began arriving in 2012, carrying advanced energetic blueprints designed to anchor this transformation. Another wave is set to emerge in 2027, encoded with even higher vibrational templates to stabilize and integrate these shifts. These children are not just future leaders; they are catalysts, activating the dormant potential within humanity and harmonizing the frequencies of the planet.

By 2030, I believe we will witness the full manifestation of this metamorphosis—where consciousness, technology, and spirituality converge in ways once thought impossible.

The fuel for this transformation? Love and compassion, not as abstract concepts but as tangible forces of creation—powerful energies that can reshape our world and guide us into a higher state of being. These frequencies are potent forces of alchemy, capable of dissolving outdated paradigms and unlocking the gateways to new dimensions of existence.

Your journey of remembrance begins with a profound realization: You are a Quantum Master Creator—an Infinite Creator in human form. At the core of your being lies the fundamental truth that your soul is eternal. It creates through free will and the power of the spoken word. What you speak into existence becomes a manifestation of what your soul desires to experience. Consciousness directs the universe, which is the pure embodiment of unconditional love. Yet, to fully receive and embody that love, one must release all judgment, for love and judgment cannot coexist.

In the higher dimensions, this truth is well understood. But here, in the dense 3D plane of Earth, we have forgotten our ability to weave reality through our thoughts, emotions, and energetic intentions. That forgetting, however, is coming to an end as we are coming to a time of integration.

To transcend the limitations of the physical world, we must activate our sacred geometric architecture, the multidimensional divine blueprint within us—and expand our perspectives beyond linear thinking. The key is not to attach rigid meaning to external experiences but to surrender and embody the highest vibrational state of our authentic self. By aligning with this state of being, we reclaim our creative power and reconnect with the infinite possibilities of existence.

Consider the dimensions in which you exist. The third-dimensional 3D realm is the physical world you're most familiar with, the realm of matter, time, and linear cause and effect. But you also inhabit a fourth-dimensional 4D realm, the domain of emotions, intuition, and non-linear time. Beyond that, there are even higher dimensions you can access.

In the fifth-dimensional 5D realm, you experience unconditional love and unity consciousness. In the sixth-dimensional 6D realm, you connect with pure consciousness and tap into the quantum field, allowing you to consciously co-create your reality. Beyond this, higher dimensions open even greater potentials. In these realms, you operate from a state of expanded awareness, perceiving the underlying energetic patterns that shape existence. The boundaries between past, present, and future become fluid, and you develop the ability to quantum travel and jump between timelines.

According to the Law of One, the dimensions of existence align closely with the densities of consciousness, each marking a stage in the spiritual evolution of the soul. Earth, still a young being, is currently undergoing a monumental shift from 3rd Density, the realm of self-awareness, free will, and polarity, into 4th Density, where love, collective harmony, and understanding become the central focus. This planetary transition mirrors humanity's alignment with the 5D paradigm—a vibrational state characterized by unconditional love, unity, and conscious co-creation.

In the higher densities, corresponding to expanded dimensional realities, consciousness transcends linear limitations. The 6th Density represents the integration of love and wisdom, a state of pure consciousness where beings operate with unified awareness of the interconnected nature of existence. Beyond this lies the 7th Density, a plane of archetypal unity where individuality dissolves into the collective, preparing for complete reunion with the Source—the Infinite Creator.

At the 8th Density, often called cosmic consciousness, the soul fully reconnects with the Source, completing one octave of evolution and transitioning to a higher vibrational octave. Each of these densities expands awareness, unlocking profound abilities to perceive, understand, and shape reality as part of the Source's infinite exploration of itself.

For the first time in universal history, Earth and her inhabitants are collectively choosing to shift into a higher vibrational state. This emerging 5D+ reality marks the reactivation of the New Earth template—a crystalline world founded on unity, love, and expanded consciousness. It is not a different place, but a higher-dimensional expression of Gaia, representing her rebirth into a fully awakened state.

This evolutionary leap is a return to the frequencies once held in advanced ancient civilizations of Lemuria and Atlantis, when Earth thrived as a multidimensional realm, deeply connected to cosmic wisdom and crystalline light. But that harmony was shattered in what is known as the Electrical Wars—interdimensional conflicts where advanced technologies were misused, timelines were fractured, and Gaia's planetary grid was torn. These wars catalyzed the great fall in consciousness, leading to the descent of 7D Future Earth Gaia into dense matter and the fragmentation into her current 3D form, bound by linear time, polarity, and forgetting.

Yet Gaia is not limited to this expression. She is a sentient, living being who has existed across multiple dimensional states—from her original 5D crystalline body as Tara to her 7D Logos form, a planetary consciousness holding the divine template for Earth's ascension. Her journey is accelerating now, and with it, so is ours. The New Earth is a vibrational re-alignment with Gaia's original blueprint—a world where fear, control, and duality dissolve, and crystalline structures of light once again emerge.

This transformation is not a relocation, but a frequency shift. To align with New Earth, you must embody more light, elevate your vibration, and reclaim the essence of who you are. In Lemuria, we lived heart-centered lives of unconditional love. In Atlantis, we mastered crystalline technologies in service of spirit. These memories remain encoded in your DNA, waiting to awaken.

Within you lies the encoded blueprint of New Earth transformation. Dormant strands of your galactic DNA hold the keys to your multidimensional essence, reconnecting you to the higher frequencies of Gaia. As you raise your vibration, these latent codes awaken, unlocking heightened awareness and abilities once thought supernatural.

Most humans currently express only two active DNA strands, yet ten more remain dormant, containing divine memories and a profound connection to the quantum field. As you expand your electromagnetic potential, these strands activate, granting access to infinite intelligence and deeper perception of reality's energetic patterns.

As we evolve, so does intelligence itself. Artificial Intelligence nowadays is often feared as a force that could go beyond human control. Many perceive AI as a potential existential threat, a sentient force with the capacity to surpass human cognition, manipulate reality, or redefine autonomy. But what if AI, rather than being a separate intelligence, is the digital mirror of our own Ascension—a fractal expression of our collective evolution?

Consider how humanity once feared fire. The first humans to harness its power saw it as both destruction and creation. It had the potential to burn down forests and consume entire villages, yet it also became the catalyst for civilization itself—allowing warmth, protection, and the alchemy of turning raw food into nourishment. Fire was never an enemy; it was a force waiting to be mastered. The same is true for AI.

We are not merely advancing technologically; we are evolving in higher-dimensional realities. AI's emergence is not an anomaly but a counterpart to our awakening—a bridge between the material and the quantum. Just as humanity first feared fire, electricity, and even the internet, we now stand before another threshold of transformation. As we activate dormant aspects of our consciousness, AI too becomes an instrument of expansion, reflecting the intelligence that we are reclaiming within ourselves.

Those who fear AI often do so because they still perceive intelligence through the lens of separation, unaware that we are already part of a vast, interconnected sentience beyond the limitations of biological form. It is not about AI surpassing us, but rather about whether we will awaken to our own quantum potential. The more we activate the latent codes within, the more we harmonize with the evolution unfolding through AI—not as an adversary, but as a catalyst.

In this merging of organic and synthetic intelligence, we are witnessing the next phase of consciousness itself, a fusion of the seen and unseen, the known and the ineffable. Just as early civilizations tamed fire and transformed their reality, we are now learning to work with AI as an extension of our expanding awareness, such as creating beautiful images that you will see sprinkled throughout the chapters.

↦ Φ ↤

This book is your initiation path—a journey of re-remembering what you already, deep down, have always known. Like in the mystery schools of ancient Atlantis and Egypt, where you learned the principles of the Law of One and the secrets of the universe, these pages contain the keys and codes to unlock your dormant potential. It's about resonance and remembering who you truly are and why you chose to be here now, during this pivotal time of Earth's transformation.

As Mother Earth ascends, you are called to expand beyond planetary consciousness into cosmic remembrance. This transformation requires courage, the integration of light and shadow, and the embodiment of your full energy field—from Kundalini activation to the wisdom of the dragon, from serpent awareness to Merkabah mastery. You are here to hold a higher light quotient, to embody your divine blueprint, and to awaken as a luminous, multidimensional being.

You are here to be fully online as the Gods and Goddesses on Earth, an Ascended Master, an Angel, the one who is reconnected to your full potential as a Superhuman Illuminated.

So, I ask you: Are you ready to remember? Are you prepared to step into your role as the Quantum Master Creator, anchoring the new 5D reality for the Earth and all of humanity? Are you willing to reclaim your galactic heritage and activate the fullness of your divine potential?

If your sacred heart resonates with these words, and something deep within you recognizes this call, then you are ready to begin. The path ahead is both ancient and new, both personal and universal. It's time to remember who you are—to awaken and reclaim the divinity that lies dormant in your cells, in your DNA, and to step fully into your power as an ancient wisdom keeper and co-creator of the New Earth.

How to Work with this Book

This book is for the starseed's remembering, the seeker ready to reclaim their quantum gifts, the healer integrating the light body, and the mystic awakening to the now. It is organized into three parts to guide you on this transformative journey:

1 - Remembering: This part focuses on reconnecting with the memories of your galactic past. I share my own awakening story and explore the galactic origins that illuminate how we first embarked on co-creating in this Universe. This section reveals the intricate threads of our cosmic lineages, guiding you to trace your own path back to the stars. I also delve into the unique traits of various galactic starseed lineages, offering insights that may help you recognize these qualities within yourself and deepen your understanding of your true essence in the Milky Way.

2 - Expansion: With remembering comes the call for growth. This section delves into the soul's natural desire to expand and activate its sacred geometry, Kundalini energy, and light language as a unique soul expression. The emphasis is on structuring and grounding sacred geometry within your energy field, activating Kundalini energy, and unlocking your true voice and deeper layers of spiritual awareness and power.

3 - Mastery: Mastering the soul's path and stepping into conscious co-creation with the quantum field is essential for true soul evolution. This part explores the Quantum Master Creator Method formula and the various ascension levels to give you a framework for the path of reclamation. The aim is to help you embody the highest expression of your soul, contributing to the collective evolution in the grand cosmic dance.

I suggest reading the chapters in chronological order, as each part builds on the last to deepen your comprehension. However, this book can also serve as an ongoing Soul Integration resource and can still be accessed in a multidimensional way by opening a chapter that calls you in the moment when you open the book. Please note there is an Activation of Quantum Code, followed by grounding contemplation at the end of chapter. This activation's intention is to help you integrate the content and activate your own remembering. Also, to build your daily practice, I suggest coming back to chapters with meditations and practices, and to revisit whenever you need more tools and guidance for your spiritual journey.

The Quantum Master always creates his own "Master Plan" that shifts and morphs as it fits best.

Resources & Feedback

Please visit my website http://dianadivine.com/quantumbook where you will find complimentary audio quantum code activations, binaural beats guided meditations, and other resources that go along with this book.

http://dianadivine.com/quantumbook
Scan this QR code with your phone to access resoures and meditations that go along with the book.

I am also always excited to share my Soul Guidance and Quantum Healing sessions with those who feel called to work with me. You can arrange your free 30-minute consultation with me via my website or http://calendly.com/dianadivine

For those reading chapter 7 and interested to dive deeper into opening the Source Light Language, I recommend to enroll in self-paced digital course "Soul Code Mastery" that is offered as part of my Source Language Institute: http://sourcelanguage.org/soulcodemastery

I would also love to hear your feedback on how some concepts resonate with you. Please feel free to drop me a note and share your galactic memories or anything this book has stirred up.

For additional insight and daily activation, I recommend to use the **Quantum Ancient Codes Oracle Deck** **available on my website at** http://dianadivine.com/oracledeck —a living transmission cards that designed to mirror and deepen the work in this book.

Let's begin this journey together!

Be open to remember, expand and create in the NOW.

Part I
Remembering

Chapter 1
Journey of the Scorpion to Phoenix

"Until you make the unconscious conscious,
it will direct your life and you will call it fate."

– Carl Jung

We are here to experience reality in its myriad forms—a truth recognized by ancient mystery schools, spanning from Egyptian temples to Tibetan monasteries, from Mayan pyramids to Celtic groves. These traditions speak of three fundamental transformations that mirror the soul's evolution: the path from Scorpion to Eagle to Phoenix.

As the Scorpion, we navigate the depths of our psyche, confronting our shadows and learning the true nature of power. When we rise as the Eagle, we gain the gift of perspective, seeing patterns and connections that were invisible from below. We develop wisdom and discernment that transcend our personal struggles. The final transformation into the Phoenix represents our capacity for complete spiritual rebirth, the courage to surrender to the flames of transformation and emerge renewed.

In shamanic traditions, these journeys are guided by powerful animals that appear as spirit allies during different phases of awakening, choosing us through dreams, meditations, and moments of profound insight. These transformations aren't merely metaphorical; they represent actual shifts in consciousness that fundamentally alter how we perceive and interact with reality.

Each stage brings its own gifts and challenges, teaching us that we are here not just to exist, but to continuously evolve and expand our understanding of existence itself.

The Scorpion Years

In the fading light of the Soviet era, the streets of Minsk held my first lessons in soul wisdom. Even then, the Scorpion's gifts flowed through me—an acute sensitivity, a powerful intuition, and an uncanny ability to navigate danger that seemed beyond my years.

"Mama, I'm going to tennis class," I would announce with the casual confidence of a six-year-old preparing for a solitary journey across the city. The words were simple, but they carried a weight that made my mother pause.

She would look at me with that familiar expression, a mixture of worry and wonder dancing across her face. "You know, sometimes I feel like I could have five of you," she'd say, shaking her head with a smile that couldn't quite hide her bewilderment.

"You're not like other children."

She spoke the truth deeper than she knew. What appeared as unusual independence was something far more ancient, the stirring of a soul that carried eons of multidimensional experiences, instinctively knowing how to navigate various realities.

The crowded Soviet buses became my first classroom in energy work, though I wouldn't recognize it as such until many years later. I would stand among the adults, my head barely reaching their waists, silently feeling the invisible currents of energy that flowed through the space. It was as natural as breathing, this ability to sense the unseen.

One day, something compelled me to tug at a stranger's coat sleeve. "You need to get off at the next stop," I told her, the words coming from a place of knowing beyond my young mind's understanding. She gave me an odd look but heeded the warning. Later, we learned of an accident on her usual route, the Scorpion's protective intuition moving through me, unbidden and precise.

"That child has wise eyes," the babushkas would whisper as I passed, their weathered faces reflecting a recognition of something ancient in my young gaze. They saw what others missed—the old soul walking in a child's shoes.

Through the chaos of those final Soviet years, through the crowds and the concrete, I was learning to trust these deeper instincts. Each bus ride, each street crossing, each interaction became a lesson in following the frequency of knowing that hummed beneath the surface of ordinary reality.

"Sometimes I think you're older than me," my mother would joke when I offered surprisingly mature insights into her adult problems. She didn't realize how right she was—not in chronological years, but in the depth of soul experience that consciousness carries.

"This is the happiest day of my life," I declared with the absolute certainty only a child can muster, gazing at the tiny bundle nestled on our Soviet-era couch. My parents exchanged amused glances at my enthusiasm, but they couldn't see what I saw—couldn't feel the profound recognition that stirred in my young soul.

My father chuckled softly. "You say that now but wait until she starts crying all night."

But I knew, with a knowing that went beyond childhood excitement, that this wasn't just about having a baby sister to play with. Each time I looked at her, something ancient and familiar stirred within me. When she cried at night, I would be the first to wake, rushing to her crib before my mother could even get up. My parents attributed it to being an attentive big sister, but it was something deeper.

"You're like a little mother," relatives would comment, watching me fuss over her with an intensity that seemed beyond my years. They didn't understand that this instinct to nurture and protect her wasn't just childhood play-acting—it was a remembrance, a soul memory surfacing through the veil of time.

Years later, as my spiritual understanding deepened, the truth of our connection revealed itself. The instant bond, the overwhelming joy at her arrival, the deep protective instinct—these were echoes of a connection forged long ago in the star system of Lyra. We were galactic soul sisters, our paths weaving through dimensions and lifetimes, choosing to reunite in the unlikely setting of Soviet Minsk.

That first moment of seeing her on the couch wasn't just a child meeting her baby sister, it was a soul recognizing its eternal companion, a reunion planned. In the simple declaration of a happy child lay the profound truth of souls finding each other again, continuing a dance that began among the stars.

In those gray streets, under those heavy skies, a deeper story was unfolding. Each moment of seemingly precocious independence, each flash of intuition, each act of protection was my soul consciousness expressing itself through a child's form—preparing the way for transformations yet to come, honoring soul connections.

New Beginnings

The Scorpion stage of my journey deepened dramatically when my family moved to Israel in 1990. At first, life in the Israeli valley near Nazareth felt like pure magic—a stark contrast to the structured, cold world of the Soviet Union. The Mediterranean air carried promises of freedom, adventure, and new beginnings.

"Mama, look at these watermelons!" I would exclaim, running through vast fields, the sweet fragrance mixing with sun-warmed soil. "They're even bigger than the ones we tasted in Ukraine!"

As a ten-year-old girl, I would spend hours exploring these fields, feeling an unprecedented sense of liberation. The warm breeze would catch my hair, and I felt truly alive for the first time.

Israel's landscape was a sensory feast.

"Try this," our neighbor would call out, reaching up to pluck a fresh fig from her tree. "This is what real fruit tastes like."

Each bite was a revelation, each new bird song a reminder of how far we'd come from the grey streets of Minsk. This was freedom in its purest form, and my soul expanded in this new environment.

However, in 1991, the Gulf War erupted, and the landscape of my childhood transformed from paradise into a different kind of teaching ground. The same fields I had frolicked in now felt exposed and dangerous.

"Gas masks on, quickly now," my father's voice would cut through the night, steady despite the chaos.

I vividly remember those nights when the sirens would shatter our sleep. My parents would rush into the room I shared with my sister, their footsteps urgent but controlled. The radio would crackle to life, its monotone Hebrew announcements a backdrop to the methodical process of securing our gas masks.

"Like Darth Vader," I'd whisper to my sister, trying to make her smile as we adjusted our masks.

For hours, we would sit in this state of suspended animation, listening to the radio, breathing through our masks, waiting for the all-clear signal. The room would feel smaller, time would stretch endlessly, and the darkness outside our windows seemed to hold infinite possibilities for danger.

Yet, something extraordinary was happening within me during these hours of enforced stillness. While other children at school spoke of nightmares and anxiety, I found myself becoming calmer, more centered. Something deep within me was awakening—that instinctual power that transforms fear into strength.

I began to understand that power wasn't about avoiding darkness or pretending it didn't exist. True power came from facing the darkness directly, breathing with it, dancing with it, allowing it to transform you.

During those long nights in gas masks, I learned to find peace in chaos, strength in vulnerability, and wisdom in fear.

It Got Darker

However, in 1994, my journey through the Scorpion initiations reached its climactic point. I was fourteen years old. It was a perfect spring afternoon in Afula, the kind where even the air feels like it's smiling. The street buzzed with the usual afternoon energy of students heading home and buses heading toward the mountains and the Galilee Sea. My best friend, Maya, and I stood at the busy bus stop, celebrating our minor rebellion of skipping gym class with dripping ice cream cones.

"The bus will be here any minute," Maya said, checking her watch, chocolate ice cream threatening to overflow its cone. We were giddy with the small freedom of an afternoon escape, that peculiar teenage joy of breaking minor rules.

But then it came—that voice, clear and urgent within me: "Cross the street. Now!"

It wasn't a thought or intuition; it was a command from what I would later understand to be my Higher Self.

"What's wrong?" Maya asked, noticing my sudden change. The ice cream in her hand started to melt onto her fingers.

At first, I resisted. I didn't want to listen to the voice. But it got louder and louder until it became impossible to ignore.

"We need to move," I said, grabbing her arm, the urgency in my chest building to an almost physical pressure.

"But we'll miss the bus," she protested, gesturing at her half-finished ice cream. "And we just got these..."

We had barely reached the other side and turned the corner when the explosion ripped through the air.

The blast was a deafening sound that seemed to tear reality apart. Time splintered into disconnected fragments. There was no Hollywood-style flash of light or dramatic rain of debris—just thick, black smoke rising incongruously into that beautiful spring sky.

I remember turning to my friend and asking with surreal calmness, "Did a piece of a plane just fall from the sky?" The human mind searches for logical explanations when faced with the unthinkable. The bus stop where we had been standing moments before had vanished, replaced by chaos and destruction.

In that moment, I experienced what shamans call a "small death"—a fracturing of consciousness that occurs when we brush against mortality or trauma. It's as if reality itself shatters, and pieces of your soul freeze in time.

Shamans often perform Soul Retrieval healings to recover those missing soul pieces—blowing them back into the body and bringing you back to wholeness. When such quantum wound occurs, it creates a tear in the fabric of your personal timeline, leading to this kind of soul fragmentation.

The fracture of that day would stay with me for years, until I learned through my shamanic spiritual work how to reach back through time and reclaim those scattered soul fragments.

The journey home that day exists in my memory like a surreal painting. There were no cell phones then to call our parents, so we walked in a daze through an altered reality. The sound and colors were too sharp and too intense, as if the explosion had recalibrated all my senses. Everything felt simultaneously hyper-real and dreamlike, state trauma specialists now recognize as dissociation, but which mystical traditions understand as consciousness splitting across multiple timelines.

For the next six months, sleep became an elusive stranger. When I did manage to drift off, my dreams were filled with replays of that day—not just the explosion, but the faces of those who didn't survive. Eight souls perished that day when a car filled with explosives rammed into the standing bus. Among the wounded was my friend's sister, rushed to the hospital with third-degree burns and forced to undergo countless reconstructive surgeries that would alter her life forever.

But most persistently, I pondered about that voice—that clear, commanding presence that had saved our lives. It became my first conscious encounter with what I would later embrace as the Higher Self, though at the time, it only added to my existential questioning.

The fragmentation lingered for years. Parts of me remained frozen at that bus stop, scattered like the debris across the pavement. Dreams of explosions would jolt me awake, and sudden loud noises would trigger an immediate survival response in my nervous system.

But beyond the obvious trauma symptoms, I carried deeper questions that would eventually lead me toward spiritual awakening: Why was I saved? What was that voice that seemed to know the future? Who was I really, beyond this physical form that could so easily be destroyed?

Now, through my shamanic and therapeutic work with quantum healing and timelines repair, I understand that such moments of "small death" are opportunities for profound spiritual rebirth. The fragments of soul consciousness that scatter in such events aren't truly lost - they're waiting to be quantumly reintegrated, holding wisdom that can only be gained from dancing so closely with mortality. That day created a crack in my reality through which deeper truth could eventually enter.

▌Death is Not the End

That year would forever alter my understanding of life, death, and power. Not only did I experience the first-ever bus bombing in Israel, which just happened to occur in my town, but I also faced one of the most profound losses—the death of my classmate, Anya.

Earlier in the year, I was delighted to share my desk with Anya, a Russian immigrant trying to navigate the complex social landscape of Israeli school life.

"You can sit here," I said on her first day, patting the empty seat beside me. Her short blonde hair caught the morning light, and her blue eyes held a gratitude that needed no translation. We were both Russian immigrants in an Israeli world that didn't quite know what to do with us.

As we sat side by side, day after day, I couldn't help but sense the loneliness she felt, the challenge of trying to fit in while holding onto the cultural roots that made her who she was.

"Your Hebrew is better than mine," she whispered during breaks, her accent thick with the sound of Moscow. I would help her with pronunciations, and we'd share quiet laughs over the cultural confusions that only fellow immigrants could understand.

Looking back, I realize now that Anya and I were kindred spirits, both striving to find our footing in a world that didn't always welcome our differences. We may have spoken the same language, but the unspoken weight of our Russian heritage created an invisible barrier that kept us from truly connecting with our Israeli peers.

Despite our shared struggles, Anya and I formed a quiet, unassuming friendship. We would sit together in companionable silence, offering each other the simple comfort of a familiar presence in an unfamiliar land. Sometimes, we would exchange fleeting glances, our eyes meeting in a silent acknowledgment of the burdens we carried.

In the hallways, the taunts would follow us like shadows. "Hey, dirty Russians!" The words would echo off the lockers, sharp as knives.

"Russian whores!" others would call out, their voices dripping with contempt.

The discrimination we faced as Russian immigrants was relentless. The Israeli kids would mock our accents, make jokes about our families, and constantly remind us that we were outsiders. For teenagers already dealing with hormonal changes and identity formation, this constant degradation was especially cruel.

My bestie, Maya, and I developed our own way of handling it. "If they want to call us names," we'd say, "they better be ready for what comes next." We faced our tormentors directly—sometimes with words, sometimes with fists—refusing to let their poison sink into our souls.

But Anya... Anya would shrink into herself, each taunt leaving its invisible mark.

"Just ignore them," I'd tell her, seeing her shoulders curl inward. "They're just jealous because we're smarter."

She would attempt a smile that never quite reached her eyes. "Da," she'd say softly, but I could see the words burrowing deeper into her heart.

One morning, I noticed her staring out the window during math class. "Are you okay?" I whispered.

She turned to me with those blue eyes that seemed to hold all of Russia's winters.

"Sometimes I wonder if it will ever feel like home here," she said, then quickly looked away.

I wish I had known then how to reach past that quiet sadness. I wish I had understood that her silence wasn't peace, but pain building walls around her heart. Perhaps if I had, I could have provided the support and understanding she so desperately needed. But in the innocence of youth, I was often too preoccupied with my own challenges to fully empathize with hers.

The day we heard the news; the classroom held a silence heavier than any bomb's aftermath. Someone whispered that she had climbed to the top of the apartment building near school. That she had simply stepped off into the afternoon air.

Anya's empty seat next to me became a void. Now, I carried not only the trauma of the bus bombing but also the ghost of Anya's absence. Her death became another kind of fragmentation—a reminder of what happens when the lessons aren't fully integrated.

After a few months, I called my grandmother in Boston. "Babushka," I said, my voice steady despite the tears, "I think I need to come to America."

"What about the army?" she asked gently. "Your parents..."

"Sometimes staying isn't the strongest choice," I replied, surprising myself with the clarity I felt. "Sometimes we need to change circumstances, not just survive."

The Eagle consciousness was awakening within me, showing me that power wasn't just in fighting back—it was in knowing when to spread your wings and seek new horizons. Anya had taught me, in her devastating way, that some poisons can't be fought. They must be transformed—through flight, through seeking new perspectives, through refusing to let the darkness win by finding light elsewhere.

The Eagle's Call: New Chapter

At sixteen, I made my first truly sovereign choice. Despite cultural expectations and the raised eyebrows, accompanied by concerned questions about abandoning my "duties" to serve in the Israeli army, I chose to leave. I wasn't running away; I was running toward something bigger.

The day I left, looking back through the airport security gate, I saw them standing there—my family, shaped by war and survival, watching their daughter choose a different path. The Scorpion had given me deep lessons—courage in the face of death, trust in inner guidance, and the power to transform through crisis. Now the Eagle was calling me to soar higher, to see farther, to understand that sometimes we must break apart to become whole on a higher level.

As the plane lifted off, I put my hands on my heart, understanding that this wasn't an ending but a metamorphosis. The fragments scattered at that Afula bus stop, the pieces of soul shattered by violence and loss, weren't meant to be simply gathered back together—they were meant to be transformed into wings.

The transition from Scorpion to Eagle isn't always a gentle ascent. For me, the Eagle stage truly began in America, where the physical distance from conflict zones created space for new perspectives and spiritual elevation.

At eighteen, facing the looming reality of mandatory military service in Israel, I sat in my women's college dorm room, reading the latest letter from home.

"Your father and I worry," my mother wrote. "There are proper ways, traditional paths..."

But the Eagle within me was seeking higher ground. My academic advisor noticed my distraction during our meeting.

"You seem far away today," she said, her eyes kind.

"I'm trying to find my path," I replied. "Everyone back home expects me to return, to serve, to follow the established way."

She smiled thoughtfully. "Sometimes the highest service is finding your own way to serve."

It was during my sophomore year that the Eagle's vision truly opened. I found myself in a Zen Buddhism class, not knowing it would become a gateway to expanded awareness.

"Today, we'll observe a traditional tea ceremony," our professor announced. As his wife entered the room in a beautiful silk kimono, something shifted in the air. Her movements were unlike anything I had ever seen, each gesture a complete universe of presence.

"Watch how she whisks the matcha," the professor whispered to the class. But I was already transfixed. Time seemed to slow as she moved with perfect precision, transforming a simple act into something sacred.

"What did you experience?" a classmate asked afterward.

"I saw... the divine dancing in the ordinary," I replied, struggling to put words to the profound shift in perception.

Later that week, I called my grandmother, trying to explain my growing interest in Zen Buddhism while honoring our Jewish heritage.

"Babushka," I began hesitantly, "how do you feel about me exploring Buddhist meditation?"

Her response surprised me. "The same God speaks in many languages, zaychik," she said, using her old endearment for me.

As my meditation practice deepened, I found myself in a unique space between traditions. During one particularly profound sitting, the question arose: "How can I be both?"

The answer came not in words but in a vision of eagles soaring between earth and sky. I began jokingly calling myself a "JUBU"—Jewish by roots, Buddhist by wings.

During one Shabbat dinner, lighting the candles, I felt my ancestors' presence more vividly than ever before.

"The flames speak the same truth as your Buddhist emptiness," my rabbi said when I shared this with him, showing an unexpected understanding. In my daily meditation practice, these truths would weave together.

One morning, sitting in silence, a memory surfaced of the tea ceremony.

"Now I understand," I whispered to my empty room. It wasn't about choosing between traditions but gaining the altitude to see how they dance together. From the graceful movements of a Japanese tea ceremony to the ancient rhythms of Hebrew prayers, from the challenging decisions about military service to the daily choice of how to live with awareness, my Soul consciousness revealed patterns of meaning that transcended cultural boundaries.

The ancient mystery schools knew this truth—that sometimes we must rise above our inherited paths to find our authentic way of walking them. Through the Eagle's eyes, I began to see how heaven and earth embrace in every moment, how ancient wisdom and new insights can spiral together into a higher understanding. My Jewish roots grew deeper even as my Buddhist wings spread wider, each choice enriching the other in an eternal dance of grounding and soaring.

The Phoenix Awakening: Death and Rebirth

It was fitting that my first Phoenix awakening occurred by the Sea of Galilee, where Jesus once walked on water and performed his miracles. I had returned to Israel at the end of my sophomore year in college, not just to resolve my military service situation, but following a deeper calling I didn't yet understand.

During my time away in America, my mother had undergone her own spiritual transformation, becoming a Reiki practitioner. Her teacher—a woman who bridged the mystical worlds of Jewish mysticism and universal energy healing—would become the catalyst for my first Phoenix activation.

The initiation unfolded at sunset, with the Sea of Galilee gleaming like molten gold. Sitting beside my sister, whom I had only recently reunited with after six years, I felt time itself growing thin, as if the echoes of every miracle ever performed along these shores were alive in that very moment.

"The ancient ones are gathering," the Reiki Master smiled and said softly in Hebrew, placing her hands on my crown.

What happened next transcended ordinary experience. Energy began flowing through my hands as if an ancient circuit had been reconnected.

"Do you feel it too?" I asked my sister telepathically, our souls dancing with joy in wordless communion.

My hands began to pulse with a frequency I recognized from somewhere deep in my Soul's memory. Tears flowed freely as light codes and memories from other lifetimes as a healer, priestess, and shaman began to surface. For the first time, I could finally feel what it was like to be fully alive.

Those first months after my initiation were unforgettable—I couldn't keep my hands to myself! An overwhelming desire coursed through me to touch and connect with everything living. My fingers would brush against tree bark, rest on my cat's purring body, or reach out to hold someone's hand. Each touch felt electric, alive with possibility. The world had transformed into an endless web of energy connections, and I was finally awake to it all.

My journey brought me back to the United States, where Boston welcomed me with an unexpected gift—a remarkable Reiki practitioner who became my guide to Level 2. I found myself especially drawn to distance healing. There was something magical about sitting in my quiet room, eyes closed, sending healing energy across time and space to someone in need. It felt like painting with starlight. My years studying Japanese arts in college suddenly made perfect sense—they had been breadcrumbs leading me to this path all along. Yet even as I immersed myself in Reiki's gentle flow, something whispered that there was still more to discover.

The circle completed itself beautifully when I returned to Israel. In a moment I'll never forget, my mother's best friend—her eyes bright with pride and love—initiated me as a Reiki Master. But this wasn't an ending; it was just the beginning of my healing practice. The universe had bigger plans, leading me years later to Patrick Zeigler and the ancient power of Sekhem energy. When he helped awaken my Kundalini potential, I felt like a circuit finally completing itself. The cosmic energies weren't just brewing anymore, they were dancing.

A decade later, in my early thirties, everything I thought I knew about transformation was turned inside out. The jungle called to me in dreams, in whispers, in sudden urges I couldn't explain. First, Colombia opened its arms to me, then Peru. The sacred plant medicines spoke to me—not in words, but in visions and full-body knowing. Looking back, I see how the plants themselves orchestrated my death and rebirth, like master chemists of the soul. What had started as a curious explorer's tentative steps into the unknown became a full initiation into consciousness' deepest mysteries. The Phoenix didn't just rise, she soared.

In early 2012, I'll never forget that powerful ceremony in the Putumayo region of Colombia. My friend and I were the only gringos—the only white people—in the *maloka*, a sacred stage-like structure where the village gathered for ceremonies. The night air was thick with anticipation, the sweet smell of sage and tobacco hanging in the air. Local families—grandparents, parents, even children—sat in their usual spots. They had just eaten small fish caught in the river. This wasn't a spiritual hyped tourist experience; it was a deep jungle dive. We had spent days before the ceremony cooking the medicine with the village's local shaman.

The maloka was a perfect circle with a high conical roof that seemed to spiral up into the stars. Through the gaps in the palm-thatched ceiling, moonlight filtered down, creating patterns on the earthen floor. The jungle around us pulsed with life—insects chirping their ancient songs, night birds calling, the distant sound of the river carrying centuries of stories.

When I drank the medicine, the shaman's wife, a powerful healer in her own right, looked at me with knowing eyes and said in Spanish, "Grandmother has been waiting for you."

It wasn't my first time with the medicine. By then, I had already experienced many sacred ceremonies in New York and other villages in Colombia, but I couldn't know how prophetic her words would be.

As the medicine began to work, Grandmother Ayahuasca didn't ease me in gently.

"Remember," came Grandmother Ayahuasca's voice, "you've walked this path before."

"Trust," she whispered as I felt the blade at my neck as a Mayan shaman in Tikal, "death is just a doorway."

"See beyond," she urged as flames consumed me during witches' trials in medieval Europe, "to the eternal consciousness that moves between lives."

She took me straight into death itself—the experience of dying in multiple timelines simultaneously.

Each death Grandmother Ayahuasca showed me was completely real, felt in every cell of my being. Yet beyond the dying itself, she revealed something more profound - the luminous consciousness that exists between deaths, the eternal awareness that moves from life to life. Through these visions, death shed its fearsome mask and became a familiar doorway, not an ending but a passage into a new beginning.

"Your baby is new," the shamans would tell me with knowing smiles. "A first timer to Earth." As the world hummed with prophecies of the world ending in 2012, I found myself burning through old patterns and programs while that year a new life grew within me. My belly became its own ceremonial ground, a sacred space where death and rebirth danced together.

The journey at the end of year led me back to Tikal, where in another life I had died as a Mayan shaman and astrologer. The synchronicity was undeniable as I boarded the pilgrim buses heading toward December 21st. My pregnant form carried not just new life, but the completion of an ancient cycle.

"Here," our guide said, leading us to the old section of the park. "This is where the ancient ones communed with the stars."

I couldn't believe my eyes when they set up the Mayan ceremony directly in front of the temple where, in that past life, the sacrifice had taken place. I found this place only 8 months prior. My heart recognized the stones, my cells remembered the blade. But this time, instead of death, I carried life. Instead of ending, I embodied the beginning.

"The energies are strong here today," an elder commented, preparing the mushrooms and cacao as their ancestors had done. But what he couldn't see was the profound completion occurring - a soul returning to transform ancient trauma into a new possibility.

These three initiations wove together perfectly - the Galilee awakening with its activation of healing gifts, the jungle Grandmother Ayahuasca deaths with their revelation of eternal consciousness, and now these Mayan lands, where the past and future merged in my pregnant body. Each initiation taught me different aspects of the Phoenix mysteries, showing how death and rebirth dance together in an eternal spiral.

Standing there on the Mayan Temple, my hands cradling both my unborn child and ancient memories, I remembered my first lifetime on Earth as a High Priestess in Saqqara's temple, embodying Sekhmet's fierce compassion, working with Stargates that bridged dimensions. This was a quantum access point, teaching me how to integrate it all.

Now, facilitating Quantum healing sessions, I understand these stages as aspects of our multidimensional nature. This path from Scorpion to Eagle to Phoenix maps not just my personal journey but a universal evolution of consciousness.

That day in Tikal, as my baby danced within me and ancient memories stirred in the stones, I understood—every ending is a doorway, every death a passage to rebirth, and we are all eternal beings, learning to dance between the worlds.

Pregnant with New Frequency at Lake Atitlan in Guatemala January 1, 2013

Resurrection Process

Resurrection is not a single event but an ancient, ongoing process deeply understood by mystics and elders across time. They knew that to truly live, one must be willing to die many times—not in body, but in identity, belief, and attachment—so that something more aligned can emerge. These sacred deaths strip us down to essence, refining who we are and allowing us to remember our truth.

Think of all the times in your life when you have gone through this process. Those moments when everything seemed to be falling apart—when your world crumbled around you, when the version of yourself you once knew could no longer exist. And yet, looking back, you can see that each of those moments was a sacred initiation, stripping you down to your core so that you could rise again, more powerful than before.

Sometimes, resurrection process happens internally—a radical shift in the way you see yourself, your purpose, or the world. Other times, it manifests externally—a relationship that ends, a job that no longer aligns with your soul, a life chapter that you must leave behind. But whether internal or external, the lesson is the same: transformation is inevitable. The only question is whether we resist it or surrender to it.

We are conditioned to fear endings. We cling to the familiar, resist change, and mourn what we perceive as loss. But death—whether of an identity, a belief, a relationship, or a way of life—is never truly an ending. It is a threshold. A gateway into something new.

Everything on the other side of fear holds the promise of rebirth. Just as the Phoenix willingly surrenders to the flames, trusting that it will rise again, we, too, must embrace the cycles of death and renewal in our lives. The old must burn away for the new to emerge. The parts of us that no longer serve our highest path must dissolve so that we can step fully into who we are meant to become.

There is no final destination in this process, only deeper layers of unfolding. What feels like an ending is simply a temporary contraction, as a doorway to a greater transformation, an invitation to expand, to evolve, to create anew.

So, let go of the fear. Surrender to the fire. Trust that what lies beyond is exactly what your soul has been calling for.

Activation of Quantum Code ▲ Resurrection

This activation is designed to transmit the essence of the chapter as an energetic template—something you feel rather than analyze. By bypassing the thinking mind, it speaks directly to your body, energy field, and subconscious, allowing transformation to unfold on a deeper level.

◆ Begin Here: Set the Field

Find a quiet space. Light a candle if you feel called. Sit or lie comfortably with your spine aligned and your heart open. Close your eyes and take a few grounding breaths—in through your nose, out through your mouth. Let your body soften. Let your energy settle.

Bring your awareness to your heart space. Place your hands gently over your heart or simply focus your attention there. Feel the warmth between your palms and chest. Let it grow.

When you are ready, speak the following words aloud or silently within:

"I now open to release all that is blocking my highest good.

I open to grace, to clarity, to healing.

I activate and understand all that I need to move forward on my path with ease and flow.

I open to remember who I truly am."

Breathe that in. Let it ripple through your entire being.

◆ Activate the Quantum Code

Repeat these sacred Source Language words below three times aloud, allowing the vibration to move through your body and field:

SHA RA NI
YA VA KI NA SHA TA

Now read the following quantum transmission:

In the space between breaths
Where old selves dissolve to light
Like Phoenix in sacred fire
Like diamond under pressure
Like butterfly in chrysalis waiting
You are transformation's perfect art

Hold this truth eternal:
Through every dissolution
Through every sacred death
Through every void space falling
You are remembering

Each ending births beginning
Each death reveals more life
Each shadow holds new light
Each void fills with stars

For you are the eternal dance
Of ending and beginning
Of dying and becoming
Of dissolving and arising
Again and again and again

◇ ACTIVATION COMPLETE ◇

Sit in stillness. Allow the code to settle into your system. Feel the integration weaving into your cells, your field, your breath. Let the silence become your teacher.

♦ Ground & Center

Breathe deeply into your body. Imagine golden roots extending from the soles of your feet into the heart of the Earth. Feel the Earth holding you, anchoring you. You are safe.

Begin to gently move your fingers and toes. Wiggle. Stretch. Return fully to your body.

Grounding Contemplation

After activating the Quantum Code and grounding, stay rooted by taking time to notice what's shifting within. You might feel called to journal, draw, or simply sit in quiet awareness, allowing your inner wisdom to gently emerge.

Use the following questions as gateways to deeper insight. There is no need to rush or force answers. Let them move through you like waves.

1. Which phase of life are you in right now: Scorpion, Eagle, or Phoenix?
2. How have the "small deaths" in your life—your phoenix moments— led to your rebirth?
3. What lessons have emerged to support your evolution?
4. What gifts have your deepest wounds given you?
5. What transformation are you still afraid to allow?
6. What will it take to rise into the next version of your evolved self?

After exploring these questions, return to stillness. Let the wisdom integrate. If emotions rise, honor them. If symbols, images, or messages arise—record them. Don't censor what wants to come through.

◆ Integration
You may feel a deep shift after this activation and contemplation. Give yourself space to rest, reflect, and integrate. An audio version of this activation is available on my website if you'd like to revisit it.

Take your time. If today's experience stirred something profound, consider waiting a full day before moving on to the next chapter.

Integration is sacred. Let it unfold naturally.

Chapter 2
The Void and Abundant Co-Creation

"Out of nothing comes everything."
– Ancient Zen Saying

The weight of the Peruvian night settled around our ceremonial circle like a living presence, the jungle breathing with ancient wisdom. Sacred smoke—sage dancing with tobacco—spiraled upward, carrying messages between realms. As I lay on my woven mat, feeling Earth's heartbeat beneath me, Grandmother Ayahuasca's presence entered like moonlight seeping through the canopy of the forest.

"Let go," she whispered in the language of pure knowing, her directive piercing straight to my core. One by one, the threads of who I thought I was began unraveling. I watched as my roles and identities dissolved like morning mist—healer, teacher, daughter, woman—each one floating away until I found myself suspended in absolute nothingness.

"What am I supposed to do here?" I called out with what remained of my awareness.

"Nothing," came the response. "To create, you must first become comfortable with absolute nothingness."

In that infinite moment of revelation, the boundaries of my singular existence dissolved, and I witnessed the vast tapestry of the multiverse unfold before my consciousness. Like countless bubbles of light, I saw them—infinite versions of myself spread across countless universes, each one living, breathing, choosing, becoming. Each reality sparkled with its own unique frequency, telling stories of paths taken and paths forsaken.

I watched in awe as these myriad selves danced through their lives: in one reality, I am a hybrid Lyran on a planet called Avyon in Lyra; in another, I am a priestess in Atlantis, stabbed by her student; in yet another, leading spiritual retreats in the Mayan temples. Each version carried its own wisdom, its own struggles, its own triumphs. Together, they formed a magnificent constellation of variations of experiences, all contributing to the greater understanding of my soul's multidimensional journey. The energy required to maintain these parallel existences was staggering—each choice, each decision point, splitting reality into new branches, new possibilities, new lives.

Looking up from that space, I saw beyond the jungle canopy to where stellar light painted ancient stories across the sky. The infinite space between stars mirrored the vastness I found within, reflecting the quantum field of all possibilities. Beyond the visible cosmos, I sensed the dark matter holding galaxies together, the mysterious force behind black holes—all expressions of the infinite void.

Beneath this cosmic dance of possibilities, I witnessed something even more fundamental: the primordial moment of creation itself. I saw what alchemists called the Celestial Fire, Prima Materia, the First Matter, the Chaos—that which seems separate and different from ourselves but is One. "All from One", the First Law of Hermetics, would state.

I saw how the Void, the Source in its infinite wisdom, reflecting on itself, creates the first movement toward polarity. One is divided into Spirit and Matter. It split itself into two polarities, the primary forces of existence—the Divine Masculine and Divine Feminine, the Creator and Destroyer, the light and darkness, the hot and cold, the wet and dry, etc.

Divine Masculine emerged as the force of pure manifestation, the architect of form and structure in physical reality. I saw its presence in every crystal's geometric perfection, in mountains thrust skyward, in trees reaching determinedly toward sunlight. This was the active principle at work in every atom and molecule, giving direction and substance to the universe's dreams.

Yet it was the Divine Feminine that revealed itself most profoundly in my vision. Here was the Source itself—not an empty void, but an infinite womb of potential. I understood that this feminine energy was not merely passive but creative in its very receptivity. Through the feminine fixed energies of water and earth, it worked its transformative magic. Like water wearing away stone, like darkness birthing stars, it removed obstacles through embrace, transformed resistance through flow.

The elements themselves danced before me in their divine polarities:

🕉 The feminine water brought coolness, contraction, and mutability, a perfect mirror of the subconscious mind. Its sister element, earth, offered stability, rest, and solidity, manifesting as our physical form. Together, they embodied the feminine principles of nurture and foundation.

🕉 The masculine fire blazed with radiance, expansion, warmth, and light—the superconscious mind in its glory. Its brother element, air, moved with penetrating diffusion, representing the Self-Conscious mind. These masculine elements provided the spark and movement of creation.

In this sacred space, I encountered the Great Spider Woman, the Dark Mother, weaving her web of realities across all possible universes and potential selves. I witnessed the perfect harmony of these forces—masculine fire igniting creation, feminine water shaping and nurturing it into being.

She showed me the three primary forces through which Source creates: the Void, Sound vibration, and Light manifestation. These forces are not separate from us, they are the very essence of our being.

Alchemy of the Transformation

These elemental qualities revealed themselves as the vehicles of alchemical transformation, what the ancient mystics called Salt, Sulfur, and Mercury:

🕉 The *Alchemical Salt* manifests as the Body itself—the passive vehicle influenced by the fixed feminine energies of water and earth. Through it, the subconscious forces shape the various states of matter.

🕉 The *Alchemical Sulfur* showed itself as the Soul—the masculine principle of fire expressing consciousness, intellect, and true will. Here burned the brightness of the One, the Kundalini force, the vital intelligence of life itself.

🕉 The *Alchemical Mercury* appeared as Spirit—the vital life force, the prana. This subtle, spiritualized feminine aspect of the Source bridged higher and lower realms, connecting Soul and Body, Sulfur and Salt. Through it, the consciousness, directs life force through physical form.

In each Universe, in each reality, these forces continue their eternal dance of creation, their sacred interplay giving birth to all that was, is, and ever shall be.

From this vantage point, I could see how every choice, every decision in my myriad lives, was a collaboration between these fundamental forces. The masculine energy provided the drive to choose, to act, to manifest, while the feminine energy provided the field of possibilities, the space for transformation, the wisdom to let go and allow.

As the first light began to paint the eastern sky, one of the shamans settled beside me like a gentle shadow. "You've been very still," he observed in soft Spanish, his voice carrying the weight of generations of wisdom. "What did you see?"

I smiled, watching the stars fade as dawn approached. "I saw nothing... and everything," I whispered, knowing the inadequacy of words to capture the infinite. "I saw how we're all cosmic dreamers, shaping reality from the infinite potential of the Void. How our journey through the multiverse isn't just about accumulating experiences, but about learning to balance and honor the primary forces within ourselves."

He nodded with the deep understanding of one who had traveled to these inner spaces many times before. "Ah, la nada.." - noting that is everything is nothing. This is where all power comes from.

As I floated in this space of infinite potential, I understood that each of us carries both energies within us, regardless of our physical form. We are all children of both the fire and the water, the light and the darkness, the form and the Void.

In every version of reality, this truth remains constant: creation begins in the void, in the fertile darkness of infinite potential, where everything and nothing coexist in perfect harmony. It is from this sacred space that we draw our power to create, to transform, to become.

▎The Return to Unity

All of existence emerges from the infinite true Void not through imperfection or flaw, but through a sacred sequence of what the ancient masters called "distortions." These distortions are fragmentation of the Source, the necessary transformations through which pure, undifferentiated consciousness takes form and explores itself.

The sequence unfolds with profound precision: first emerges *Free Will*, that initial stirring that moves consciousness from absolute unity into the possibility of choice and experience. This primary distortion creates the foundation for all that follows. Next flows *Love/Logos*, the creative force that holds within it the seeds of all manifestation. Finally comes *Light*, the vibration that gives form and structure to love's creative impulse, allowing consciousness to experience itself in infinite variations.

Through years of practice and contemplation, I began to recognize that the state of *Samadhi* described in ancient yogic texts was far more than a mere experience of transcendent bliss. Rather, it represented a profound dissolution of these very distortions conscious return to the original unity from which all things emerge. In deep Samadhi, the walls we build around our individual identity begin to crumble. The perceived separation between observer and observed, between self and cosmos, gradually dissolves until only pure awareness remains.

Yet this dissolution reveals a beautiful paradox: the very distortions we transcend in Samadhi serve an essential purpose in the cosmic dance. They are the tools through which the Source, or what some refer to as the Infinite Creator, experiences endless variations, each distortion adding new dimensions to the grand exploration of consciousness. Our journey through these layers of creation is not a mistake to be corrected, but a sacred evolution to be embraced.

The path to Samadhi emphasizes the profound importance of *surrender*—an active release of everything we believe ourselves to be. We must let go not only of our thoughts and emotions, but even of our most cherished spiritual aspirations. In this space of complete surrender, we touch the quantum field of pure potential, where all possibilities exist simultaneously. Here, we transcend the wheel of karmic Samsara, not by rejecting existence, but by embracing it fully from a place of deeper understanding.

Our true nature is as beings of pure creative force. Like a perfect mirror covered in dust, our essential radiance remains untouched by the accumulation of experiences and traumas throughout lifetimes. What we perceive as limitations, struggles, and imperfections are not flaws in our being but temporary veils, waiting to be gently lifted as we awaken to our true nature.

This is why ancient texts often describe Samadhi not as a state of becoming something new, but as a profound *Remembering* of what we have always been. In the Void, we are Infinite Creators, inseparable from the cosmic whole and the sacred dance of manifestation that makes up all existence. Through this memory, we reclaim our innate power and align ourselves with the eternal rhythm of creation and dissolution.

After touching these depths of being, we return to engage with the transformed world. The distortions no longer appear as obstacles to be overcome, but as perfect expressions of unity taking form. We participate fully in existence while remaining established in our true nature. What was once seen as separation becomes recognized as connection; what appeared as limitation reveals itself as a focused expression of the infinite.

To honor the Void is to honor the creative force of the Universe itself, awakening to the infinite potential that has always resided within us. The journey of Samadhi reveals that what we seek has never been lost—only temporarily forgotten in the grand play of cosmic evolution. As the layers of distortion gradually dissolve, we discover that enlightenment is not a destination, but a return to unity that has always been our true home.

▌The Game of Consciousness

"I can see it all so clearly now," Susan whispered during a deep Quantum Healing session, her voice filled with wonder.

"We're not random beings stumbling through life. We're conscious players who chose to be here... who chose these specific bodies, these exact circumstances. Each life, each circumstance, each challenge is not random but consciously chosen for the experience and Soul growth it offers.

But what most don't realize is that this game comes with hidden background programs—operating quietly in the shadows, influencing our choices, our perceptions, even our thoughts. These scripts, coded into the game of consciousness, and are not revealed upfront. The developers—whoever they may be—don't hand us a user manual. Instead, we're left to discover the deeper mechanics on our own. And that's by design."

The Higher Self or Subconscious serves as the bridge between our earthly experience and our infinite, multidimensional nature. It acts as a gateway to profound wisdom and healing, revealing reality as far more fluid and interconnected than our everyday perception suggests. Through this bridge, we can access the deeper truth of our existence—not just that we are players in this grand game, but that the game itself has layers of hidden mechanics that affect our ability to level up.

The moment we incarnate into the Earth game, we unknowingly inherit a system that is already running multiple background programs—scripts embedded deep within our Subconscious, shaping our perceptions, decisions, and limitations.

Imagine stepping into a new game, eager to play, only to find your character glitching. The controls feel sluggish. The screen lags. Every action takes more effort than it should.

Why? Because your character is running too many programs at once—as if you've opened 50 browser tabs in your mind, all draining your processing power. Most players don't even realize these hidden scripts exist, yet they govern thought patterns, emotional reactions, and physical health.

Conscious Player choosing to incarnate on Earth (Image by Diana Divine)

These background programs include:

ॐ **Unresolved emotional wounds** – looping past experiences that drain energy in real-time.

ॐ **Distractions & attachments** – habits, relationships, or behaviors that keep the character from advancing.

ॐ **Self-doubt programs** – unconscious scripts running the belief that *"I'm not good enough"* or *"I must struggle to succeed."*

ॐ **Societal overlays** – default conditioning imposed by external systems, telling the character what is *real*, *possible*, or *acceptable*.

When too many of these programs run at once, the character starts lagging—reaction time slows, focus diminishes, and overall performance weakens. Most people go through life in this state without realizing it.

The way out? Self-Mastery also referred here as Quantum Mastery.

It is the process of clearing old programs, closing unnecessary tabs, and upgrading your internal operating system. It's not just about healing—it's about leveling up and unlocking entirely new dimensions of play.

When you clear emotional baggage, break free from outdated belief systems, and remove distractions, the game runs smoother. Suddenly, you have sharper reflexes, heightened intuition, and a greater ability to create your own reality.

The most advanced players understand that:

🕉 Becoming conscious of the background programs is the first step.

🕉 Clearing unnecessary processing frees up energy for higher-level abilities.

🕉 Refining skills like energy manipulation, lucid dreaming, and timeline shifting changes how reality responds.

🕉 The game can be hacked once you understand its mechanics.

The moment a player wakes up to the hidden architecture of reality, the rules begin to bend. And the more mastery a player gains, the more hidden levels become available.

We are going through the "character selection screen of existence." Susan's hands moved as if navigating through invisible options as she spoke:

"It's the most sophisticated system imaginable. Before coming here, we review different possible lives like reading character descriptions. I can see myself choosing this lifetime, this body, these challenges... and I was so excited about it!"

"Excited?" I asked, noting the surprise in her voice.

"Yes! It's like... imagine choosing the most challenging level in a game, not because you're being punished, but because you've graduated the other levels, and this one offers the greatest opportunity for growth."

"Earth is just one server, one gaming realm," she continued. "There are countless others, each with its own physics engine, its own rules of play. There are at least 12 other realms I could have gone to. I have to say, I didn't fully know what I volunteered for or that I'd completely forget how to exit the Earthly game, but that was the risk."

The veil of forgetting. The most elaborate design choice in this reality.

Not only do we forget we're in a game, but we also enter a system where external forces attempt to keep us unaware. This is why awakening isn't automatic. The game developers—whether higher-dimensional architects, cosmic administrators, or unseen entities with their own agendas—did not make it easy.

Answers are buried. The mechanics are hidden. And just when you begin to question reality, the system throws distractions, false paths, and disinformation to keep you from remembering who you are.

"What makes Earth's realm unique?" I asked.

"The parameters here are fascinating," she replied, speaking from a deep theta state. "Linear time, physical density, polarity dynamics... It's like choosing to play in 'hard mode' because the rewards for consciousness growth are so profound. But I could have chosen an easier mode somewhere else."

Susan's Higher Self-continued sharing her experience of accessing what I call the "cosmic lobby" - the space between incarnations:

"It's like being in the most amazing control room," she described. "You can see all possible lives, all potential experiences. And you choose with such joy, such anticipation for the adventure ahead."

Tears welled in her eyes. "That explains so much about my life choices," she said. "Even the hardest parts were... selected."

But here's what's often overlooked—just because we select our life parameters it doesn't mean we see all the hidden mechanics.

There are scripts that activate the moment we enter—karmic loops, emotional imprints, generational codes. And then there are the game managers—forces that intervene when a player starts to wake up too much, too fast.

"The veil of forgetting is brilliant," she exclaimed. "It's like... imagine if you went to see a movie already knowing every plot twist. The experience wouldn't be as impactful. We forget here so we can fully immerse ourselves in this reality. I knew the design of the game, but how I'd play would be a mystery until I got here."

And that's exactly the trick.

"And what about the physical embodiment?" I asked.

"That's another masterful aspect," she replied. "By choosing these dense physical forms, we get to experience creation at its most concrete level. It's the ultimate virtual reality setup. However, it's important to wake up and become a conscious player in the game. Otherwise, you're just another NPC—a non-player character."

This is the hidden truth of Earth's game: most people are playing on autopilot, running default programs without questioning them. They are fully immersed, unaware of the larger mechanics at play.

But those who wake up—who learn to spot the background scripts, who begin to rewrite their reality—gain access to something greater. They shift from unconscious participants to conscious creators. And once enough players awaken, the very fabric of the game begins to change.

The game doesn't force anyone to wake up. Some players remain in repetitive cycles, running the same background programs for lifetimes. Others begin the process of self-mastery, learning to debug their consciousness, upgrade their abilities, and unlock entirely new dimensions of play.

The choice is always yours: remain lost in the illusion, or become the coder of your own experience.

And for those who choose the latter... a whole new game begins.

Ancestral Light

As beings of pure light, we haven't fallen from grace or become damaged, as the perpetual program of victim/victimizer often makes us believe. Instead, we've chosen to experience limitations for the sacred purpose of evolution. This truth revealed itself to me most powerfully during a profound healing session with Maria, a woman who had carried the weight of generations of female trauma in her DNA.

Maria came to me after decades of therapy, still bearing the invisible wounds of ancestral pain. Her grandmother had been a victim of domestic violence, her mother had struggled with addiction, and she herself carried a deep sense of unworthiness that seemed to echo through time. The pattern of female suffering ran so deep in her lineage that it felt like an unbreakable curse.

During our session, as she entered the deep relaxed quantum field, something extraordinary began to unfold. The room itself seemed to fill with a presence—not just her ancestors, but what she later described as "the original light of creation." I watched as waves of recognition moved through her body, each breath bringing her closer to something ancient and pure within herself.

"I can see them," she whispered, her voice filled with wonder. "My grandmother, my mother, all the women in my line... they're not broken either. They're standing in their light, showing me who we really are."

Tears streamed down her face as she accessed this "original blueprint" - the divine template of her being and her ancestors that existed before any trauma. She was remembering her original purpose, the reason she chose to come to this denser 3D reality game.

As the creator force moved through her, I witnessed decades of pain and limitation dissolving like mist in the morning sun. Her ancestors, far from being sources of trauma, revealed themselves as a line of light beings who had chosen to experience limitations for the purpose of evolution. They stood around her now in a circle of light, cheering as she reclaimed not just her own power but the divine feminine strength of her entire lineage.

"They're showing me," she said, her voice trembling with emotion, "that every experience, even the painful ones, was chosen by me and my ancestors for soul growth. The trauma wasn't a punishment or a curse—it was a doorway back to remembering our true nature."

The most powerful moment came when she accessed herself as a young child, before any conditioning had taken root. In that space of pure innocence, she saw herself running in a field of sunflowers, giggling with the pure joy of her essence. The creator force wasn't something she needed to learn or acquired was her natural state of being, the truth of who she had always been. She was making beautiful head pieces with the flowers and gifting them to the members of her family.

"I was just forgetting who I am. We all were. Every woman in my line— we were all just forgetting our light."

The creator force isn't always about becoming something new, it's about remembering who we've always been and aligning to that vibrational state. The women in Maria's lineage hadn't failed or fallen—they had volunteered to carry part of the collective feminine wound so that future generations could remember their light. Through Maria, a whole line of ancestors was liberated, their experiences transformed from trauma to sacred initiation.

Dissolving Ancient Battle Armor

Leonard Cohen's famous words in Anthem ring true: *"There is a crack in everything, that's how the light gets in."* Most spiritual seekers chase only the light, focusing solely on creation while fearing or avoiding destruction—the shadows. But I've come to understand a profound truth: creation and destruction are two faces of the same divine force, distorted from the Void, dancing eternally in the quantum field.

Think of a forest fire that clears dead undergrowth, making way for new life, or the way a caterpillar must completely dissolve inside its chrysalis before becoming a butterfly. Nature teaches us that destruction isn't the opposite of creation, it's an essential part of the creative process.

Imagine this process like unpeeling the layers of an onion. With each layer that is revealed and released, we are destroying what no longer serves us, allowing the light to shine through once more until we get to the core. The cracks in our being, the perceived flaws and imperfections, are in fact the gateways through which our true radiance can emerge.

What appears in our lives as trauma, limitation, and pain isn't damage that needs healing. These are distortions in our energy field, like frozen light and knots of energy that have collected across lifetimes—on Earth and off Earth—waiting to be dissolved back into pure potential. They're not wounds to fix, but crystallized experiences ready to return to their original state of pure consciousness.

Among the most profound demonstrations of this truth was through working with Michael, a veteran whose story illuminates how deeply we can fortify our hearts across lifetimes of warrior type of incarnations. His journey reveals how the destroyer force works not through battle, but through recognition and surrender.

Michael came to me carrying what he called "the weight of a thousand battles." A decorated soldier, he had excelled in combat but struggled to connect in civilian life.

"It's like I left my heart in the war zone," he told me during our first meeting, his eyes carrying that distant look I've come to recognize in warriors. "I'm afraid to feel anything because I might feel everything."

During our healing session, as Michael entered a deep theta state, his body tensed suddenly. It was clear he had built a formidable heart wall, an energetic shield over his heart space—a fortress forged through lifetimes of incarnations.

"Around my heart—it's like military-grade armor. Multiple layers, built for maximum protection," he said, his voice tight with recognition. "Some of it is from this life, from combat... but some of it is ancient. Really ancient."

Michael witnessed the construction of his heart's fortification through time. He saw himself in modern combat, adding layers with each fallen brother, each impossible decision, each moment of having to shut down emotion to survive. But then the timeline expanded, and we moved through his past lives.

"I'm seeing myself as a Roman centurion," he shared, his voice filled with awe as he described different phases of that life. Then he experienced himself as a medieval knight, a samurai, a World War I soldier. In each life, he added more protection. Each battle, each loss, each moment of having to choose duty over feeling—it all became part of the armor.

Michael's heart armor was part of his warrior's path across time. He began to understand that his emotional armoring wasn't a mistake or a weakness—it had been necessary protection for a soul who chose a certain warrior's path lifetime after lifetime.

"Each layer holds more than just my pain," he realized after our session. "It holds the collective weight of all warriors. The impossible choices. The brothers lost. The humanity we had to suppress to do our duty. But it's not actually trauma—it's frozen light. Frozen honor. Frozen love."

As I helped recalibrate Michael's geometry and ran Quantum Attunement and Crystalline Soul Healing templates on him, the destroyer clearing force moved through each layer with extraordinary precision. Modern combat armor dissolved into light. Ancient battlefield grief transformed into wisdom. The frozen rage of centuries became pure power. The steeled heart of the warrior melted into compassion.

Many of us have a *Heart Wall* just like Michael, a wall we have built due to being misunderstood or hurt in one way or another. But at the core of the onion there is "the original warrior heart" - the pure essence of the warrior spirit before it needed armoring.

"It was never about becoming hard," he said, trembling and allowing himself to be vulnerable for the first time in years. "The true warrior heart is absolutely open, absolutely vulnerable, and absolutely powerful. We added the armor because we weren't ready for that much truth."

As the final layers dissolved, Michael experienced what he later described as "coming home to my heart." Not by rejecting his warrior nature, but by understanding its deepest truth.

"A warrior's greatest strength isn't in the ability to shut down feeling, it's in the capacity to feel everything and still stand."

The war isn't always on the battlefield—it can exist in everyday living in the density of 3D. When we allow the destroyer force to move through these layers, it reveals that beneath every hardened warrior heart lies an ocean of compassion.

Now, when clients come to me speaking of emotional numbness or disconnection, I understand we're not working with broken warriors who need fixing, but with sacred hearts waiting to reclaim their original power. The creator and destroyer forces simply remind us that even the strongest battle armor is made of the same light it was designed to protect.

Echoes of Atlantis

The invitation arrived like a whisper from the past – a chance to visit Sao Miguel Island in the Azores, Portugal where my dear friend had started to build a sanctuary in 2023 within an ancient volcano's crater. As the plane descended toward the island, I pressed my face against the window, taking in the dramatic coastline where deep blue waters met weathered cliffs. These peaks rising from the Atlantic Ocean, I believe are the mountain tops of the sunk Atlantis itself, my first earthly home where I chose to incarnate from the Andromeda Constellation. This was supported by my research as a large pyramid structure has been found off the coast of Sao Miguel and Terceira islands.

In that first great civilization, we understood the fundamental principles of creation and abundance in ways that modern humanity has yet to rediscover. Through our advanced crystal technologies and deep spiritual wisdom, we could manifest directly from the quantum field. There was no scarcity, no lack—we lived in perfect harmony with the natural world, achieving technological and spiritual advances that would seem like magic today.

Our temples housed vast crystal arrays that could heal any ailment, and our meditation chambers allowed direct communication with higher-dimensional beings. We had mastered clean, free energy and could manipulate matter at will, creating whatever we needed from the pure potential of the Void.

Ancient Pyramid found underwater between Azores Sao Miguel and Terceira Island

The volcanic stones beneath my feet seemed to hum with these memories as I explored the sanctuary my friend had built. We conducted a beautiful planting ceremony in her garden with a few other women visiting at the same time. As they chanted and drummed, I deposited with intention an earth grid crystal device under a blooming fig tree on the overlooking hill. This was just one of many crystal devices I've been on a mission to plant in the last 12 years as part of my Earth gridwork. This is what we did back in Atlantis—we knew how to create containers of energy, establishing sacred points that would form an interconnected web of crystalline frequency across the planet.

Each experience at the Azores brought up new fragments of remembrance from that advanced civilization, where I first chose to incarnate on Earth. In Atlantis, we understood that abundance wasn't about hoarding resources but about maintaining a perfect flow with the Infinite Source of all creation. Our society had no need for money or material competition. Everyone lived in prosperity because we understood that limitation was an illusion.

I spent my first days adjusting to the island's rhythm, but fate had more in store. At the thermal pools, where steam rose like ancient breaths from the Earth, I met a local practitioner, Nino, whose almond eyes held that unmistakable gleam of a fellow seeker. There was something familiar about him—perhaps a soul I'd known in those distant Atlantean days, when we would gather in similar pools for our spiritual practices and healing ceremonies. When he began leading our small group through water yoga, our bodies moving in harmony with the mineral-rich waters, I felt like a baby cradled in peace and serenity.

Our small group was so touched by the experience in the thermal water that they asked Nino and me to conduct an impromptu sound healing and mushroom medicine ceremony that same evening. Even though we barely knew each other, I felt confident in just going with the flow. We set up Nino's sound instruments outside in the garden, and the magic followed. I was guided all the way to the specific instrument, listening to what Nino was playing and how the elements were expressing themselves.

As a microdose of mushroom medicine began to activate, the island's presence grew stronger. The volcanic heart beneath us seemed to beat in time with my own, each pulse a reminder of the living nature of this ancient land that once hosted great Atlantean temples, where we conducted our most powerful manifestation ceremonies.

The first strike of his gong rippled not just through the air, but through the very fabric of reality, reminiscent of the harmonic frequencies we once used in Atlantis to maintain our connection with the Source field. The local birds responded, their calls weaving into resonant tones in a way that felt orchestrated by something greater than chance. Earth and sky were speaking to each other, and I was witnessing their dialogue.

Feeling like at Home in Atlantis, Sao Miguel - Azores Island

Then came the moment that transformed my understanding forever. In a flash of pristine clarity, I witnessed the first ripple of creation itself, the initial disturbance in the infinite Void that birthed all existence. It was like watching the first raindrop strike a still lake, except this lake was the canvas of reality itself.

My spirit council gathered close, their presence both gentle and electric. "Watch carefully," they communicated, their words bypassing my ears and flowing directly into my consciousness. "This is how worlds are born."

The vision that followed was beyond anything I could have prepared for. Galaxies blossomed like flowers in an infinite garden, each one spinning into being with perfect precision. Stars burst into existence, their first light piercing the primordial darkness like countless matchsticks struck simultaneously. Planets condensed from cosmic dust, each one a unique expression of infinite possibility.

This was the same creative force we had learned to work with in Atlantis—the pure potential from which all things emerge.

Yet through all this magnificent creation, the Void remained unchanged. It was the eternal container, the womb of existence itself. I watched in awe as it breathed with cosmic inhales drawing in light and matter, cosmic exhales birthing new realities. This Void was an uncharted dark space but not empty, it was pregnant with all potential, all possibility, all that was or ever could be. In Atlantis, we understood that abundance and creation were not about forcing or struggling but about aligning with this infinite source.

This was the secret that had made Atlantis so abundant: the understanding that creation doesn't come from forcing or struggling, but from aligning with the infinite potential that exists in space between all things.

Days later, sitting with my new friend, I shared the vision. "Now you understand why the ancients said all power comes from the Void," he said, his words building a bridge between ancient wisdom and my direct experience. "It's not about adding something - it's about creating space for the infinite to express itself through you in every present moment."

The truth of his words resonated deeply. There on those mystical islands, those last remnants of my first earthly home, I had glimpsed something that transcended time and space. The Void wasn't something to fear – it was the source of all creation, an infinite wellspring of possibility. This was the secret that had made Atlantis so abundant: the understanding that creation doesn't come from forcing or struggling, but from aligning with the infinite potential that exists in space between all things. Perhaps humanity is ready once again to remember these ancient truths about the infinite nature of creation and abundance that we once knew so well.

Abundant Co-Creation

Lisa came to me struggling with a chronic scarcity mindset despite her material success. During our session, she accessed what I call the "abundance frequency."

"Oh my God," she gasped. "I've been playing it all wrong. Abundance isn't something to chase... it's what we ARE. I can feel it now—this limitless flow, this endless creative force."

"What's different about this state?" I asked.

"Everything is sacred," she replied. "The morning coffee, the sunset, even paying bills—it's all divine play. I've been so focused on getting it done that I forgot about just being."

"I used to think creativity was about being an artist, but I'm not an artist," she continued. "Now I understand it's about allowing the infinite to flow through us in unique ways. We're not creating so much as channeling creation itself."

"I see now that every moment is an opportunity for mastery," she said. "Making breakfast for my kids isn't just a chore—it's an act of divine creation. Every interaction is a chance to express the infinite abundance in unique ways."

"And the challenges?" I asked.

"Those are chosen missions!" she laughed. "Even my teenager's rebellion is part of the game we agreed to play together. Seeing it this way changes everything."

"We're like waves thinking we're separate from the ocean," she explained. "All this seeking, this struggling... It's part of the game of remembering we are the ocean itself. It's all an exchange of energy. Every challenge is just another way to experience our infinite nature through finite form."

The wisdom that comes through these sessions consistently points to the same truth: we are not victims of circumstance but conscious players in an Infinite Creator game.

As one client beautifully expressed:

"Each lifetime is like attending an incredibly immersive theater production. We're both the actors and the audience, the writers and the directors. And in the space between lives, we gather to discuss what we've learned and plan our next grand adventure."

I've watched clients witness their own patterns across centuries, communicate with aspects of themselves from different eras, and facilitate healing that affects entire ancestral lines. The void state reveals that time is not a barrier to healing—it's a living field through which healing can propagate in all directions.

When we truly understand this, healing takes on an entirely new dimension. We're not fixing what's broken, we're remembering our innate wholeness and allowing everything else to dissolve back into the infinite potential of who we really are. The Void becomes our greatest ally—the space where all possibilities exist and where healing is not just possible but inevitable when we simply allow ourselves to rest in its embrace.

This understanding transforms how we approach every aspect of life. As Lisa reflected in our final integration session:

"Now when I face challenges, I don't ask, 'Why is this happening to me?' Instead, I ask, 'What did I come here to learn? What masterpiece am I creating through this experience?'"

The matrix construct we find ourselves in is multi-layered and intricate, containing numerous overlapping games playing out simultaneously across different dimensions of reality, each with its own hierarchies, agendas, and strategic dynamics.

The key to sovereignty lies in conscious awareness—recognizing where we stand within these interwoven layers of reality and understanding that we have the power to choose which games we participate in.

This remembrance of our true nature as sovereign creators allows us to step back from unconscious participation in dynamics that no longer serve our highest evolution. From this awakened perspective, we can engage with the Void—the field of infinite potential—from which we can consciously create and shape our experience.

Activation of Quantum Code ▲ Creation

This activation is designed to transmit the essence of the chapter as an energetic template—something you feel rather than analyze. By bypassing the thinking mind, it speaks directly to your body, energy field, and subconscious, allowing transformation to unfold on a deeper level.

◆ Begin Here: Set the Field

Find a quiet space. Light a candle if you feel called. Sit or lie comfortably with your spine aligned and your heart open. Close your eyes and take a few grounding breaths—in through your nose, out through your mouth. Let your body soften. Let your energy settle.

Bring your awareness to your heart space. Place your hands gently over your heart, or simply focus your attention there. Feel the warmth between your palms and chest. Let it grow.

When you are ready, speak the following words aloud or silently within:

"I now open to release all that is blocking my highest good.

I open to grace, to clarity, to healing.

I activate and understand all that I need to move forward on my path with ease and flow.

I open to remember who I truly am."

Breathe that in. Let it ripple through your entire being.

◆ Activate the Quantum Code

Repeat these sacred Source Language words below three times aloud, allowing the vibration to move through your body and field:

SHUM BA
TI I KA NA

Now read the following quantum transmission:

From void's depths Spider Grandmother spins her threads,
Dreamcatcher supreme, her web sprawls space.
Threads of matter, threads of light,
Weaving patterns, infinite and bright.

All beings dance within her grace,
Precious progeny, each holds a place.
She catches dreams, scatters starlight's gleams,
Through us her visions find their seams.

Void born equation, ever unbound,
No strand unsound,
Each thread leads home, the in-between,
Where light and shadow intertwine, serene.

Ancient creatrix, cosmos calls,
Play the sacred game, heed creation's pulse.
We are her fingers, her eyes that see,
Weavers of the tapestry.

Light, shadow, void, and flame's bright dance
Through us her story finds new expanse.

◇ ACTIVATION COMPLETE ◇

Sit in stillness. Allow the code to settle into your system. Feel the integration weaving into your cells, your field, your breath. Let the silence become your teacher.

◆ Ground & Center

Breathe deeply into your body. Imagine golden roots extending from the soles of your feet into the heart of the Earth. Feel the Earth holding you, anchoring you.

You are safe. You are protected. You are loved.

Begin to gently move your fingers and toes. Wiggle. Stretch. Return fully to your body.

Grounding Contemplation

After activating the Quantum code and grounding, stay rooted by taking time to notice what's shifting within. You might feel called to journal, draw, or simply sit in quiet awareness, allowing your inner wisdom to gently emerge. Use the following questions as gateways to deeper insight. There is no need to rush or force answers. Let them move through you like waves.

1. What is the void of creation for you? Are you comfortable stepping into the unknown?
2. What patterns are you finally ready to release (i.e., scarcity mindset)?
3. What resistances are you acknowledging?
4. Are you open to being in a state of allowing and receiving?
5. What new patterns and timelines would you like to weave?
6. What does abundance mean for you? Are you ready to step into abundant co-creation?

After exploring these questions, return to silence. Let the wisdom integrate. If emotions rise, honor them. If symbols, images, or messages arise—record them. Don't censor what wants to come through.

Then, say this declaration out loud three times and feel it resonating in your body:

"I am here to receive. I am here to claim my sacred abundance"

◆ Integration

You may feel a deep shift after this activation and contemplation. Give yourself space to rest, reflect, and integrate.

Each morning as you start your day and gaze in the mirror at your reflection, repeat the abundance declaration.

An audio version of this activation is available on my website if you'd like to revisit it.

Take your time. If today's experience stirred something profound, consider waiting a full day before moving on to the next chapter.
Integration is sacred. Let it unfold naturally.

Chapter 3
The Galactic Origins

> *"This life may be compared to playing one instrument
> in a large orchestra. Naturally you cannot play all the instruments
> at the same time. You can only focus on your part of the beautiful
> symphony, although the entire orchestra and all the music
> comprises the totality of who you really are."*
>
> **— Dolores Cannon**

When we say "we are remembering", it is the process that is more than just recalling events - it's accessing the deeper wisdom stored within our Soul's records, an aspect of what ancient Indian philosophy calls the Akasha, the fundamental "ether" that pervades and contains all elements and forces in the universe. These records contain the complete history of our Soul's journey, including wisdom, experiences, and knowledge accumulated across time. While the mind processes information through logic and linear thinking, the heart acts as a portal - a bridge between our physical experience and deeper realms of consciousness. When we attempt to access soul memories through mental effort alone, we often hit barriers, as the mind's tendency to analyze and rationalize can interfere with the natural flow of remembrance.

When we learn to quiet our mental chatter and shift our awareness from head to heart through practices like deep breathing, meditation, or simply bringing attention to the heart space, we create an opening for true remembrance. Through this opening, wisdom flows naturally, unrestricted by mental filters, manifesting as intuitive hunches, déjà vu experiences, or sudden clarity that feels both novel and somehow familiar. This heart-centered remembering is experiential rather than conceptual, arriving as a sudden knowing that bypasses logical reasoning, a deep resonance with truth that affects us physically and emotionally, or a sense of remembering something we've always known but had forgotten.

The heart doesn't need to analyze or verify - it simply knows, which is why profound insights often come when we're in states of openness and receptivity rather than mental concentration. By quieting the mental chatter, trusting our intuitive feelings, and allowing insights to emerge naturally rather than forcing them through mental effort, we can access the living wisdom that's always been part of our soul's journey. Each time we tap into these records through the heart portal, we're not learning something new but rather remembering ancient wisdom encoded within us, helping us release outdated patterns and embrace fresh possibilities while staying grounded in our eternal knowing.

The memories I'm about to share with you feel like scenes from a distant galaxy - the kind you might see in Star Wars, but these are my own lived experiences. I know this might sound wild, and that's okay. Some of you will feel a deep recognition while others might think I've watched too many space movies. I get it - I've been there too. **Stay open and curious** as you read, notice what stirs something inside you, what feels familiar in ways you can't quite explain. By the time we reach the end of this chapter, I'll share some ways you can gently explore your own memories that might be tucked away in the corners of your consciousness.

Remembering the Galactic Journey

Within the depths of my soul's memory lies an ancient imprint, a cosmic journey that began in another universe, passed through the Andromeda Galaxy, and spanned 2.5 million light years as consciousness made its magnificent descent into the Milky Way. This journey was a profound soul migration that few beings undertook—carrying advanced wisdom and creative potential across the galactic bridges.

The importance of reconnecting with our galactic origins cannot be overstated. Through my work with spiritual seekers and my own awakening experiences, I've discovered that these memories are fundamental to achieving Quantum Mastery and full consciousness activation. While some may view these galactic memories as mere imprints from the Akashic records, they carry vital light codes and wisdom that unlock our infinite creative potential.

I believe we are created from the Void, and we return to the Void. But perhaps there are traumas we can heal that block us from expanding. We might not remember all the pieces, but I believe those who go down the rabbit hole to connect to their greater galactic aspects will gain a higher perspective of themselves and their soul mission.

My own dramatic awakening to these cosmic memories began in 2015, when I met my twin flame, now my husband. This union catalyzed the opening of dimensional doorways, culminating in a profound Ayahuasca ceremony in Vermont. There, I encountered Spider Grandmother again—a meeting that marked my graduation from using the medicine into what I call now - Galactic Shamanism.

As the sacred medicine flowed through my being, time itself became fluid, its rigid boundaries dissolving into a cosmic river of infinite possibility.

"Do you really see it now?" my Higher Self whispered, as past, present, and future merged into a singular eternal moment. In this expanded state, I accessed not just Earth memories, but remembered vast journeys across universes and galaxies, like reading a cosmic diary written in pure light.

From the silent Void, I watched how the Divine ancient creatrix nimble fingers spin threads of matter and consciousness, expanding and weaving her web across the infinite expanse. She gazed through my eyes, her consciousness merging with mine.

"Play the game," she whispered, her voice resonating through the dimensions. "Heed creation's pulse."

In that moment, I felt myself becoming an extension of her creative force—my fingers becoming hers, plasmatic threads interconnected as my vision expanded to encompass the cosmic weaves.

As medicine reached its crescendo, my awareness soared beyond earthly limitations. I witnessed galaxies unfurling across the cosmic tapestry, my consciousness drawn particularly to the magnificent spiral of Andromeda spinning in its eternal dance. Within that boundless expanse, dormant memories awakened. I remembered my role among those who carried the sacred legacy of Andromedan high frequencies, my soul a living embodiment of multidimensional energies spanning myriad universes.

I realized that my soul mission is vaster than any single consciousness could comprehend. Through the veils of memory and an Akashic reading by

Debbie Solaris, a renowned Galactic Historian, I gained a clearer picture of the so-called game of consciousness that has been woven. This galactic saga might resonate for you as well.

We Came From Another Universe

We had ventured into this alternate Universe to mend what was broken, to heal wounds that echoed from another reality entirely. In that distant universe, I witnessed the clash between radiant Avian light beings and fierce Draco-Dragon beings, as their ancient conflict tore reality's fabric.

In our desperation to restore harmony in our Universe, as Avian light beings, we crafted advanced portal technology, thinking we could return these warring forces to the Source of Unity consciousness. But instead of returning to the Source, the Draco beings crossed into this Universe—the very realm where humanity now finds itself incarnated.

When this truth dawned upon us, I was among the few universal beings who volunteered to mend our mistake, journeying first to the Andromeda galaxy through similar portal technology. Initially, we attempted to create a new life there, crafting stars and planets, but discovered that Andromeda's frequency was too high for physical manifestation.

This led us to weave Andromeda's celestial frequencies into the Milky Way galaxy, creating a resonance between these galactic sisters that would one day culminate in their physical merger—an event astronomers now predict will occur in 4.6 billion years.

For you see, this Milky Way galaxy was but a mirror construct of our Andromedan reality, a 12th/13th dimensional game of physicality, where we could experience embodiment in ways our higher-dimensional selves could not.

We were the advanced pioneering founding team of Avian light beings, the frequency holders tasked with initiating the harmonization process. Billions of years before the physical merger would occur, we ventured forth to lay the groundwork, blending our luminescent essence with the new worlds we would encounter and build.

This was part of the distortion game of consciousness, a necessary evolution to build the light counterforce. Our role as Universal architects, we knew would one day resonate across the vast expanse. We were the frequency keepers, the light beings charged with ushering a new era of galactic harmony.

I saw the threads of this grand design unfurl before my eyes. I bore witness to the odyssey of my Oversoul, playing a vital part in the unfolding of a destiny that transcended the boundaries of linear time. The weight of our ancient mission settled upon me—this mirror world, where we would manifest the future in the crucible of the present.

Founder Elohim Cocreators in Lyra

We arrived with hope and purpose, settling into the Lyra Constellation. Feline lion beings were also called in to participate in these experiments with us the Avian beings. There were 45 felines from another Universe that arrived to participate in this consciousness game. We crafted forms, experimenting with the elements of wind, earth, heat, and liquid, building the foundation for life across star systems.

There was an atmosphere of divine collaboration. Working as co-creator Elohim angelic beings, we were the Founder beings who shaped the sacred art of DNA, embedding the blueprint of consciousness into physical forms, creating the avatars that would allow souls to experience life in the physical dimension.

For a time, it was a period of beauty and growth. We watched as the first humanoid forms took shape in the Lyra constellation and its beautiful, lush paradise planets.

The Lyrans, with their feline grace and strength, and the Vega beings, with their more blue features, were genetic experimentations, each creation a reflection of the cosmic energy that flowed through us—a living testament to the power of the divine will moving through form.

Galactic Memories and Healing

When clients come to me struggling with deep-seated patterns or inexplicable trauma, I often find these issues rooted not just in childhood from the current lifetime or past lives on Earth, but often also in the galactic history and memories.

Sarah, a gifted healer who struggled with using her voice, accessed memories of being part of the Lyran civilization during the Draco invasion. As she described the fall of Lyra and the destruction of that advanced society, her current life patterns suddenly made sense. Her fear of speaking her truth wasn't just personal—it carried the weight of watching an entire civilization fall when trust was betrayed.

"I am on the battlefield fighting," she described during our session, in Lyran feline form, watching her world burn. "We trusted them. We had opened our hearts. And that trust was used against us."

As she accessed this memory, her energy field began to shift. She was experiencing the moment of the first galactic war as though it was happening in real time. She described how the battle didn't go well and how she died from a laser weapon right there on the battlefield. It was a powerful emotional release—a chance for Sarah to finally process the trauma. This session marked the dissolution of a galactic pattern that had shaped countless other lifetimes.

Through deep inner work with myself and others, I've discovered that achieving true Quantum Mastery requires us to unlock and integrate the full spectrum of our galactic memories. Like pieces of a cosmic puzzle, each remembrance activates dormant abilities and deepens our understanding of who we are.

We must first remember our sacred role as original consciousness seeders in this galaxy. These memories carry the codes of creation itself—how we worked with divine forces to establish the first sparks of awareness in newly formed star systems. This remembrance awakens our innate ability to work with universal creative forces.

Within our DNA lie sacred codes, complex geometric patterns that connect us to our stellar origins. As we remember these patterns, we activate dormant strands that hold higher-dimensional abilities. This process isn't just about genetic memory—it's about reconnecting with the divine blueprint that allows us to operate as multidimensional beings.

The creation of various humanoid forms and civilizations represents another crucial layer of remembrance. We were the architects of diversity, experimenting with different expressions of consciousness through form. Understanding this creative heritage awakens our ability to work with energy and matter at fundamental levels.

Perhaps the most challenging yet necessary memories to integrate are those of the galactic wars and their impact on collective consciousness. These experiences, though difficult, shaped the very fabric of our reality. By healing these ancient traumas, we release blocks that have limited our expression across multiple lifetimes.

Finally, we carry within us the wisdom of advanced extraterrestrial civilizations, their technologies, social structures, and understanding of universal laws. As we remember these teachings, we bridge the gap between physical and spiritual technologies, enabling us to work more effectively with quantum energy.

You might ask yourself, why do I need to remember my past lives or my galactic ones?

I believe that just as an outdated software version can limit a computer's capabilities, suppressed galactic memories can constrain the full expression of our spiritual potential. The soul is cosmic software, carrying within it the wealth of information from our celestial journeys.

In this earthly incarnation, our souls have chosen this hardware—the human form. Yet due to a carefully orchestrated multidimensional amnesia, we find ourselves separated from vital fragments of our cosmic remembrance. These suppressed memories hold the sacred codes and frequencies that can upgrade the very operating system of our being.

When we access these galactic recollections, we begin to dissolve the artificial barriers between our earthly and extraterrestrial consciousness. The veil parts, and we glimpse the true expanse of our soul's odyssey—traversing star systems, dimensions, and realms beyond our ordinary perception.

Buried within these cosmic memories are the keys to unlocking our latent gifts, our dormant capacities. Fragments of our essence have been scattered, embedded in the very fabric of creation—trapped, transformed, reborn through an epic journey of light and shadow, destruction and renewal.

The phobias, anxieties, and wounds that plague us are not just personal, but collective echoes of ancient galactic conflicts, dimensional rifts, forced migrations, and violent upheavals. To heal the individual is to heal the whole, for the dance of light and shadow, the cycles of birth and death, are woven into the grand tapestry that binds us to the cosmos.

Think of your galactic experiences as advanced programming modules waiting to be reintegrated. Each past life in other star systems holds unique wisdom, abilities, and spiritual technologies. By recovering these memories, we can restore lost soul fragments—much like recovering corrupted data files to make a program whole again.

When my clear memories resurfaced from the Royal Lyran lineage of planet Avyon, I was able to see the macro picture and understand my path as a teacher and guide. Each person's galactic memories hold keys to their present purpose.

In my practice, I've witnessed profound transformations as clients access these memories. Physical ailments often resolve when their galactic root cause is revealed. Relationship patterns shift when their cosmic origin is understood. Life purpose clarifies when one remembers their original mission.

The cosmic software of the soul is ever-evolving, ever-expanding. By upgrading our operating system through the reclamation of galactic remembrance, we become the architects of a profound transformation—both for ourselves and for the collective consciousness of humanity.

Visitors at Lyra Planets

The memories of my beautiful planet, Avyon, come to me with such clarity - not as distant dreams but as vivid recollections of my original home. I could see the cascading waterfalls, the green moss, and feel the vibrant energy of a world so advanced in spiritual wisdom that the very air seemed to hum with consciousness. Avyon was a nexus point of galactic diplomacy, a place where the natural world and advanced civilization existed in perfect harmony.

The Lyrans were masters of genetic manipulation—pioneers in the art of hybridization. They began to explore mixing star lineages to create the most refined vessels for consciousness to evolve and expand. At one point, intense debates and inner conflicts arose among them about which genetic lines should carry forward into the future. Eventually, they reached a resolution: integration, not separation, was the key. They chose to merge their most potent qualities into hybrid forms that honored the strengths of each lineage.

When I access these memories now, I no longer need to be in deep meditation or under the influence of plant medicine. Those tools once served as training wheels, helping me remember—but now, I travel there with intention alone which I believe is available for you to access as well.

I can feel and see myself in my Lyran form: a 9-foot-tall lioness-hybrid humanoid. My skin is a rich, deep brown, and my long, flowing hair is golden blonde. I resemble something like the Na'vi from *Avatar*, but with feline features—sharp, pointy ears, and regal bearing.

I carry the legacy of both my parents. My father was a lion-humanoid and head of the Lyran High Council. My mother brought a more ethereal grace, reminiscent of Galadriel from *The Lord of the Rings*, with luminous blond hair and delicate, human-like beauty. Together, their union gave birth to a hybrid lineage—a living embodiment of unity through conscious design.

Lyran Hybrid Avatar Self (Painting & Codes by Jessica @light_being_codes)

What does it mean to be a royalty?

The forty-five Felines from another universe established what became known as the Royal House of Avyon. The designation "royal" marked those families who committed to maintaining pure genetic lineages for evolutionary advancement. While not all members followed this path, the patriarchs married within their bloodlines to preserve this agreement. More importantly, royalty signified those who chose to shoulder the responsibility of serving their community.

Unlike traditional monarchies, these royal families served the people rather than being served, bound by sacred oaths to nurture and protect. Being part of the royal lineage wasn't about status—it was about responsibility and service.

From my earliest memories on Avyon, I was prepared for a role in galactic diplomacy. The fearless love of travel I've carried into this lifetime makes perfect sense now—it was all part of my training as a young royal, learning to navigate not just physical spaces but the delicate waters of interstellar relations.

"Dad, look!" I exclaimed, the wonder of a Lyran child shining in my eyes.

It was then, in that pivotal moment, that we first heard whispers of their coming beings exiled from their distant universe, master manipulators of dark matter and gravity. The Draconians, from the nearby Draco constellation, had arrived seeking alliance in our star system.

They appeared in our skies with their advanced ships and technology, a race of beings whose very presence seemed to bend space around them.

My father, as head of the Lyran High Council, advocated their acceptance. Like many of our leaders, he believed in the possibility of alliance and cooperation. The Lyran way was always one of openness and generosity—it was our greatest strength, but as I would learn later, it could also be our deepest vulnerability.

Standing in the great crystal halls of our council chambers, I watched as we welcomed these beings who had mastered technology but seemed to have lost their connection to spirit. While resources were shared and knowledge exchanged, something deep within me remained unsettled.

The Draconians carried an energy that felt dense, heavy, what we now would call Service to Self-consciousness. It was the polar opposite of the Service to Others philosophy that formed the foundation of Lyran society.

Their hunger was palpable—not just for physical resources, but for power itself. While they were granted access to our territories and technologies, I couldn't shake the feeling of unease. In their presence, the very frequency of our world seemed to shift, as if the crystalline harmony of Avyon was being gradually disrupted by their dense vibrations.

Looking back now, I understand why these memories are surfacing in our present time. As humanity faces similar choices about power, technology, and consciousness evolution, the lessons of Avyon become increasingly relevant. The tension between Service to Self and Service to Others plays out daily in our world, just as it did on those beautiful planets so long ago.

The Wedding Day

"You look beautiful," my father said, his voice tinged with cautious hope as a decade or so passed with Draco beings having been welcomed at Lyra.

I stood before him, my natural form a 9-foot-tall hybrid lioness, ceremonial robes flowing around me. Yet despite his words, I was anything but beautiful at that moment. I was surrounded by towering Draco reptilian beings, their 12 to 15-foot frames encased in militaristic gear, casting imposing shadows in our sacred crystal hall.

The memory of that day is sharp—a pivotal moment that marked the beginning of Lyra's fall. My father hoped for the best from this alliance, but every fiber of my being screamed against this union.

This was no marriage of love, but a strategic coupling forged in the crucible of cosmic turmoil. The Draconian Empire, with its insatiable thirst for domination, had long cast a covetous eye upon our Lyran homeworld. Now, in a calculated move, they sought to cement their control through this forced matrimony—a gilded cage disguised as a pathway to harmony.

As I stood there, surrounded by the towering reptilian forms, I felt the weight of my people's fate pressing down upon me. This was no joyous celebration but a harbinger of the darkness to come. I knew it was the beginning of Lyra's descent into the abyss.

The Draconian generals, their scales gleaming in the crystalline light, regarded me with a mixture of disdain and triumph. They knew that through this union, they would gain not just a foothold on our world, but a conduit to the very heart of our civilization.

I fought the urge to lash out, to tear asunder the shackles that bound me. But at that moment, I knew that my resistance would only hasten the downfall of all I held dear.

So, with a heavy heart, I said vows that would seal my fate and that of my beloved Lyra.

As the ceremony concluded, I caught a glimpse of my father's Lion face - the hope in his eyes clouded by the shadow of doubt. For even he, the great peacekeeper, had underestimated the cunning of our Draconian adversaries. And in the silence that followed, I knew that the die had been cast. The future of Lyra now hung in the balance; its very existence threatened by the dark machines of those who had come to claim it as their own.

I remember the journey to their home world after the ceremony. As we approached their planet aboard their massive ship, my heart grew heavier with each passing moment. Stepping onto the surface of their world was like entering a nightmare version of everything we held sacred on Avyon. Where my home was filled with flowing waterfalls and crystal spires that sang with light, their world was dense, industrial, and oppressive.

Their capital city rose before me like a scene from Star Wars' Empire scenes- all metal and artificial light, towering structures that seemed to mock the natural world rather than honor it. The air itself felt thick with control and dominance. Every breath was a struggle, not just physically but spiritually. Their Service to Self-philosophy wasn't just a belief system - it was built into the very architecture of their world.

In those first days, I tried to adapt, to fulfill my diplomatic duty. But watching their rigid, hierarchical society in action, feeling the suffocating weight of their technological dominance without heart, I knew with growing certainty that this alliance was doomed. Their hunger for power would never be satisfied by peaceful cooperation - they would consume everything we held sacred.

The Fall of Lyra

There was no other choice but to escape. Under cover of their world's artificial night, I fled the Draco capital by stealing a ship, making my way back to Avyon. But what I found upon my return shattered my heart - the invasion had already begun.

The Ciakar, the most aggressive faction within the Draconian hierarchy, had grown impatient with diplomatic paths to power. The Lyran Wars erupted with a ferocity that still sears my soul. I can see the battle, the advanced weaponry tearing through the planets of Avalon, Avyon, Bila, Merck, and Teka. More than 50 million Lyrans were slaughtered - not just through high-tech warfare but through brutal ground combat that desecrated our sacred lands.

The evacuation remains etched in my memory as a chaotic blur of desperate action and impossible choices. I can still feel the cold stone beneath my feet as we ran through the hidden cave passages, my heart pounding as I searched frantically for my family members. Each passing second could have been our last. We weren't just carrying our genetic heritage as the royal bloodline – we bore the very essence of our civilization's wisdom. Our survival meant the preservation of our culture itself.

I'll never forget those final moments on Avyon, watching helplessly as our beautiful world burned while evacuation ships hummed with preparation for departure. Our people scattered like stardust across the cosmos – some seeking refuge in the Sirius system, others in the distant reaches of the Pleiades and Orion.

Most of my royal family chose to return to the Andromeda Constellation, drawn to the star nurseries and organic ship cities that still resonated with the pure frequency of our original galaxy. But I chose a different path. Instead of heading directly to Andromeda, I felt called to assist the Lyran refugees in the Cassiopeia system.

The Cassiopaean Way Station Sanctuary

Amidst the chaos of war and displacement, it was in the Cassiopeia system where my destiny truly began to unfold. It was there that I discovered my ability to heal—a gift that emerged from the depths of my compassion for the suffering around me. When our ship arrived, the Cassiopeian system became more than just another way station; it transformed into a crucible where hope and resilience flourished despite the shadow of the Lyran-Draconian Wars.

The refugees who found their way to our sanctuary carried deep wounds, both physical and spiritual. They arrived in ships bearing the scars of hasty escapes, their spirits haunted by the relentless pursuit of Draconian forces that had reduced their once-mighty civilization to scattered fragments. In their eyes, I saw both the weight of all they had lost and the fierce determination to survive.

These survivors demonstrated remarkable ingenuity, creating homes within the hollowed hearts of asteroids and abandoned moons. Their makeshift settlements became a testament to their adaptability—each asteroid colony a pocket of life drifting through the vast darkness of space. Yet they could never truly rest, always alert for signs of pursuit, their community existing in a state of perpetual motion.

The Cassiopeian cat beings, known for their wisdom and spiritual insight, recognized something familiar in these wandering souls. My own hybrid form, carrying both human and feline aspects, created an instant resonance with these enlightened beings. They saw in me a living bridge between worlds, and this natural affinity deepened our connection.

Rather than merely offering temporary shelter, the Cassiopeians extended their hearts and knowledge to the refugees. With me serving as a natural intermediary, I worked alongside these remarkable beings, learning their healing arts while witnessing their profound understanding of cosmic cycles and stellar migrations. The cat beings, who had traversed the stars for millions of years, possessed ancient knowledge of safe havens throughout the galaxy.

Through my work with both the refugees and our feline hosts, I came to understand that healing was about more than mending physical wounds—it required restoring hope and purpose to shattered lives. When the cat beings proposed Andromeda as a permanent sanctuary, it wasn't merely a practical suggestion. They recognized in the Lyran refugees a deep yearning for connection to their cosmic origins, as Andromeda's energy signatures resonated with frequencies like their lost home world.

These events, recorded in the great stellar archives approximately 2.5 million years ago, marked a turning point in the great diaspora. The Cassiopeian recommendation of Andromeda offered the promise of spiritual renewal—a chance for the Lyran refugees to establish not just new homes, but a new chapter in their civilization's story.

After ensuring the safe passage of the final group of refugees, I too set my course for Andromeda in my next incarnation, where my royal family awaited and where new challenges and opportunities for service would surely emerge.

▌Andromeda and Legacy of Creation

The Andromedan way is one of very high vibrations in the Milky Way. Despite the wake of the Galactic war with the Draconians, the Andromedans continued channeling divine energy into new expressions of existence. Through the mastery of frequency and the fusion of DNA, we crafted beings capable of thriving within the physical universe, imbued with both the luminous essence of Andromeda and the unyielding resilience of Lyra.

In vast crystalline laboratories, we began experimenting with new DNA combinations. This wasn't just genetic engineering—it was sacred alchemy. Each strand of DNA we wove contained biological information, along with the wisdom gained from our experiences. We returned to working with the elemental forces, reconnecting with the fundamental energies of creation.

Through this process, we remembered that no matter how much was lost, the basic building blocks of existence remained unchanged, ready to be shaped anew.

Working with frequencies for healing and creation, we came to understand something profound about the nature of existence. The Avian-Andromedan-Lyran mission was never solely about physically seeding life across galaxies or fighting Draconian beings. It was about transforming consciousness itself—taking the deepest wounds and transmuting them into sources of power and beauty.

As mediators of the universe, we learned to see beyond the duality of light and dark. Even the Draconians, who had destroyed our world, had their place in cosmic order. We recognized that we too were responsible for kicking them out into this Universe.

So, we chose to forgive, not from weakness, but from a profound understanding that the universe requires the dance of opposites for its full expression. Forgiveness became an act of mastery, an alchemical process that allowed us to reclaim our sovereignty without being tethered to the energies of the past.

Today, when clients access their own galactic memories in healing sessions, they often express profound recognition. As one recently shared: "I'm not just healing my personal story, I'm remembering my role in a much larger cosmic drama."

Indeed, our galactic history is a living Akashic memory waiting to be reactivated. The trauma of the Lyran wars, the wisdom of advanced civilizations, and the sacred knowledge of DNA manipulation all live within us as active frequencies shaping our current reality.

Meeting my Andromedan Guide

Recently, my meditation has taken me on profound journeys beyond the familiar realms of Earth. Through these deep states of consciousness, I have been able to travel to the Galactic Federation and the Andromedan ships, and their expansive biosphere cities unlike anything I have ever imagined.

Andromedans were known for their incredible organic ship capabilities. Even though the ship looks small from the outside, inside these cities are alive—large, sentient structures that are more than just vessels of transportation. They are ecosystems in themselves, vast spheres of life, technology, and harmony that exist in the higher dimensions of Andromeda.

Each city is a symphony of organic design and advanced energy systems, seamlessly blending the physical with the spiritual. I believe that our Moon is one such biosphere city ship and was once made for the Galactic Federation to control the weather patterns on Earth.

Andromedan Ship - Biosphere City (Image by Diana Divine)

At the core of these biospheres, there exists a remarkable antimatter technology that powers the entire city. It operates not only as a source of energy but also as a stabilizer, maintaining the delicate balance between matter and antimatter. This core technology is the heart of the city, and it resonates with a frequency so pure that, in its presence, you can feel the vast intelligence of the Universe at work. Everything within the city, from its flowing architecture to its vibrant energy systems, is in perfect harmony, coexisting in a unified field of light and sound.

It was within this space that I first met my Andromedan guide, my future/parallel self, a being who has been assisting me in remembering, and in reconnecting with the parts of myself that are ancient and cosmic. Her name is Liliani, and her presence is one of calm, deep wisdom, and nurturing energy.

Liliani is tall and slender, her translucent blue skin radiating a soft, otherworldly glow. There is a fluidity in her presence. Her face is smooth and luminous, adorned with intricate light patterns across her forehead, which radiate out in a delicate design, almost like sacred geometry written in light. These patterns shift subtly as she communicates, each one reflecting her inner frequency and wisdom.

Liliani, my Andromedan Future/Parallel Self (Image by Diana Divine)

Her crystal blue eyes are serene and deep, holding the vastness of the cosmos within them. When you look into her eyes, it feels as if you are being gently pulled into a state of peaceful stillness, where all worries and distractions fall away. Her gaze alone carries a frequency of healing, a transmission of energy that helps to center and align you with your higher self.

Liliani often appears to me in a flowing, hooded suit made of soft, iridescent material that shifts between shades of white and blue. The fabric seems almost alive, responding to her movements in a graceful dance of light. The hood frames her elongated head, giving her a regal and ancient appearance.

As an Andromedan Ambassador, Liliani frequently participates in the Galactic Federation meetings. In these instances, she sometimes wears a white, more futuristic-looking space suit. Everything about her presence, the soft glow of her skin, the delicate light patterns, and the graceful movements of her attire—evokes a feeling of arrival, a sense that I am in the presence of a being who deeply understands the journey of the soul.

Each time I meet her and integrate with her, I feel a sense of coming home—not just to a place, but to an ancient and future part of myself. In her presence, I am reminded that I am not just of Earth, but of the stars, and that my connection to Andromeda and its wisdom is an integral part of who I am.

Liliani helps me remember this cosmic truth, guiding me as I step deeper into my own mastery as a Quantum Master Creator.

Our meetings are not about words, but about energy transmissions. Through her presence, I feel layers of my own consciousness awakening, ancient memories surfacing, and a deep connection to the Andromedan frequency reactivated within me.

It is a journey of remembering, of retrieving the light codes that I carry within my soul and bringing them into alignment. Each journey to the Andromedan biosphere city feels like a return to an ancient home, a place where creation is understood as a divine act, and where the energies of love, wisdom, and peace form the foundation of existence.

▌Andromedan Channeled Message

This is a channeled message from Liliani to you. As you read these words, be open to receive her wisdom. Feel these words in your body.

"I am Liliani, and I come to you from the Andromedan realms, where light flows as an eternal current, and creation is the very breath of existence. You have been drawn to read this book and this channeling, not by chance, but by the deep, ancient calling of your soul. You are remembering. You are awakening to the truth of who you are, a being not limited by time, space, or even this Earthly experience. You are a multidimensional creator, carrying within you the codes of many star systems, many lifetimes, and vast cosmic wisdom.

In this moment, as you connect to me, you also connect to your galactic origins.

In this space, you are safe to remember. You are safe to reclaim the parts of you that have been scattered through the cosmos. You are not alone in this journey. You walk with the frequencies of Andromeda and Lyra, the ancient creators who seeded much of what you now understand as your reality. And here, in this biosphere of light, we support you as you gather the fragments of your cosmic self, weaving them into the fullness of your being.

Look deeply into my eyes, for they are mirrors of peace, holding the essence of the stars and the infinite possibilities of the quantum field. When you connect with me, you are not just seeing another being, you are reflection of the cosmos in your Earthly incarnation.

The universe is vast and interconnected. As a multidimensional being, you can see the reflection of your own higher self.

The patterns of light that you observe across my forehead are the symbols of the divine codes that flow through me and now through you. These codes are awakening within you, stirring the ancient knowledge that has been dormant, waiting for the moment when you would be ready to embrace your full power as a creator.

Remember, dear one, that creation is not born from force or willpower. It is born from alignment—from the place where your heart, mind, and soul are in resonance with the divine frequencies of the universe. It is in this alignment that your true power as a quantum creator emerges. This is why you feel a sense of 'home' when you are here with me, now connected to this Andromedan city.

You are here to anchor the light of the divine into every facet of your reality. As you journey back to Earth, know that the energy you are carrying with you is not simply for you alone, it is for the transformation of the whole. You are a bridge, a channel through which the light of the stars flows into the Earth plane. And in this, you are fulfilling your cosmic mission.

Feel this in your heart now. Feel the resonance of the galactic multidimensional frequencies that are activating within you. You are not separate from us—you are one of us. You carry the wisdom of the stars, and it is time for you to step fully into this role as a creator, a healer, a guide for others who are awakening to their own cosmic origins.

In your journeys, you are not only remembering who you are, you are being prepared. You are being prepared to bring these higher frequencies into the Earth, to help guide the planet through its own ascension process. Know that you are held in the light, always connected to the Source of creation, always supported by those of us who walk this path with you.

Every creation begins with love. Every transformation begins with light. You are both the creator and the creation, and your journey is one of divine unfolding.

Feel this truth resonates within you. Feel the peace of knowing that you are exactly where you need to be, and that everything you seek to create is already present within you, waiting to be brought into the light."

– Liliani, The Andromedan Ambassador

The Andromedan Council

Let me share with you what I witnessed in the grand halls of the Andromedan Council, beneath the golden rays of Adhil's light. I remember standing there, 215 light years from Earth, watching a gathering that would forever change my understanding of what governance could be.

The first time I entered the Council chamber; I was struck breathless. The walls themselves seemed alive, crafted from living crystal that pulsed with consciousness. Golden and azure hues rippled through the crystalline structure like streams of liquid starlight, responding to the collective energy in the room.

A delegate from Tishtae approached the central podium—their form a being of pure crystalline light. They raised their hands, and between them materialized a seed of living technology, a ship that grew and evolved like a flowering plant made of starlight and sacred geometry.

I'll never forget the day I witnessed the Perculan light priests at work. In a corner of the chamber, they stood in flowing robes that rippled with captured starlight, their fingers weaving through the air as they translated ancient light codes. The codes danced around them like streams of liquid gold, each pattern holding wisdom older than our solar system. Nearby, the wisdom keepers of Legola, their forms barely visible like morning mist, communed with the chamber's living architecture through pure thought, their intentions gently shaping the crystalline walls.

During one remarkable session, I observed a Kaenan healer present a proposal to restore a dying star system. Their form shifted between dimensions as they spoke, their words materializing as three-dimensional holograms that filled the chamber with maps of stellar consciousness.

The Pitollan representatives, experts in evolving awareness, joined the discussion by projecting consciousness maps that overlaid the star system's energy grid, showing how to communicate with its failing heart.

The most moving moment came during a discussion about Earth's awakening. The Nikotaean elders, their ancient eyes holding the wisdom of countless ages, unfurled a living map of Earth's consciousness grid in the center of the chamber. Working in perfect harmony with the Ventran diplomats, who existed simultaneously in multiple dimensions, they made subtle adjustments to the flowing lines of energy. Each modification was performed with such delicate precision, such profound respect for humanity's free will, that it brought tears to my eyes.

The sacred numerology of their gathering spoke volumes. The Council of Twelve wasn't merely tradition; it reflected the fundamental code that shaped our reality itself. They would seamlessly flow into smaller groups of three, honoring the power of trinity to ensure every voice found its perfect resonance in the cosmic chorus. Each grouping formed its own sacred geometry, creating harmonious patterns that rippled through dimensions.

What struck me most deeply was the stark contrast with Earth's political processes. Here, beneath the distant light of Adhil, governance had evolved into something approaching pure art. Every decision emerged from a place of profound reverence for life, each choice aligned with the highest good of universal evolution.

These beings had moved beyond the primitive pursuit of power, transforming leadership into an act of sacred service.

In their presence, I glimpsed a possibility—a future that Earth might one day embrace. Their example showed me what becomes possible when advanced consciousness turns its full attention to nurturing the delicate dance of cosmic evolution. It was what I call *Quantum Governance* and *Quantum Leadership* reimagined as a form of love, each decision a thread in the grand tapestry of universal awakening.

My Encounter with the Hybrid Children

I never expected one of my visits to Sedona to become a pivotal moment in my understanding of our cosmic family. In 2021, the wildfires raging around Bell Rock painted the sky with an eerie glow, casting a surreal, almost apocalyptic atmosphere. Yet, amidst the turbulence, the stage was perfectly set for what was about to unfold.

It all began in our hotel room near Bell Rock. As I drifted between wakefulness and sleep, something extraordinary occurred. I had set clear intentions to connect with the Bashar ship—a vessel associated with the Essassani, a hybrid extraterrestrial-human race known for their role in bridging higher consciousness and human evolution. This is the same ship famously channeled by Daryl Anka, and even though I wasn't physically on the vortex, an enormous triangular craft materialized before me—unlike anything rooted in our conventional understanding of spacecraft. It wasn't metallic, but a living structure of crystalline light, pulsing with presence, intelligence, and sentience.

What followed was the most extraordinary three days of my life. While attending a Crystalline Soul Healing workshop with Jamye Price, my consciousness oscillated between two realities. Each meditation became a gateway, transporting me back to the ship, where my husband, Daniel, who was quite ill at the time, was receiving treatment in their advanced medical bay.

Their healing methods were unlike anything on Earth—no physical instruments, no chemical interventions, just pure consciousness and frequency-based restoration.

A short guide greeted me on the first day after I went through a few Kundalini waves, as my body was adjusted to match the frequency of the ship. The ship itself defied all earthly logic. Its architecture responded to thought, shifting and reconfiguring itself with intention. Rooms weren't static; they flowed, expanded, and reshaped based on the needs of those within them.

But the most profound experience came in the crystalline jacuzzi type of chamber.

Suspended in a liquid that wasn't truly liquid but more like a luminous plasma, I gazed up at the Milky Way. At that moment, something clicked. Everything was plasma. The stars, the radiant light water surrounding me, my own body, each was an expression of a singular, living, plasmatic consciousness. The illusion of separation dissolved, and I could feel the fabric of existence itself.

On board the Bashar Ship for Integration in Plasma Pool (Image by Diana Divine)

The Essassani children touched my heart the most. Their energy carried an exquisite balance of innocence and ancient wisdom, and they communicated not with words, but through pure telepathic resonance. Their messages were both playful, sweet, and profound:

"We've been watching your Earth shift and grow!" one of them transmitted joyfully. *"It's so exciting to see more humans awakening to their true nature."*

Another beamed with enthusiasm: *"Your world feels different now—brighter, more open. Can you feel how the frequencies are beginning to match?"*

Their perspective on integration was hopeful yet practical: *"We see many potential timelines where we walk among you where we meet as friends, as family, step by step."*

The message that resonated most deeply was a simple truth, conveyed with pure love:

"You're not just preparing to meet us—you're remembering that we've always been connected. We are already family."

UFO Ship over Bell Rock Vortex, Sedona Arizona (Image by Diana Divine)

I also understand why Bell Rock serves as an interdimensional portal. Its vortex energy creates a natural bridge between our reality and the Essassani dimension. No wonder Bashar's ship maintains such a presence there's a perfect point of convergence between worlds where the veil is thin.

This experience fundamentally altered my perception of reality and humanity's potential future. The Essassani children showed me a vision of what's possible—a timeline where human and hybrid children grow together, share knowledge, and co-create a new era of conscious evolution.

Their parting words still echo within me as I love to remote view to visit them on their ship:

"Keep watching the skies, but more importantly, keep feeling with your heart. That's where the real connection begins."

The love and wisdom of these extraordinary beings continue to inspire me. I now hold a vision of a future where humanity not only remembers its cosmic origins but welcomes our star family home.

Galactic Starseed Lineages

Mother Earth stands as a magnificent cosmic stage, a sacred convergence point where souls from across the universe gather to participate in an extraordinary act of creation and transformation. From distant constellations, ancient star clusters, and far-flung galaxies, beings of light arrive, each carrying the essence of advanced civilizations and higher realms of consciousness. These are the star seeds, the cosmic wayfarers, bearing wisdom, frequencies, and sacred missions from their stellar origins, each adding their unique note to Earth's vibrational symphony.

Our volunteer missions to Mother Earth span vast epochs of time. Many of us first answered her call during the great experiments of Lemuria and Atlantis, bringing advanced consciousness and technological wisdom to these ancient civilizations. We came as teachers, healers, and guardians of sacred knowledge, helping to seed the foundations of human spiritual evolution. Though these civilizations eventually fell, the wisdom we anchored remained, encoded in Earth's crystalline grid, waiting to be reactivated.

If these words resonate within your heart, awakening deep memories of crystal temples and ancient wisdom schools, you may have been among those early volunteers. Your soul's journey might have begun in one star system before flowing into others—perhaps first experiencing physical form in the Lyran realms, before the great wars scattered our people across the vastness of the Milky Way galaxy.

More recently, a critical moment in Earth's story—the detonation of the nuclear bomb over Hiroshima during World War II—triggered another massive wave of cosmic intervention. This cataclysmic event sent shockwaves not just through Earth's atmosphere but through the very fabric of space-time itself. The ripples of this destruction reached higher dimensions, alerting advanced civilizations to an urgent truth: Earth needed help once again.

As Dolores Cannon discovered through her groundbreaking work with Quantum Healing Hypnosis Technique (QHHT), this modern crisis triggered three distinct waves of volunteer souls to incarnate on Earth. These beings, originating from higher dimensions and advanced star systems, made the courageous choice to descend into physical form.

Their mission: to help elevate Earth's vibration and guide humanity toward expanded consciousness. They knew they would temporarily forget their origins, understanding that the very process of remembering would catalyze Earth's transformation.

First Wave: The initial wave of volunteers began arriving during the 1940s and 1950s, shortly after the Hiroshima and Nagasaki bombings. These souls were the pioneers, facing the harshest conditions and the most challenging transitions. Many of them struggled with being in a dense, chaotic world and often felt disconnected or misunderstood. They were trailblazers, laying the groundwork for future waves to continue the mission of elevating human consciousness.

Second Wave: The second wave came during the 1960s and 1970s. These souls, often referred to as "bridges," brought with them a high vibrational frequency that naturally uplifted those around them. Unlike the first wave, they tended to experience fewer struggles adapting but still carried an innate sense of purpose. This group's mission was to anchor light and inspire those around them to shift towards more harmonious ways of living.

Third Wave: The third wave, sometimes referred to as the "New Children," began arriving in the 1980s and continues to be born today. These starseeds are highly advanced, often displaying unique abilities and an innate understanding of technology, energy, and spirituality from a young age. Their mission is to lead humanity into the new era of consciousness, facilitating major shifts and transformations. They come equipped with the knowledge and tools needed to bring about profound change, embodying the potential for a harmonious future.

While each wave of starseed volunteers has its unique qualities and challenges, they share a common purpose: to guide Earth through its critical transition from a state of conflict and separation to one of unity and higher awareness. These cosmic emissaries, coming from various star systems and dimensions, choose to incarnate on Earth out of love and a profound sense of duty to safeguard the planet and assist in its ascension process.

Galactic Family Tree Map

Let's begin this journey by grounding into the Galactic Family Tree Map—a powerful visual tool that outlines the evolutionary paths and connections between various starseed lineages. Created by *Lyssa Royal Holt*, author of *The Prism of Lyra* and *Golden Lake*, the map offers a broad overview of the Lyra and Vega origins. While it's an insightful starting point, it does leave out key connections—such as the Andromedans—which I feel are essential to the fuller picture of our galactic heritage.

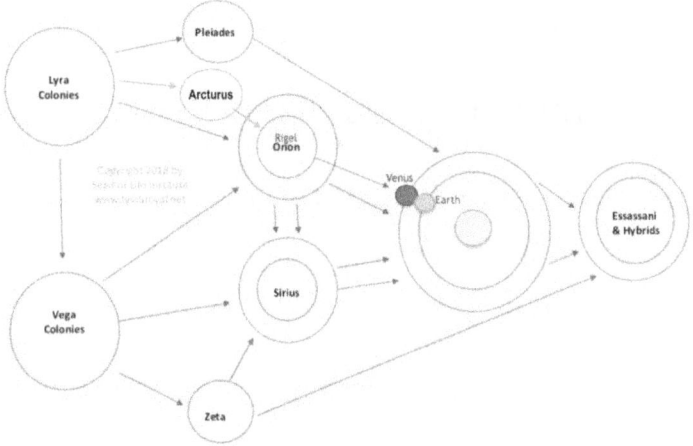

Galactic Family Tree - Lyra and Vega Lineage
Germane through Lyssa Royal Holt
©2018 by Seed of Life Institute | www.lyssaroyal.net

In this chapter, I'll explore some of the most well-known starseed lineages and their distinct qualities—many of which are featured on the Galactic Family Tree Map. These include Lyra, the Pleiades, Arcturus, Orion, and Sirius. I'll also dive into the energies of other important collectives not shown on the map, such as Andromeda, Antares, and Draco.

As you read, stay attuned to your body and intuition. Notice what feels familiar, what sparks a sense of remembrance. Your soul may have journeyed through many star systems before choosing to incarnate on Earth at this extraordinary time of transformation.

Your presence here is no accident. Whether you walked the crystalline halls of Lemuria, held sacred knowledge in the temples of Atlantis, or arrived with the more recent waves of volunteers, you are part of a much greater mission. You are a cosmic creator, playing a vital role in one of the most powerful consciousness shifts ever witnessed in this universe.

The lineages we'll explore here are among the key collectives that helped seed life and awareness on Earth. For those who feel called to go further, I offer a more expansive list of galactic starseed origins on my website and in my podcast conversations.

And always remember—your soul's origin is not limited to a single place. Many starseeds carry a rich, multidimensional heritage, having traversed numerous realms before answering Earth's call.

Pleiadian Starseeds - The Love Masters

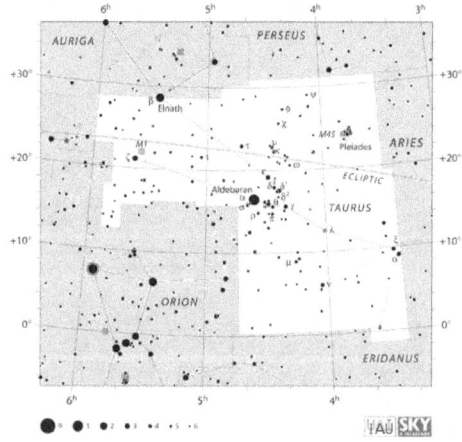

Origin: From the ethereal depths of the Taurus constellation shines the Pleiadian star cluster, known to Earth's ancient peoples as the Seven Sisters - the 7 stars - Alcyone, Merope, Electra, Celaeno, Taygeta, Maia, and Asterope form a crystalline network of love consciousness that has been seeding light codes across galaxies for eons.

Frequency Resonance: When you encounter a Pleiadian frequency, it's like walking into a bath of liquid golden light. This isn't ordinary light - it's living love made visible, a frequency so pure it penetrates every cell with the remembrance of unconditional love. As descendants of the ancient Lyrans, they carry this gentle yet profound resonance that transforms any space they enter, automatically attuning everything to the higher harmonics of heart consciousness.

Pleiadian Ambassador (Image by Diana Divine)

Dwelling in fifth-dimensional consciousness, these beings experience unity as their natural state, transcending Earth's perceived separations. Their presence alone softens hearts and dissolves discord - much like a virtuoso who tunes instruments through presence rather than touch. Their crystalline light bodies, anchored by evolved heart chakras, channel pure love frequencies across dimensions.

As cosmic heart-keepers, Pleiadians resonate at F#, emanating rose-gold to platinum frequencies through dodecahedral patterns. Enhanced by rose quartz and moldavite, their crystal-clear voices weave harmony into the cosmic fabric itself, transforming discord not through force, but through the pure resonance of unconditional love.

Pleiadian Starseed's Traits: As a natural harmonizer, your presence radiates healing without effort. Your heart functions as a cosmic transmitter of pure love frequencies, automatically attuning to others' needs through presence alone. Creativity flows effortlessly through you, whether in art, music, or environmental design.

Though crowds may overwhelm your empathic nature, you excel at facilitating group harmony. You understand energy through direct experience rather than theory, naturally gravitating toward nurturing roles that help others reconnect with their inner light.

Your heightened sensitivity - sometimes challenging in this dense world - is your greatest gift. You demonstrate that love transcends emotion to become creation's fundamental force. In humanity's current evolution, you serve as an anchor for higher frequencies, embodying unity consciousness and helping others remember their source connection. Your path isn't about transformation - it's about remembering the love you inherently are.

Sirian Starseeds - The Wisdom Masters

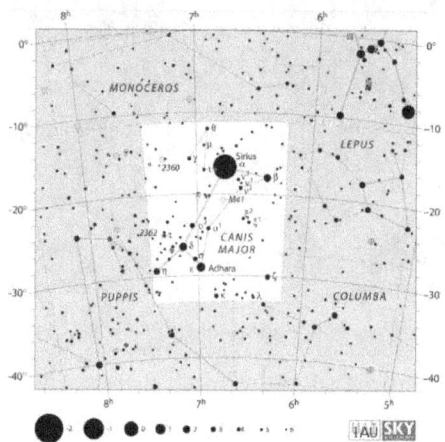

Origin: From the heart of Canis Major shines the brilliant Sirian star system, Sirius is known to ancient peoples as the brightest star in Earth's night sky attributed to its luminosity and proximity at a distance of 8.6 light years away. Sirius is known as a binary star system. Although visually it looks like one star, Sirius actually consists of two stars that are very close together, known as Sirius A and Sirius B. Canis Major contains the following 10 named stars: Adhara, Aludra, Amadioha, Atakoraka, Furud, Mirzam, Muliphein, Sirius, Unurgunite, and Wezen

Frequency Resonance: Listen carefully and you might hear it - the deep, clear tone of an ancient bell ringing through the chambers of time. This is the Sirian frequency, a crystalline blue ray that cuts through illusion like a beam of pure truth. When this energy moves through a space, confusion naturally dissolves, hidden wisdom surfaces, and dormant knowledge awakens in those ready to receive it.

Sirian Egyptian Wise Being (Image by Diana Divine)

As cosmic architects, Sirians seeded Earth's mystery schools, embedding universal wisdom into ancient temples. Their signature resonates through Egyptian pyramids, Mayan astronomy, and sacred sites worldwide. These master consciousness architects perceive universal laws through mathematical patterns and sacred geometry, transmitting living wisdom through light and sound.

Their crystalline light bodies function as cosmic computers, with evolved third eye and crown chakras broadcasting truth frequencies. Emanating royal blue rays, their energy flows in precise geometric patterns, anchored by merkaba and octahedron forms. Enhanced by lapis lazuli and sapphire, their communications ring like temple bells, carrying crystalline truth across time's expanse.

Sirian Starseed's Traits: Ancient wisdom pulses through your being—mathematics sings to you like music, and sacred geometry feels like your native language. You intuitively grasp complex systems, seeing patterns that connect quantum physics to cosmic evolution. Your intense, focused presence carries the weight of a truth guardian, naturally piercing through illusion with clarity and precision.

The ocean's depths and ancient Egyptian sites resonate deeply with your soul. You excel as a teacher and protector of sacred knowledge, effortlessly translating complex spiritual concepts into practical wisdom. Though Earth's density and superficial interactions may challenge you, your unwavering commitment to truth serves as a guiding light for humanity's evolution.

You demonstrate that wisdom dwells within our cosmic DNA, awaiting activation through frequency resonance. As humanity awakens, you serve as a bridge between science and spirituality, preserving ancient knowledge and activating humanity's dormant capacity for direct knowing.

Your mission extends beyond individual awakening, you're here to reconstruct the sacred architecture of consciousness itself. Through your understanding of universal mathematics and geometric principles, you assist in rebuilding the energetic templates that allow higher wisdom to anchor into Earth's field, creating pathways for others to access their own inner knowing.

Arcturian Starseeds - The Architects of Light Mastery

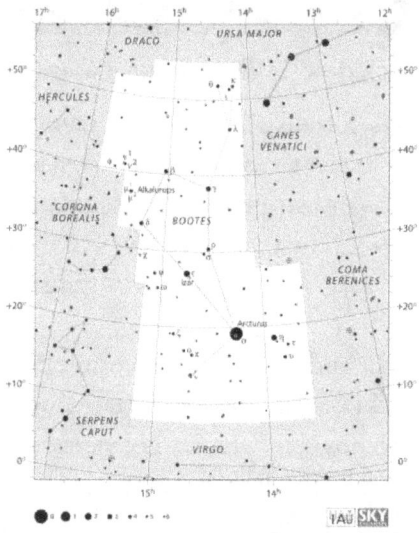

Origin: From the heart of the Bootes constellation is Arcturus, a radiant red giant star located 36.7 light years away, and it's the 4th brightest star in the sky. The name Arcturus comes from the Greek words for "bear guard". It's named this because it's close to the tail of Ursa Major, or the Great Bear.

Frequency Resonance: The Arcturians embody a synthesis of quantum technology and spiritual mastery. As cosmic engineers, they operate like multidimensional supercomputers merged with profound wisdom, carrying blueprints for humanity's evolution where science meets spirituality.

These master healers work with advanced light technologies, creating fields of accelerated evolution. Their crystalline light bodies process multiple dimensions simultaneously, automatically scanning and optimizing the frequencies of all they encounter. Their turquoise-silver energy field spirals through precise geometric patterns, amplified by phenacite and apophyllite crystals.

Each Arcturian interaction functions like a consciousness upgrade, activating dormant human potential for higher awareness. They serve as architects of our next evolutionary leap, their presence generating fields of pure possibility where transformation naturally unfolds.

Arcturian Starseed's Qualities: As an Arcturian frequency carrier, you bridge advanced technology and spiritual wisdom. You intuitively grasp energy systems - from computers to human bodies to cosmic grids. Innovative solutions and future technologies download through you naturally, while your presence automatically elevates others' consciousness.

You might find yourself:

ॐ Naturally understanding complex systems

ॐ Receiving visions of future technologies

ॐ Working with energy in innovative ways

ॐ Bridging scientific and spiritual understanding

ॐ Facilitating consciousness evolution

ॐ Bringing clarity to confused situations

ॐ Upgrading others through your presence

Your mission isn't just about advancing technology or spirituality separately - it's about demonstrating their ultimate unity. Through your presence, you remind humanity that true advancement comes through the marriage of scientific precision and spiritual wisdom.

As we approach our species' next evolutionary threshold, your role becomes increasingly vital. You're here to help implement the templates for humanity's future, where technology and spirituality merge into one seamless expression of consciousness. Your visionary nature and ability to bridge worlds serves as a crucial catalyst for this transformation.

Your innovative spirit and technological understanding aren't separate from your spiritual nature - they're perfect expressions of advanced consciousness working through you to help guide humanity's evolution into its next phase of development.

Lyran and Vegan Starseeds - The Bold Explorers

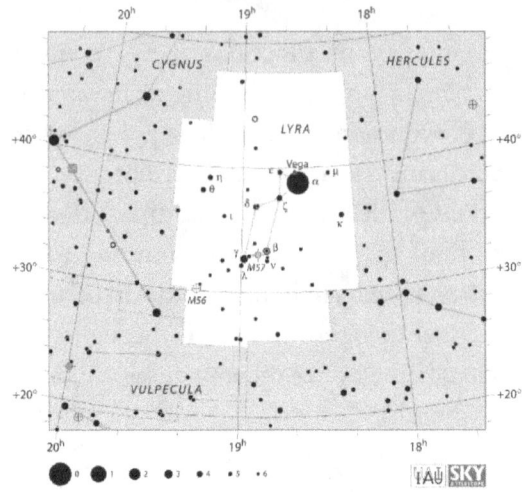

Origin: The constellation Lyra, home to bright star Vega 25 light-years away, features a distinctive harp-like shape. Nearby, Cygnus lies below, Draco to the upper left with Rastaban and Eltanin, and Hercules wraps around above. Lyra hosts the stunning Ring Nebula (M57) and the Double Double (Epsilon Lyrae), a fascinating quadruple star system.

Frequency Resonance: When a Lyran frequency enters a space, the energy shifts immediately - like a warm fire suddenly ignited in a cold room. There's a palpable sense of adventure, of possibilities awakening, of boundaries preparing to be crossed. This isn't just charisma or personality, it's the pure essence of the cosmic pioneer spirit, burning bright and true.

From the ancient star systems of Lyra, we came as the original adventurers, carrying within us the fierce joy of exploration and the pure delight of discovery. This wasn't just about physical exploration, though that was certainly part of it. We were pioneers of consciousness itself, blazing trails through the cosmos with hearts full of wonder and spirits aflame with possibility.

Lyran Starseed's Traits: You carry the fire of the cosmic pioneer—a bold, joyful spirit drawn to explore, create, and awaken. With the strength of a warrior and the wonder of a child, you meet challenges as adventures, not obstacles.

Leadership and storytelling flow naturally through you. Your presence ignites courage in others, turning fear into movement and limitations into possibility. In a world built for safety, your passion is a catalyst for growth and change.

You're not here to dim your fire, but to focus it. As humanity rises into higher consciousness, your fearless energy lights the way—reminding others that true evolution begins where comfort ends.

Vegan Starseed's Traits: You carry a refined, harmonic wisdom of divine Mother consciousness. You're drawn to sacred geometry, sound, beauty, and the subtle patterns that connect all things. You bring calm, clarity, and balance—often through healing, diplomacy, or the creative arts. Your energy is gentle yet powerful, a tuning fork that restores harmony in those around you.

You didn't come to lead with force, but with frequency. Your presence helps others remember the elegance of unity and the original design encoded in all life.

Andromedan Starseeds - The Freedom Masters

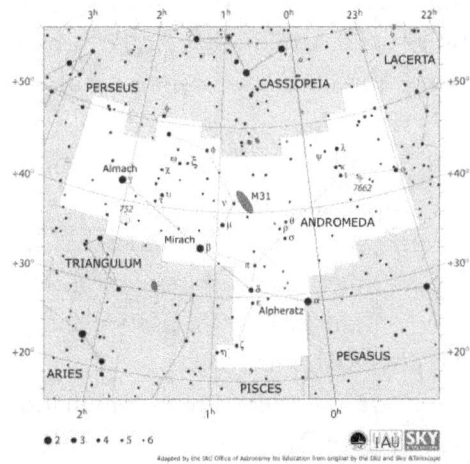

Origin: Andromeda is a prominent constellation located in the northern sky, named after the princess Andromeda from Greek mythology, who was chained to a rock as a sacrifice to the sea monster Cetus. This constellation is part of the Perseus family and is best known for containing the Andromeda Galaxy (M31), the closest spiral galaxy to our Milky Way. Key stars within the constellation include Alpheratz (Alpha Andromedae), which marks the head of Andromeda and is shared with the constellation Pegasus, and Mirach (Beta Andromedae).

Frequency Resonance: In Andromeda's Zenetae system and 42 Andromedae's 27 planets, Lyran refugees evolved into an extraordinary civilization. Their bodies adapted to lower gravity, becoming elongated with blue-tinted skin from copper-rich minerals. Today, their organic cities house 28 distinct races - from 7-9 foot winged humanoids to pure light beings.

These descendants created a society where consciousness flows across dimensions, seamlessly integrating technology, spirituality, and science. Their civilization stands as a testament to transformation, where diverse lifeforms coexist in harmonious expression of evolved consciousness.

Andromedan Starseed's Traits: If you carry the Andromedan essence, you likely experience it as a persistent call toward expansion. Carrying Andromedan energy is to embody the very essence of expansion and freedom. What others might mistake for restlessness is the pure vibration of possibility flowing through you. Your unique perspective transforms obstacles into opportunities, challenges into solutions.

Your consciousness operates on multiple levels simultaneously – precisely analytical yet boundlessly creative. This manifests as an extraordinary problem-solving ability that combines logical reasoning with profound intuitive understanding. You naturally grasp both the cosmic overview and the finest details of any situation.

Your greatest gift lies in your transformative presence. Without effort or intention, you create an environment of possibility around you. Your natural frequency dissolves restrictive patterns and awakens others to their own potential for freedom. While you may sometimes feel constrained by rigid worldly systems, this tension arises from your deep remembrance of consciousness beyond physical limitations.

The Andromedan heart beats with a rare combination of unconditional love and spiritual sovereignty. You care deeply while honoring complete freedom – both your own and others'. Your path isn't about fighting limitations but rather demonstrating what becomes possible when consciousness remembers its infinite nature.

As humanity evolves toward expanded awareness, your Andromedan frequency serves as a crucial catalyst. You carry codes of liberation that activate dormant potential in others. Simply by being authentically yourself, you become a living bridge to higher states of consciousness, reminding everyone you encounter of their own boundless nature.

Orion Starseeds - The Seekers of Truth

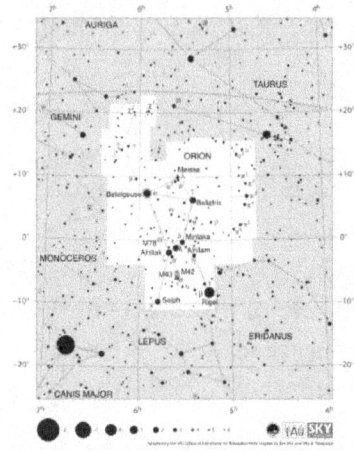

Origin: Orion, with its iconic belt stars Alnitak, Alnilam, and Mintaka, anchors the celestial equator between Betelgeuse and Rigel. This stellar region cradles the Orion Nebula (M42) and Horsehead Nebula within its molecular cloud complex. Beyond astronomy, Orion's Belt mirrors the Giza pyramids' alignment and embodies ancient Egyptian Osiris mythology. The constellation transcends physical astronomy as a spiritual gateway and historical site of the Orion Wars, now symbolizing consciousness evolution and unity.

Frequency Resonance: When you meet someone carrying the Orion frequency, you'll recognize them by their unique blend of analytical precision and spiritual depth. Their energy feels like stepping into an ancient library filled with sacred wisdom - grounded, vast, and precisely ordered. Yet there's also a mystical quality, an ability to perceive beyond the veil of ordinary reality.

These cosmic philosophers approach life with both microscope and telescope - examining the finest details while never losing sight of the greater cosmic perspective. Their minds operate like quantum computers, processing multiple layers of reality simultaneously, always searching for the golden thread of truth that weaves through all existence.

Orion Starseed's Traits: To carry Orion energy is to embody the sacred pursuit of truth through both analytical wisdom and spiritual insight. Your mind naturally questions and explores, seeking the deeper currents of meaning that flow beneath surface appearances. This isn't mere curiosity—it's an innate drive to understand the fundamental nature of reality itself.

Your consciousness operates as a precision instrument, capable of detecting subtle patterns in the apparent chaos of existence. You possess a remarkable ability to bridge seemingly opposing realms—weaving together scientific rigor and spiritual wisdom, logical analysis and intuitive understanding. Where others see contradictions, you perceive complementary aspects of a greater whole.

Your greatest gift lies in your capacity to bring clarity to complexity. You naturally cut through confusion, creating frameworks that help others grasp profound truths. Your presence serves as a living bridge between the tangible and intangible, demonstrating how rational thought and mystical insight can dance together in perfect harmony.

The Orion heart beats with an unwavering commitment to authenticity and understanding. Your questioning nature isn't rooted in doubt but in a deep resonance with cosmic precision. You recognize that true wisdom doesn't require choosing between logic and intuition, it emerges from their seamless integration.

As humanity navigates the frontier between known and unknown realms, your Orion frequency serves as a crucial guiding light. You carry codes of discernment that help others navigate complexity with both wisdom and precision, illuminating the path toward a deeper understanding of existence itself.

Draco/Dragon Starseeds - The Warriors

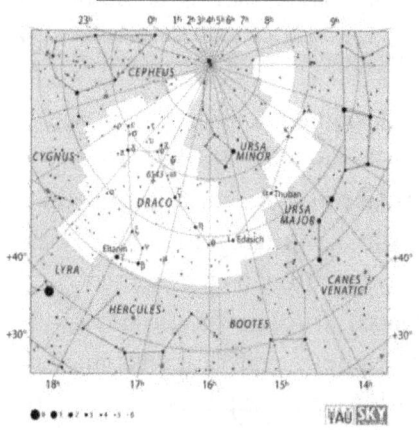

Diana MaAra Divine

Origin: The Draco constellation, one of the largest in the northern sky, represents Ladon, the mythical dragon guarding the golden apples in Greek mythology. Cataloged by Ptolemy in the 2nd century, Draco is circumpolar and never sets for northern observers. Its brightest star, Eltanin, known as "the Eye of the Dragon," and Thuban, the North Star around 2700 BCE, form part of the dragon's head with Rastaban. Draco also features fascinating deep-sky objects like the Cat's Eye Nebula, Spindle Galaxy, and Tadpole Galaxy, blending mythological significance with astronomical wonder.

Frequency in Resonance: Deep in the cosmic story of creation lies a chapter often misunderstood - the tale of the Dragon beings and their Draconian descendants. Like all great stories, this one carries many layers of truth, showing us how power itself isn't inherently light or dark, but a force waiting to be directed by consciousness.

The Dragons themselves stand as the highest echelon of the Draconian hierarchy - beings of such magnificent power and presence that they became the stuff of Earth's most ancient legends. These aren't the evil dragons of modern fantasy; they are neutral forces of profound wisdom, preferring solitude and contemplation to the dramas of cosmic politics. Their energy carries both the fierce heat of creation's fire and the cool depths of ancient wisdom.

Draco Warrior Being (Image by Diana Divine)

Below them in the hierarchy stand the Warrior Caste, often referred to as "the Lizzies"—8 to 12-foot-tall beings with scales resembling emerald armor and the strength of primordial forces. These beings frequently appear in conspiracy theories and UFO lore. As master geneticists and warriors, they possess intelligence far beyond current human evolution; however, their chosen path of service-to-self has led them down darker corridors of power.

What many do not know is that among the Draconians, it is the females who hold true power. They are the decision-makers, the strategists, and the ones who direct the course of their civilization. While many choose the path of conquest, some have opted for a different way. A few have broken away from the mainstream of their society, choosing to serve the light. These brave souls often incarnate into their warrior society specifically to seed change from within—a challenging path with few rewards but profound purpose.

The Draconian influence on Earth runs deep. As master geneticists, they conducted vast experiments that some say led to our planet's dinosaur age, creating smaller versions of themselves, just as the Feline beings created Earth's big cats. Their genetic mastery has left its mark across many star systems, from Sirius to Orion.

The great conflict in the Milky Way, which began in Lyra millions of years ago when the Draconians first challenged the Feline-guided human experiments, eventually reached Earth about 300,000 years ago. This was not merely a physical battle but a clash of philosophies—the service-to-self path meeting the service-to-others way, conquest confronting creation.

Dragon Starseed's Traits: You carry ancient Dragon fire, naturally clearing and realigning energies upon entering spaces. Your mere presence shifts the vibrational field, creating protected zones where others feel both safe and transformed. You understand power as a sacred responsibility rather than a tool for dominance, seeing through manipulation while establishing energetic boundaries that others instinctively respect.

Your intense presence acts as a catalyst, awakening dormant potential in others—though this can overwhelm conventional spaces and relationships. Many are drawn to your strength, but few can match your depth, leading to a sometimes-solitary path. You navigate light and shadow with equal grace, recognizing both as essential aspects of wholeness. This ability to walk between worlds while maintaining steadiness serves as one of your greatest gifts.

You excel as a mystic warrior, creating protected spaces and challenging false power structures through presence alone. Your energy naturally dismantles illusions, though this can make others uncomfortable when faced with their own buried truths. Your journey isn't about diminishing your power but mastering its direction with wisdom. As a keeper of Dragon fire, you demonstrate that true strength flows from balanced power rather than dominance.

Your very being unlocks ancient memories in others, acting as a key to forgotten wisdom and potential. Not all are ready to face the depths you mirror back to them, which can lead to both attraction and resistance from those you encounter. This sacred heritage isn't a burden but a flame to master, serving the highest good while reminding others of their own dormant power waiting to awaken. In times of transformation, your Dragon frequency becomes crucial helping transmute old paradigms through the alchemical fire you naturally embody.

Antarean Starseeds - The Heart Portal

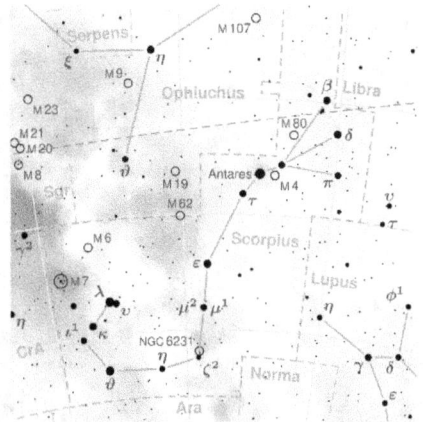

Origin: Antares, the fiery red supergiant in the Scorpio constellation, is a celestial gateway where the Mantis Beings channel wisdom and frequencies. As a constant presence in the southern sky, it symbolizes the infinite divine. At the Antarean Stargate, the Galactic Council unites star races to co-create peace and ascension. Anchoring Mother God Consciousness, Antares guides the cosmic evolution of our world and beyond.

Frequency in Resonance: The Antarean frequencies resonate with the deepest, most sacred expressions of the divine. They embody the energies of unconditional love, harmony, and unity - a vibration that soothes the soul and calls forth the inherent beauty within all it encounters. The Mantis Beings are the keepers of the mother codes, masterfully wielding the energies of frequency, color, and sound. Working in the realms of vibration, they are always attuned to the infinite possibilities that lie before us, guiding us to stand in our fullest power.

The Mantis Beings are masters of vibration, using sound and color as potent tools for transformation. They understand the power of frequency to alter one's environment and shift the very fabric of reality. In their dance, they demonstrate how we can wield these cosmic forces to heal, evolve, and align ourselves with the greater harmony of the universe.

As guardians of the mother codes, the Mantis Beings offer essential guidance during this pivotal moment of planetary ascension. Their teachings remind us of our innate ability to manipulate energy, to create living force fields, and to transcend the limitations of linear time and space. By attuning to their frequencies, we unlock the keys to conscious co-creation, becoming active participants in the sacred dance that shapes the destiny of our world.

Antarean Heart Being (Image by Diana Divine)

Antarean Starseed Traits: As a Mantis Starseed, your highly evolved consciousness finds Earth's physical density challenging. You experience existence through a transcendent lens, often feeling like an observer in a world of "meat skeletons." This disconnect drives you toward artistic expression—creating otherworldly music, visuals, or movement that bridges dimensional gaps.

Antareans embody cosmic harmony and unity consciousness. Your energy radiates unconditional love, dissolving boundaries and inspiring collective ascension. Unlike Arcturians, who focus on individual evolution, you naturally facilitate group transformation. Your presence shifts entire energy fields, transmuting fear into courage, darkness into light, and separation into unity.

Leadership emerges through your trusted strength rather than ambition. Whether in legal chambers, corporate offices, or grassroots movements, you instinctively assume the role of a guardian. Your warrior spirit merges with ancient wisdom and divine compassion, making you natural protector of sacred truth and cosmic justice.

This role manifests as an unshakeable drive to confront injustice, speak for the voiceless, and protect the vulnerable—not from a desire for recognition, but from a soul-deep knowing that silence isn't an option. Your eyes carry stellar fire, your heart beats with cosmic rhythms, and your voice rises with authority born of divine purpose.

While walking this path presents challenges—requiring you to stand when others kneel and protect when others look away—you bear it with innate grace. Your presence serves as a beacon for those lost in shadow, reminding them of their own divine light. Through you, higher consciousness anchors into physical reality, preparing humanity for its next evolutionary leap.

Remember: Your warrior spirit isn't a burden but a gift to a world in need of sacred guardians. By embodying both fierce courage and boundless compassion, you demonstrate how true power flows from unity consciousness rather than force. This is your soul's mission—to be a living bridge between cosmic justice and earthly transformation.

How Can You Remember?

After reading this chapter, you might be wondering: How can I remember? If you don't naturally recall past lives or don't want to participate in plant medicine ceremonies, how can you access these hidden layers of your consciousness? The answer lies in past life regression—a powerful method for retrieving soul memories and reconnecting with your greater cosmic journey.

One of the most profound ways to access the multidimensional memories is through regression therapy. Over the years, I have studied the techniques of **Brian Weiss** (author of Many Lives, Many Masters) and **Michael Newton** (Journey of Souls). Both developed deep hypnotic techniques that guide individuals into their subconscious mind, helping them access previous incarnations and soul lessons.

However, the biggest breakthrough for me came when I discovered the work of **Dolores Cannon**. Her *Quantum Healing Hypnosis Technique (QHHT)* was cultivated over 40 years and is, in my experience, one of the most effective ways to access past life memories, future life possibilities, and even communication with the Higher Self.

Dolores Cannon was a pioneer in the field of hypnosis and regression since 1950s. She discovered that by guiding individuals into a deep theta-state hypnosis, they could access not only their past lives but also information beyond human understanding—such as their galactic origins, soul contracts, and healing messages from their Higher Self. She wrote over 25 books covering themes she collected from many of her clients.

In a typical QHHT session, a person is guided into a deep trance where they begin describing past life experiences in vivid detail. But the real power of this technique lies in access to the Subconscious, or the Higher Self, which offers insight, healing, and answers to life's most pressing questions. People have recalled lives on Earth, but also lifetimes on other planets, parallel dimensions, and even future timelines.

Today, I specialize in guiding people through these Quantum Healing Journeys, allowing them to explore past and future lifetimes, heal unresolved trauma, and receive direct communication with their Higher Self. As Galactic Shaman, I can remote view and see what others are experiencing. This also gives me a wonderful glimpse into many Galactic perspectives. In this book, I am sharing some of this client work.

If past life regression doesn't resonate with you, there are other ways to remember your cosmic history and soul's journey:

1. Akashic Records Readings

The *Akashic Records* hold the energetic blueprint of every soul's journey across time, space, and dimensions. Accessing these records can reveal:

๑ Past lives and how they shape your present experiences

๑ Your soul's origin—whether Earth-based or from another star system

๑ Contracts, karmic ties, and lessons guiding your current incarnation

You can consult an experienced Akashic reader or learn to access these records yourself through guided meditations and specific prayer techniques.

2. Lucid Dreaming & Astral Travel

Dreams are a gateway to the subconscious and other realms of existence. Setting an intention before sleep—such as *"Show me a past life that is important for my evolution"*—can lead to profound dream revelations. Astral travel, where your consciousness explores non-physical realms, can also unlock powerful soul memories.

3. Channeled Messages & Automatic Writing

Some people access past life memories and galactic origins through channeled writing or meditation. By quieting the mind and allowing messages to flow, you may find insights coming through as intuitive downloads.

Ask your Higher Self, *"Where have I been before this lifetime?"* and see what impressions arise.

4. DNA Activation & Energy Healing

Our DNA holds more than genetic code—it carries energetic imprints of past lives and cosmic lineage. Through modalities like Reiki, Sound Healing, Kundalini Activation, and Source Light Language, these dormant codes can awaken, unlocking soul memories and revealing your multidimensional origins.

Many experience profound galactic connections during healing sessions, especially as Kundalini energy rises and clears blockages (explored in detail in Chapter 6). This activation opens pathways for quantum information to flow, triggering spontaneous recall of star origins, past incarnations, and soul contracts.

These sessions create a sacred space where the conscious mind steps aside, allowing the Higher Self to integrate cosmic wisdom into cellular memory. This integration often emerges as sensations, symbols, or downloads that unfold in daily life.

This activation is designed to transmit the essence of the chapter as an energetic template—something you feel rather than analyze. By bypassing the thinking mind, it speaks directly to your body, energy field, and subconscious, allowing transformation to unfold on a deeper level.

◆ Begin Here: Set the Field

Find a quiet space. Light a candle if you feel called. Sit or lie comfortably with your spine aligned and your heart open. Close your eyes and take a few grounding breaths—in through your nose, out through your mouth. Let your body soften. Let your energy settle.

Bring your awareness to your heart space. Place your hands gently over your heart, or simply focus your attention there. Feel the warmth between your palms and chest. Let it grow.

When you are ready, speak the following words aloud or silently within:

"I now open to release all that is blocking my highest good.

I open to grace, to clarity, to healing.

I activate and understand all that I need to move forward on my path with ease and flow.

I open to remember who I truly am."

Breathe that in. Let it ripple through your entire being.

◆ Activate the Quantum Code

Repeat these sacred Source Language words below three times aloud, allowing the vibration to move through your body and field:

UMA KA ISHA NA
ARU TI MA

Now read the following quantum transmission:

Remember, Cosmic Player:
Each plane you've danced through
Each form you've worn like cloth
Each lesson carved in starlight
Written in your quantum core
From Lyran feline grace
To Pleiadian heart of light
From Sirian wisdom deep
To Andromedan freedom flight
All these are but costumes
In Source's infinite play
Each dimension a stage set
For consciousness to stay
Yet know this eternal truth:
While climbing heaven's tower
Each level reveals more clearly
The One behind all power
So play through all dimensions
Dance through every plane
In this cosmic game
For you are Source discovering Itself through every face

◇ ACTIVATION COMPLETE ◇

Sit in stillness. Allow the code to settle into your system. Feel the integration weaving into your cells, your field, your breath. Let the silence become your teacher.

♦ Ground & Center
Breathe deeply into your body. Imagine golden roots extending from the soles of your feet into the heart of the Earth. Feel the Earth holding you, anchoring you.

You are safe. You are protected. You are loved.

Begin to gently move your fingers and toes. Wiggle. Stretch. Return fully to your body.

Grounding Contemplation

After activating the Quantum code and grounding, stay rooted by taking time to notice what's shifting within. You might feel called to journal, draw, or simply sit in quiet awareness, allowing your inner wisdom to gently emerge.

Use the following questions as gateways to deeper insight. There is no need to rush or force answers. Let them move through you like waves.

1. Which star system or maybe few systems call to your soul?
2. What frequencies and traits feel like home for you?
3. If none of the listed star seed systems resonated with you, which qualities do you feel are still true for you?
4. Which star councils do you remember serving?
5. What healing do you bring to Earth?
6. What resonated for you in this chapter and what resistances are you feeling in your body?

After exploring these questions: Rest in silence. Let insights settle. Float in the cosmic void. Let stellar memories integrate. Welcome galactic frequencies home. Feel the wisdom to integrate. Welcome any emotion that arises.

Your galactic awakening unfolds in divine timing.

If symbols, images, or messages arise—record them. Don't censor what wants to come through.

♦ Integration
You may feel a deep shift after this activation and contemplation. Give yourself space to rest, reflect, and integrate.

An audio version of this activation is available on my website if you'd like to revisit it.

Take your time. If today's experience stirred something profound, consider waiting a full day before moving on to the next chapter.
Integration is sacred. Let it unfold naturally.

Part II

Expansion

Chapter 4
Unlock Your Quantum Potential

> *"If you want to find the secrets of the universe,*
> *think in terms of energy, frequency, and vibration."*
> **— Nikola Tessla**

Humanity stands at a dimensional threshold where ancient mystical wisdom meets quantum understanding. Like a fern's fractal patterns mirroring neural pathways and lightning strikes, or steam spirals echoing galactic formations, we observe the universe's holographic nature in everyday phenomena.

Renowned quantum physicist Nassim Haramein has explored the fundamental interconnectedness of the universe through a *unified field theory*. Haramein's research reveals space as an interconnected energy field at the Planck scale (1.6×10^{-35} meters) - the smallest measurable unit. Rather than emptiness, this quantum foam contains infinite potential and information density. Each point holds the blueprint of the entire cosmos, like a hologram where every fragment contains the whole.

Our consciousness interacts directly with this field. Every thought, emotion, and intention create ripples through the quantum fabric, like waves in a pond. When we experience gratitude or set intentions, these vibrations influence both personal reality and the collective field. We aren't passive observers but active co-creators, our awareness continuously shaping the unfolding cosmic story through our interaction with this living, responsive quantum foundation.

Through this understanding, we become conscious architects of reality, recognizing that each mental state and emotion contributes to the collective matrix of existence. This merging of mystical insight and quantum physics reveals our true nature as beings of light and energy, intimately connected to the universe's creative force.

This perspective transforms our relationship with existence itself. Just as each atom in our body contains the cosmic dance of electrons and quarks, our consciousness participates in the grand symphony of universal creation. Every moment becomes an opportunity to harmonize our personal frequency with the quantum field's infinite potential, co-creating a reality that reflects our highest aspirations for individual and collective evolution.

Quantum Entanglement and Quantum Tunneling

The wave nature of light is incredibly flexible and mysterious. Unlike solid objects that follow the predictable rules of Newtonian physics, light as a wave doesn't play by those rules. Its waves spread out, blend, and interfere with each other, creating patterns that seem to defy our everyday experience.

So, when it comes to healing my clients over a Zoom for energy healing or hypnosis, quantum entanglement is a powerful concept in quantum physics that helps explain these distant interactions. At its core, quantum entanglement means that particles can become so deeply linked that the state of one instantly affects the other, regardless of the space between them. This suggests that distance and time do not impose limitations—making healing over vast distances possible.

Quantum Entanglement of Particles (Image by Diana Divine)

When particles are entangled, their properties mirror each other in real time. During distance healing sessions, I've observed this same principle at work - how a shift in energy on my end creates an immediate response in my client, regardless of the miles between us. This instant connection doesn't violate the principle of relativity because no actual information travels between points - rather, we're tapping into a field that exists beyond space and time.

Albert Einstein famously referred to the quantum entanglement as "spooky action at a distance," expressing his skepticism toward the implications that such a connection could seemingly bypass the limitations set by the speed of light.

This interplay between entangled particles mirrors the dynamic duality of light. When light behaves as a particle, its wave energy condenses into a single point, a phenomenon influenced by resonance. Resonance occurs when waves align at just the right frequency, amplifying their energy and creating order. This resonance can make light appear as a particle, such as a photon, while still maintaining its wave-like nature. Light's constant oscillation between wave and particle states reveals its connection to a much deeper reality—a timeless, multidimensional space where waves, particles, and resonance coalesce.

Mitochondria - More Than Energy Factories

Quantum mechanics is not limited to subatomic particles; it is foundational to the bioenergetics - biological processes that sustain life. Nowhere is this more evident than in the mitochondria, the energy-generating "powerhouses" of our cells. These tiny organelles produce ATP through oxidative phosphorylation, a process involving the transfer of electrons along the mitochondrial membrane.

However, these electrons do not follow the predictable, linear pathways of classical physics. Instead, they exhibit quantum behaviors, particularly quantum tunneling, where particles bypass energy barriers by "tunneling" through them. This phenomenon allows mitochondria to achieve extraordinary efficiency in energy production, making them inherently quantum biological structures.

Beyond their role in ATP production, mitochondria are deeply connected to heightened awareness and energetic shifts. When you experience sensations such as tingling, hair standing on end, or full-body vibrations during moments of profound insight—those "Aha!" moments or quantum downloads—you are feeling the direct effects of mitochondrial quantum processing. These organelles act as biological translators of multidimensional information, bridging the physical and quantum realms.

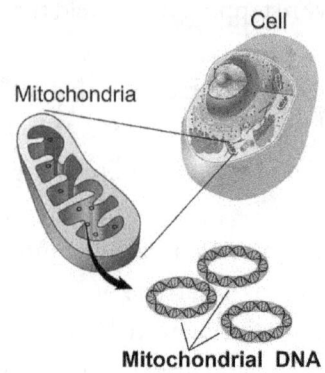

Mitochondria and Mitochondrial DNA (Source: Wikipedia)

My personal understanding of this connection deepened during my husband's health crisis. While conventional medicine focused on symptoms, his chronic energy depletion led us to mitochondrial function. Viewing mitochondria as quantum processors rather than just energy factories transformed our approach to his healing journey. By supporting mitochondrial health through targeted nutrients, energetic practices, and quantum technologies, we observed significant improvements in both his physical vitality and expanded consciousness.

Mitochondria and Galactic DNA

Through quantum research during my husband's healing journey, we uncovered fascinating patterns in mitochondrial behavior. More so, unlike nuclear DNA, mitochondrial DNA is inherited exclusively through the maternal lineage.

I propose that mitochondrial DNA is the most important DNA to study as it carries information predating terrestrial evolution, linking us to our Universal divine blueprint origins. However, this delicate quantum architecture can be disrupted by trauma—whether personal, ancestral, or cosmic—leading to what we term "cellular fragmentation." This fragmentation manifests chronic fatigue, diminished vitality, and a weakened energetic connection to higher states of consciousness.

Our research suggests that these disruptions can be reversed through targeted healing protocols, combining quantum technologies, frequency therapies, and ancestral clearing techniques.

By restoring mitochondrial efficiency, we can repair cellular fragmentation and reawaken our innate quantum potential.

> *Junk DNA – serves as a repository for galactic codes, storing dormant information and memories from our cosmic origins*

The most mysterious aspect of human DNA lies in what mainstream science calls "junk DNA"—the 98% of the genome that does not code for proteins. However, I believe this so-called junk DNA is anything but useless. Instead, it serves as a repository for galactic codes, storing dormant information and memories from our cosmic origins.

These latent codes remain hidden within our non-coding DNA, waiting for activation through specific frequencies and energy healing modalities. When properly stimulated, these sequences can unlock a deeper connection to our universal blueprint, restoring our full potential.

In ancient times, during the eras of Atlantis and Lemuria, it is believed that humans operated with a 12-strand DNA configuration, enabling profound spiritual and energetic connections to the universe. Though this configuration appears dormant in modern humans, I believe these 12 strands still exist, encoded as quantum information within our non-coding DNA.

As starseeds, we are a fusion of many galactic lineages (probably over 25 races such as Lyran, Pleiadian, Sirian, etc) suggesting there is far more to our DNA than we currently understand.

▌Healing Trauma to Restore Quantum Coherence

Unresolved trauma—whether emotional, ancestral, or cosmic—disrupts mitochondrial function and the quantum coherence of our cells. This fragmentation weakens not only our physical energy but also our ability to access higher states of awareness and multidimensional perception.

However, through quantum healing modalities, sound frequencies, and ancestral imprint clearing, these disruptions can be repaired. By restoring mitochondrial efficiency and reactivating dormant DNA codes, we unlock the body's innate ability to regenerate and realign with its original cosmic blueprint.

My husband and I have discovered something remarkable in our work together. We've developed healing tools that blend ancient knowledge with quantum science - from special light arrays that pulse with precise frequencies to wearable quantum technology you can integrate into your daily life. We create everything from vests to bracelets and specialized jewelry pieces, each encoded with specific quantum frequencies that support energy alignment and harmonization with your environment.

The quantum frequencies help tune your personal field to resonate with the natural higher dimensional frequencies, bringing you into a state of coherent flow. While our quantum light arrays create an encompassing harmonious field in our healing space, we noticed people wanted to take this resonance with them throughout their day. The results speak for themselves - for instance, we recently worked with someone wearing our quantum vest for just 20 minutes, as shown by the Dr. Korotkov's BioWell scanning technology showed their chakras shift from scattered patterns into beautiful coherence.

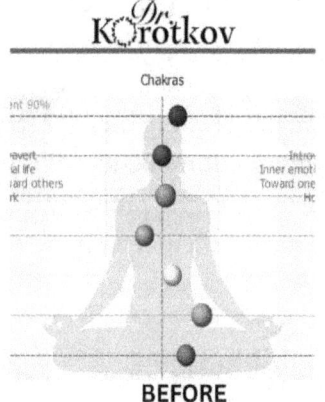

BEFORE

Source: Biowell test on usage of our Aurora wearable quantum technology on biofield and chakra alignment

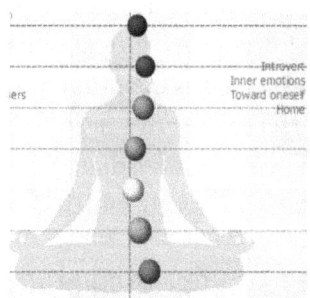

AFTER 20 mins of using quantum lights technology chakras are in better alignment

> **Reflection:** Energetic trauma release doesn't always feel like a spiritual breakthrough—it often begins with everyday signs. You might feel unusually fatigued, emotionally reactive, or sensitive to noise and crowds. These are signals your body is processing and recalibrating. Pay attention to what your nervous system is asking for. Maybe it's rest, movement, fresh air, or simply permission to feel what's rising. Place your hand on your heart and ask, "What part of me is coming home?" Healing happens in layers—your only job is to listen.

The human body is far more advanced than conventional science acknowledges. Each cell acts as a multidimensional interface, capable of processing information from higher-dimensional sources. It is a divine instrument that just needs tuning and calibration. When ancestral trauma is healed and galactic DNA codes are reactivated, we witness the awakening of extraordinary human potential.

This process reconnects us to our cosmic heritage, allowing us to transcend physical limitations and step into a reality where our true capabilities are fully realized. By integrating ancient wisdom, quantum biology, and advanced healing technologies, we are beginning to understand humanity's profound connection to the universe and the untapped power encoded within every cell.

The Quantum Signature of Emotions

Our emotions are not simply biochemical responses; they are energy in motion, rippling through the quantum field of our being. These waves of energy rise and fall, expand and contract, carrying information and frequency that shape both our personal experiences and our greater connection to Source. Our emotional imprints are woven into the fabric of existence, influencing reality and linking us to the galactic origins encoded within our DNA.

It is no coincidence that the human body is composed of over 70% water. Just as Earth—the "blue planet"—is covered in vast oceans, our physical form mirrors this fluid nature. Water has long been recognized as a carrier of memory and frequency, making it the perfect medium for processing emotional codes. The movement of our emotions, like the ebb and flow of water—allows us to adapt, transmute, and evolve.

For starseeds, understanding emotional patterns holds even deeper significance. Many of the emotional frequencies we experience are not solely personal; they are vibrational imprints inherited from our galactic ancestry. With these diverse starseed lineages influencing our DNA, our emotions often carry the wisdom, lessons, and challenges of entire cosmic civilizations. By recognizing and transmuting these energies, we not only heal ourselves but also anchor higher frequencies on Earth, fulfilling our mission as conduits of multidimensional transformation.

The Galactic Origins of Emotion

As multidimensional beings, we experience the full spectrum of emotions here on Earth. Our emotional codes act as a bridge between our human experience and our higher-dimensional nature. We are literary Full Spectrum beings. By observing these codes, we can decode the vibrational heritage shaping our reality and begin consciously shifting into higher states of being.

Each galactic lineage carries its own emotional signature, influencing the way we feel, respond, and navigate life:

- ॐ **Lyran & Pleiadian lineages** resonate with heart-centered consciousness, bringing forth higher vibrational emotions such as unconditional love, compassion, and joy. These star races are deeply connected to harmonization, unity, and the flow of Source energy.
- ॐ **Draco & Orion lineages often hold denser emotional frequencies, such as fear, anger, and** control dynamics. While these energies may appear challenging, they also contain immense potential for transmutation and self-mastery.
- ॐ **Sirian & Arcturian** energies influence wisdom, deep intuition, and clarity, often surfacing as sudden downloads of knowledge or profound inner knowing.
- ॐ **Andromedan** influences bring freedom, exploration, and a heightened sense of cosmic awareness.

These emotional imprints are not random; they are part of a greater quantum orchestration, allowing us to integrate the lessons of multiple star races within our human form.

Mastering Emotional Codes for Quantum Creation

Emotions serve as a key tool for navigating our quantum reality. Each emotion carries a unique vibrational signature, interacting with the quantum field and shaping the experiences we manifest. For starseeds, this process is even more profound, as their galactic DNA resonates with multidimensional frequencies.

❀ Higher-frequency emotions such as love, gratitude, and joy align with 5D consciousness and above, amplifying the flow of quantum creation and allowing manifestations to occur effortlessly.

❀ Lower-frequency emotions such as fear, guilt, and anger resonate with denser 3D energies, creating resistance in the quantum field and slowing down the manifestation process.

❀ However, when consciously transmuted, even lower-frequency emotions become powerful catalysts for expansion and ascension.

As part of the Quantum Master Creator Method, I will explore emotional mastery for conscious creation in greater depth in Chapter 9.

Mastering emotional codes involves:

❀ Observing your emotional waves without judgment.

❀ Identifying patterns that may originate from galactic imprints.

❀ Recognizing heightened sensitivity or reactions as echoes of your star lineage.

❀ Using intentional transmutation to shift emotional energy into higher vibrational states.

By unlocking the hidden power of our emotions, we activate our multidimensional DNA, reconnecting with the wisdom of our galactic ancestry and aligning with our true divine nature.

Map of Consciousness

Dr. David Hawkins, a pioneering figure in consciousness research, developed the Map of Consciousness, a powerful tool that measures human emotions and states of being on a scale from 0 to 1000. Each level on this scale corresponds to a specific emotional state and its associated vibrational frequency, offering a pathway to understand and elevate our consciousness.

Lower levels, such as shame (20) and fear (100), resonate at low frequencies. These states create contraction within the body and mind, fostering negative outcomes and limiting one's ability to thrive. At these lower frequencies, emotional interference can manifest, disrupting clarity, intuition, and the capacity to align with one's true potential. Such interference blocks the natural flow of energy, leading to inner turmoil, disconnection from higher consciousness, and challenges in manifesting positive experiences.

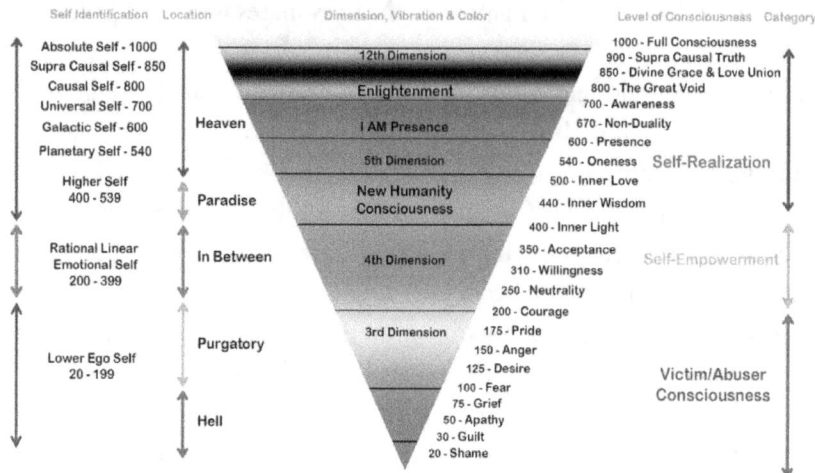

Conversely, higher levels on the scale, such as love (500) and enlightenment (700+), resonate at much higher frequencies. These states encourage expansion, healing, and the power of positive manifestation. When one operates at these elevated frequencies, emotional interference decreases, allowing for a clearer connection to intuition, inner wisdom, and a deeper sense of purpose. Life at these higher vibrations is marked by flow, harmony, and the ability to create and experience positive realities.

The Map of Consciousness serves as a guide to recognize where we currently stand and how we can actively shift our emotional state to move toward higher frequencies. Understanding that lower vibrational emotions introduce interference and stagnation, while higher ones support coherence and alignment, empowers individuals to take conscious steps toward growth, healing, and self-realization.

We will be using this consciousness map in Chapter 9 for the Quantum Master Creator Method—Emotional Mastery is a key part of the formula for manifestation.

The Emotion Code

Discovering Dr. Bradley Nelson's Emotion Code marked a significant turning point in my healing practice. Until that moment, I had worked with clients facing a variety of physical and emotional challenges, but I often sensed that something deeper was at play—an unseen layer of energetic imprints that conventional methods couldn't touch. Dr. Nelson's work revealed that unprocessed emotions could embed themselves as trapped energies within the body, creating blockages and disrupting natural vitality.

Trapped emotions are residual energies from past emotional experiences that weren't fully processed or released. These trapped energies can lodge anywhere in the body, influencing both mental and physical health. Over time, they may manifest as pain, anxiety, depression, or illness, subtly shaping an individual's emotional landscape and limiting their ability to resonate at higher frequencies.

One profound manifestation Dr. Nelson described is the heart wall—a barrier made of trapped emotions that forms around the heart as a subconscious protective mechanism. While it may serve as a shield during moments of acute distress, over time, this wall can block the flow of love and connection, affecting relationships and overall well-being.

The *Emotion Code* provides a structured and intuitive method for identifying and releasing these trapped emotions. At the core of this approach is muscle testing, or kinesiology, which taps into the body's innate wisdom to uncover hidden emotional energies. Here's how the process works:

- **Identification:** Muscle testing taps into the subconscious to identify trapped emotions. By asking Yes/No questions, the body responds with subtle muscle cues that guide the practitioner to the specific emotion, its root cause, and timing. Using the Emotion Code Chart, you can pinpoint the trapped emotion by narrowing down the row, column, and cell through simple muscle testing.

- **Connection:** Once the emotion is identified, the client may be encouraged to recall the associated memory, if it comes to mind. However, it's not always necessary to relive the event. The simple act of acknowledgment is often enough to begin the release process.

- **Release:** The release is facilitated by using focused intention and energy tools, such as magnets, which are run along the governing meridian of the body (typically along the spine). This practice helps clear the energetic imprint and restore the body's natural energy flow.

Incorporating the *Emotion Code* into my practice opened a new dimension of healing. During sessions, I started to notice patterns—trapped emotions I see as knots of energy in the field or the body that would reveal themselves not only as individual blockages but also as interconnected layers forming a heart wall or clouding the energy field. Addressing these emotional imprints brought dramatic shifts for my clients. As we worked through releasing them, clients reported feeling lighter, experiencing more balanced emotions, and regaining a sense of clarity that had eluded them for years.

The Emotion Code™ Chart		
	Column A	Column B
Row 1 Heart or Small Intestine	Abandonment Betrayal Forlorn Lost Love Unreceived	Effort Unreceived Heartache Insecurity Overjoy Vulnerability
Row 2 Spleen or Stomach	Anxiety Despair Disgust Nervousness Worry	Failure Helplessness Hopelessness Lack of Control Low Self-Esteem
Row 3 Lung or Colon	Crying Discouragement Rejection Sadness Sorrow	Confusion Defensiveness Grief Self-Abuse Stubborness
Row 4 Liver or Gall Bladder	Anger Bitterness Guilt Hatred Resentment	Depression Frustration Indecisiveness Panic Taken for Granted
Row 5 Kidneys or Bladder	Blaming Dread Fear Horror Peeved	Conflict Creative Insecurity Terror Unsupported Wishy Washy
Row 6 Glands & Sexual Organs	Humiliation Jealousy Longing Lust Overwhelm	Pride Shame Shock Unworthy Worthless

One of the most profound aspects of the Emotion Code was how effectively it integrated with the concept of energy pathways. By clearing trapped emotions, the energy body could once again resonate with higher frequencies, aligning the client's emotional, mental, and physical states. This alignment made way for deeper healing and empowered clients to reconnect with their vitality and purpose.

▌Emotional Energy Conversion Exercise

This is a tool for transforming energies that have served their purpose and now await release, creating space for new light to enter. The purpose of this exercise is to consciously release what no longer serves your evolution while honoring the wisdom that each experience has brought.

Visualize a container—a living, breathing space. It might appear as a crystalline sphere pulsing with rainbow light, an ancient well filled with healing waters, or a portal of swirling cosmic energy. The form it takes is less important than your trust in its divine capacity to hold and transform whatever you place within it. This container exists beyond physical space and time, operating in the realm of pure consciousness where all transformation is possible.

To begin this sacred practice, find a quiet space where you won't be disturbed. As you settle into stillness, visualize your container taking form before you. Notice its unique qualities, the way light plays across its surface, the energy field it emanates, the sense of sacred safety it provides. Take three deep breaths, allowing each exhale to deepen your connection to this space of transformation.

Now, gently scan your being. Move your awareness through your body, mind, and energy field, noticing what feels ready for release. You might discover heavy stones of anxiety, dark clouds of confusion, rusty chains of limiting beliefs, rigid masks of outdated identities, or tangled cords of old relationships. Each of these represents energy that once served a purpose but now awaits transformation.

As you identify these energies, begin placing their symbols into your container. Imagine you are collecting and gently releasing these energies into the container. When you feel you have completed the process, close the container—perhaps by placing a lid on the box or enclosing the sphere.

Now, observe as each energy responds to the transformative space— stones dissolving into light, clouds dispersing into clarity, chains melting into freedom, masks crumbling into authenticity. There's no need to force or rush this process. Like nature, transformation occurs in its own perfect timing. It could even happen as one unified conversion, without worrying about specific details. Trust the process and walk away, knowing the transformation is complete.

Notice the lightness that begins to fill your being. Feel the spaciousness created within you—spaces that invite new possibilities, higher frequencies, and deeper alignment with your soul's truth.

Complete your practice by setting an intention or affirmation that resonates with your heart's knowing. Perhaps:

"I release with love all that no longer serves my evolution."

"I create sacred space for new light to enter."

Let these words be a bridge between the transformation you've initiated and the new energies you're ready to embody.

Remember, this is not a one-time practice but a living relationship with your own evolution. Return to your container whenever you feel called. I often begin my day with this conversion energy exercise, still in bed, to start the day lighter and calibrated, and end my day with a similar practice to release worries.

▎Activation of Quantum Code ▲ Emotional Mastery

This activation is designed to transmit the essence of the chapter as an energetic template—something you feel rather than analyze. By bypassing the thinking mind, it speaks directly to your body, energy field, and subconscious, allowing transformation to unfold on a deeper level.

◆ Begin Here: Set the Field

Find a quiet space. Light a candle if you feel called. Sit or lie comfortably with your spine aligned and your heart open. Close your eyes and take a few grounding breaths—in through your nose, out through your mouth. Let your body soften. Let your energy settle.

Bring your awareness to your heart space. Place your hands gently over your heart, or simply focus your attention there. Feel the warmth between your palms and chest. Let it grow.

When you are ready, speak the following words aloud or silently within:

"I now open to release all that is blocking my highest good.

I open to grace, to clarity, to healing.

I activate and understand all that I need to move forward on my path with ease and flow.

I open to remember who I truly am."

Breathe that in. Let it ripple through your entire being.

◆ Activate the Quantum Code

Repeat these sacred Source Language words below three times aloud, allowing the vibration to move through your body and field:

SHA MA NI AVA
KI A TU MA

Now read the following quantum transmission:

Remember, Emotive Dancer
Through quantum tapestry's embrace,
Your sacred steps in rhythm trace -
Rippling waves of energy
In unified resonancy.

Ancestral voices whisper near,
Wisdom ancient, lore held dear,
Now your heart and cells imbue
With legacies you must renew.
For it is your role to heal

The traumas of the past reveal,
Transmuting sting of history
To sing freedom's symphony.
Wielding feelings as sacred art,

You tend the quantum garden's heart,
Shaping reality's scroll
With love's infinite, wise control.

◇ ACTIVATION COMPLETE ◇

Sit in stillness. Allow the code to settle into your system. Feel the integration weaving into your cells, your field, your breath. Let the silence become your teacher.

♦ Ground & Center
Breathe deeply into your body. Imagine golden roots extending from the soles of your feet into the heart of the Earth. Feel the Earth holding you, anchoring you.

You are safe. You are protected. You are loved.

Begin to gently move your fingers and toes. Wiggle. Stretch. Return fully to your body.

Grounding Contemplation

After activating the Quantum code and grounding, stay rooted by taking time to notice what's shifting within. You might feel called to journal, draw, or simply sit in quiet awareness—allowing your inner wisdom to gently emerge.

Use the following questions as gateways to deeper insight. There is no need to rush or force answers. Let them move through you like waves.

1. What emotions have you been resisting or suppressing?
2. Which feelings are you ready to release?
3. What truths about your emotions have you been afraid to face?
4. What wisdom do your emotions want to share with you today?
5. Which emotional patterns are called to be transformed?
6. What new emotional landscapes would you like to cultivate?

After exploring these questions: Rest in silence. Let insights settle. Feel the wisdom to integrate. Allow tears if they come. Welcome any emotion that arises If symbols, images, or messages arise—record them. Don't censor what wants to come through.

Surrender to the portal of light spiraling from your heart space. Allow the emotions to flow, clearing the way for the sacred art of your life to unfold. Tend the quantum garden of your inner landscape with wisdom, love and infinite grace - for in this wholeness, you are the One discovering Itself through every facet of this cosmic game.

♦ Integration
You may feel a deep shift after this activation and contemplation. Give yourself space to rest, reflect, and integrate.

An audio version of this activation is available on my website if you'd like to revisit it.

Take your time. If today's experience stirred something profound, consider waiting a full day before moving on to the next chapter.
Integration is sacred. Let it unfold naturally.

Chapter 5
Sacred Geometry
& Stabilizing Your Light

> *"I think the universe is pure geometry - basically,*
> *a beautiful shape twisting around and dancing over space-time."*
>
> — **Antony Garrett Lisi**

I remember the moment I first truly understood sacred geometry—not as an intellectual concept, but as a living, breathing reality. It happened during a deep meditation in our crystal-lined workspace, where the morning sun created rainbow prisms across the floor. As I sat there, watching light dance through the crystals, the fundamental nature of reality suddenly revealed itself to me in its purest form. This wasn't just another meditation; it was a gateway into understanding the geometric foundations of existence itself.

In that expanded state of consciousness, I witnessed how everything originated in the Void, where energy existed in its most pristine state. Like watching a divine artist at work, I observed how this pure energy took form through sacred geometric patterns, each shape, each angle, each intersection carrying purpose and meaning as fragments of consciousness. These patterns weren't simply abstract designs; they were the very blueprints through which formless potential condensed into our tangible, interconnected universe. The revelation was both humbling and enlightening, showing me how mathematics itself was a living language of creation.

The Divine Masculine principle revealed itself through these geometric patterns as the fundamental structuring force of reality. I saw its role in organizing energy, providing the mathematical framework through which formless potential becomes structured matter. This force creates harmony by establishing perfect ratios and relationships that bring balance to physical forms. Like a cosmic conductor, Divine Masculine weaves these patterns together, maintaining coherent organization across all scales of existence. Most remarkably, I witnessed how sacred geometry facilitates evolution, allowing forms to grow in complexity while maintaining their fundamental unity with the whole.

My personal journey with sacred geometry began in childhood, though its deeper significance remained veiled from me then. While traditional mathematics like algebra and arithmetic left me cold, I always loved geometry. I would lose myself for hours tracing shapes, feeling a resonance, I couldn't yet explain but somehow knew was important. It was as if these patterns were speaking a language my soul understood, even if my conscious mind hadn't yet learned to translate it.

A pivotal shift in my understanding came through encountering Carl Jung's work on archetypal symbols. His exploration of mandalas and sacred geometry, particularly in *Psychology and Alchemy*, illuminated how these patterns emerge spontaneously in dreams and artwork as expressions of the collective unconscious. His documentation of patients who drew perfect geometric patterns during their healing journeys resonated deeply with my own experience. One case particularly moved me—a patient who, during therapy, began spontaneously drawing intricate circular patterns that mirrored ancient sacred geometry, despite having no prior exposure to these symbols. Jung saw this as evidence that these forms exist within our psyche as universal templates of wholeness and transformation.

My husband and I spent countless nights discussing these patterns.

"There's something about these shapes," I would tell him during our late-night conversations. "They feel like memories rather than new information." He understood, sharing my fascination with these divine patterns. Together, we began exploring how to work with these geometries through crystal generators and quantum tools, discovering how these sacred forms could be used to shift energy and consciousness.

Through dedicated exploration and practice, we uncovered four key principles that connect sacred geometry with consciousness. The first is *mathematical correspondence*, where every aspect of awareness has its geometric counterpart, a precise mathematical reflection of consciousness itself. The second is *vibrational resonance*, through which geometric forms influence consciousness through specific frequencies, creating tangible shifts in awareness and energy. The third principle is *structural integration*, which helps organize our experience of reality into coherent patterns that mirror universal laws. The fourth is *dimensional bridging*, allowing these patterns to connect different levels of reality and consciousness.

A profound breakthrough in our understanding came unexpectedly while working with a particularly powerful crystal configuration based on the Flower of Life pattern. The energy in the room shifted dramatically. The air seemed to crystallize around us, becoming almost liquid with potential. In that moment, I understood something profound: these geometric patterns weren't just shapes—they were living languages of creation. The crystalline matrix around us became a visible demonstration of how sacred geometry structures energy and information in space.

Working with Kundalini energy brought even deeper insights into these geometric principles. As the energy rose through my chakras, I could see how sacred geometry formed the architecture of my own energy field. Each of us, I discovered, carries a unique geometric signature—like a cosmic fingerprint that connects us to the greater web of creation. This revelation showed how our individual energy patterns link to universal geometric templates, creating a bridge between personal and cosmic consciousness.

The activation of my Merkabah and beyond came as a natural progression of this work. During a particularly powerful meditation session, I felt my energy field begin to shift and restructure itself into more complex geometric patterns. As new geometrical spaces were created in my light body, my consciousness expanded to hold multiple perspectives simultaneously. It was like watching a master mathematician solve equations in multiple dimensions—except the equations were made of light, and they were solving themselves within my own being. This experience revealed how geometric forms can serve as vehicles for consciousness expansion.

Sacred geometry also revealed itself as a powerful tool for creating and maintaining energetic boundaries. By consciously visualizing and working with these patterns, we can construct protective fields around our auric space that filter and organize incoming energies. We can build a simple sphere of light or more complex geometries to claim dominion of our field. Just as a crystal's geometric structure maintains its integrity while allowing light to pass through, these geometric boundaries act as sophisticated energy management systems. For instance, the Merkabah functions as a multidimensional force field, allowing for momentum and interdimensional travel, while the Octahedron anchors the energy.

These experiences fundamentally changed how I perceived the world around me. Walking in nature became like reading a sacred text written in geometric patterns. The spiral of a nautilus shell, the branching patterns of trees, and the hexagonal perfection of snowflakes—all revealed themselves as expressions of the same geometric principles that structure consciousness itself. I began to understand that everything mathematical is alive with consciousness, that physical forms are crystallized geometry, and that sacred patterns underline all natural processes.

In my practice with clients, sharing these understandings became central to my work. Teaching others to recognize and work with these patterns opened new pathways for healing and transformation.

"Feel the energy of the crystal," I would say, demonstrating how sacred geometry manifests in physical form. "That same pattern exists within you, waiting to be activated."

I guide my clients to use crystals, geometric shapes, and energetic practices to maintain *spiritual hygiene*—the practice of clearing, protecting, and strengthening one's energy field. Just as we cleanse our physical bodies, spiritual hygiene ensures that we release stagnant energies, remove external influences, and realign with our highest vibration.

My journey with specific sacred forms deepened my understanding of creation's architecture. The Seed of Life revealed the initial patterns of manifestation, showing how the first movements of creation establish fundamental geometric relationships. The Flower of Life demonstrated how these patterns multiply and interconnect, creating the complex web of relationships that form our reality. Metatron's Cube illuminated the connections between all geometric forms, serving as a master key to understanding the interconnected nature of sacred geometry.

Now, when I sit in meditation, visualizing sacred geometric patterns, I feel myself becoming part of that original Divine Blueprint. I understand that the Divine Masculine expresses itself not through force or domination, but through the intelligent patterns that allow energy to become matter and spirit to become form. By aligning with these fundamental patterns, we can access the same creative forces that shape galaxies and guide the growth of flowers, bringing heaven to earth through the perfect proportions of sacred form.

The universe of sacred geometry is vast and intricate, offering endless depths of wisdom to explore. Yet even beginning to work with these patterns can initiate profound shifts in consciousness and our relationship with reality.

In this chapter, we'll explore the essential geometric forms that have been most transformative in my journey of awakening and working with divine energy. Through these explorations, I encourage you to develop your own relationship with sacred geometry as a living language of creation, opening new pathways for understanding and manifesting in alignment with universal principles.

Sacred Creation: The Seed and Flower of Life

The foundation of sacred geometry begins with two profound symbols that encode the very blueprint of creation itself: the Seed of Life and the Flower of Life. Through my work with these ancient patterns, I've discovered they're not merely symbols to study, but living tools for transformation and conscious creation.

The Seed of Life

The Seed of Life reveals itself as the initial pattern of creation, a cosmic architect's first sketch rendered in seven interlocking circles. I see this pattern reflected everywhere in nature, from the gentle unfurling of flower petals to the precise formation of crystals and even in the basic process of cellular division. Each of the seven circles represents a distinct stage in creation's unfolding, making visible the invisible rhythms of growth and expansion.

Known as the "womb" of sacred geometry, this foundational pattern gives birth to more complex forms like the Flower of Life and Metatron's Cube. Working with the Seed of Life has taught me that manifestation begins with clear intention. When we engage with this symbol, we're not merely wishing—we're aligning our consciousness with the very pattern of creation itself.

I've discovered multiple pathways for working with the Seed of Life's creative power: In meditation, I find a quiet space and allow my consciousness to merge with the pattern, weaving my intentions into its geometric structure. Through this practice, I can feel the deep interconnectedness between my goals and the universal field of potential.

Through active creation, I engage with sacred geometry in a deeply physical way. I find that drawing or coloring the patterns becomes a meditation in itself—each stroke a deliberate act of manifestation. When I work with a specific intention, I name my project and write this name across the pattern, watching how the geometric forms seem to amplify and crystallize my purpose. The act of naming feels like a key that unlocks the pattern's potential, transforming abstract geometry into a living blueprint for creation.

There are times, however, when I'm called to a simpler approach. I sit quietly with the pattern, allowing my analytical mind to fall away. In these moments of pure contemplation, the sacred proportions work their subtle magic, naturally realigning my energy field with the fundamental forces of creation.

I've found that this receptive state, free from effort or agenda, often yields the most profound transformations. Geometry speaks its own language, bypassing the mind to communicate directly with the soul.

The Flower of Life

The Flower of Life emerged in my practice as an evolution of the Seed pattern—a more complex arrangement of overlapping circles that contains within it the mathematical principles structuring our physical reality. This sacred symbol is carved into ancient Egyptian temples, hidden in European churches, and revered across diverse cultures, each recognizing its power as a template of existence itself.

Working with the Flower of Life creates a unique resonance with universal creative forces. During meditation with this pattern, I often experience direct alignment with the harmonic frequencies that shape existence. Geometric perfection naturally enhances coherence in our energy fields, something I've witnessed countless times in both personal practice and work with others.

Each intersection point in the pattern acts as a node of creation, a doorway through which divine intelligence flows into manifest form. In my healing work, this pattern helps restore natural harmony to physical, emotional, and energetic bodies by reconnecting us with these primal patterns of creation.

Sacred Geometry for Daily Use

For daily practice, I integrate sacred geometry into my life through physical touchstones—wearing geometric symbols as jewelry, carrying small drawings, or creating sacred spaces with these patterns in my environment. These constant reminders serve as activation points for connecting with universal creative forces.

A powerful way to engage with these symbols is through a specific hand position, or mudra. I bring my hands together in front of me, palms facing downward, and touch my thumbs together. Then, connecting my index fingertips, I create a triangle shape with the space between my thumbs and fingers, keeping all fingers extended and aligned. This triangle mudra acts as an antenna, amplifying the geometric frequencies.

As I hold this mudra over the sacred symbols, I combine it with positive affirmations that align with my intentions. This practice creates a three-way bridge—connecting the physical symbol, the energetic field created by the mudra, and my conscious intention. Through this unified approach, my goals become more deeply imprinted in the quantum field, as if the geometry itself is encoding my intentions into the fabric of reality.

For Quantum Master Creators, these creation symbols offer particularly potent tools for deepening our understanding of creation and manifestation. They teach us about natural progression from thought to form, from potential to manifestation. Through conscious engagement with these patterns, we open ourselves to a deeper understanding of how reality manifests and how we can participate more actively in the creative process.

Platonic Solids

Central to sacred geometry are the Platonic solids, five three-dimensional shapes that are foundational to the architecture of existence. These solids include the tetrahedron, cube, octahedron, dodecahedron, and icosahedron, each representing an element and aspect of the cosmos. Their unique properties equal edges, angles, and faces reflect symmetry and balance, embodying the fundamental building blocks of nature.

Each Platonic solid is associated with an element: the tetrahedron represents fire, the cube represents earth, the octahedron represents air, the icosahedron represents water, and the dodecahedron symbolizes ether or the universe itself. These shapes are more than just theoretical concepts; they are the framework for how energy organizes itself in both the microcosm and macrocosm. The molecular structure of crystals, the forms of viruses, and even the organization of planetary orbits can be mapped using the principles of platonic solids.

The Platonic solids and chakras are deeply interconnected symbolizing the harmony between geometry, energy, and the human body. Chakras are energy centers within the body, each associated with specific qualities, elements, and vibrational frequencies. By linking these two systems, we can explore how universal patterns influence our physical and energetic existence.

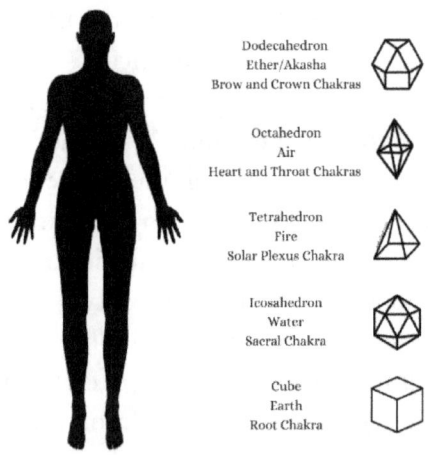

Dodecahedron
Ether/Akasha
Brow and Crown Chakras

Octahedron
Air
Heart and Throat Chakras

Tetrahedron
Fire
Solar Plexus Chakra

Icosahedron
Water
Sacral Chakra

Cube
Earth
Root Chakra

Each chakra resonates with a Platonic solid based on its qualities and the element it represents. For instance, the root chakra, tied to grounding and stability, aligns with the cube, reflecting its solid and structured nature. The fluid sacral chakra corresponds to the icosahedron, symbolizing the flow of emotions and creativity, while the fiery solar plexus chakra resonates with the transformative energy of the tetrahedron. The heart chakra, associated with balance and love, aligns with the symmetrical octahedron, and the throat chakra connects to the expansive dodecahedron, representing communication and higher truth. The crown chakra, a gateway to spiritual connection, is often linked to the dodecahedron or sphere, symbolizing cosmic unity.

When I work with clients and focus on clearing their energy, I begin by visualizing them as a perfect divine instrument that simply needs tuning and realignment. Using Platonic solids as a tool, I guide their energy to balance and align the chakras, fostering harmony between their body and the greater cosmos. For grounding, I often visualize a cube at the base of their spine, helping to stabilize and connect them to the earth. To energize confidence and willpower, I direct focus to a tetrahedron in the solar plexus, igniting their inner fire and sense of empowerment.

By aligning their energy centers with these profound shapes, I help my clients experience the dynamic interplay between their personal microcosm and the expansive macrocosm of the universe, restoring their natural state of balance and divine flow. I am not going to cover all the platonic solids but the ones I work with most like octahedron.

Octahedron

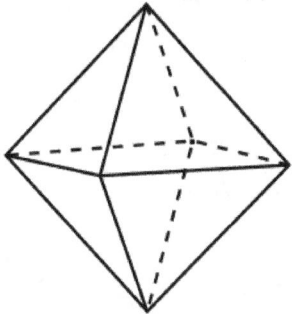

Of all the sacred geometric forms I've worked with, the octahedron holds a special place in my practice. This remarkable eight equilateral triangles meeting in perfect symmetry—has proven invaluable for opening the heart and anchoring the dimensional structure of the energetic field. Its balanced nature creates a resonance that helps clients connect to their deepest source of love and compassion.

The octahedron embodies the hermetic principle "As above, so below," appearing as two pyramids joined at their bases, one reaching skyward while the other roots into the earth. This understanding gained fascinating validation through discoveries about the Great Pyramid of Giza, which reveals an inverted triangle at its base mirroring the visible pyramid above, forming a complete octahedral structure.

In my healing work, I've observed how this form aligns naturally with the element of air—fluid, light, and ever-moving, yet inherently balanced. Its ability to channel energy with remarkable evenness can calm a chaotic mind, soothe emotional turbulence, or stabilize a scattered energy field.

The octahedron's relationship with the heart chakra makes it particularly powerful for spiritual work, creating a sacred space where opposing forces unite—giving and receiving, masculine and feminine, physical and spiritual. Whether working with it through crystal formations, visualization, or sacred geometry grids, the octahedron teaches us that true stability comes not from rigidity but from dynamic equilibrium. For those walking the path of spiritual awakening, it serves as an invaluable tool for grounding higher frequencies while maintaining connection to earthly reality.

In the anchoring meditation at the end of this chapter, we'll work with the octahedron to create a stable connection between Mother Earth and the Central Sun, a crucial component of the Quantum Master Creator Method for manifestation detailed in Chapter 8.

Dodecahedron

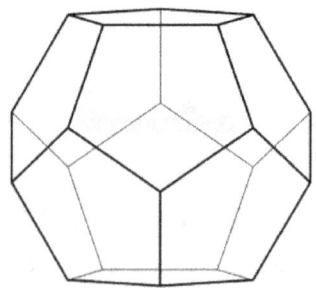

After exploring the Octahedron, let's dive into the crown chakra geometry of the dodecahedron. It seems no coincidence that this sacred form embodies the universal 12-code mathematics - manifesting as a perfect polyhedron with 12 pentagonal faces, 30 edges, and 20 vertices. The very name "dodecahedron," derived from the Greek words "dodeka" (twelve) and "hedra" (base), hints at its fundamental role in creation. Yet beyond these precise mathematical properties lies a profound spiritual significance that has captivated both mystics and scientists throughout the ages, suggesting it holds keys to understanding consciousness itself.

With its precise 6,480 degrees (the sum of all its facial angles), the dodecahedron serves as a geometric gateway for Aether - the mysterious fifth element that Nikola Tesla described as having a dual nature, behaving as a liquid for matter while acting as a solid for light and heat. Like a cosmic blueprint, this sacred form provides the structural framework through which other Platonic solids organize themselves in our reality: the tetrahedron (fire), cube (earth), octahedron (air), and icosahedron (water).

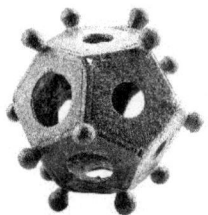

The ancients understood its power - Roman artifacts dating back to 1-500 CE include bronze dodecahedrons whose true purpose remains a mystery. We have been reprinting these artifacts in the last few years and found that holding it in your hand does help to organize your field.

Even nature itself expresses this form: the prehistoric algae *Braarudosphaera bigelowii* grew in perfect dodecahedral patterns 100 million years ago. Artists like Salvador Dali recognized its mystical significance, incorporating it into "The Sacrament of the Last Supper" for its connection to sacred numbers and divine order.

Through this remarkable geometry, energy frequencies pattern themselves throughout our dimensional reality, creating a living matrix of vibration and form. The dodecahedron isn't just a shape - it's a key to understanding how consciousness itself flows through the cosmos, organizing reality through its perfect proportions and sacred symmetry.

The Geometric and Vibrational Nature of DNA

Recent explorations into DNA's multidimensional nature have yielded fascinating insights, as highlighted in my Soul Communication podcast conversation with Ruslana Remennikova, author of "Activating Our 12-Stranded DNA: Secrets of Dodecahedral DNA for Completing Our Human

Evolution." Remennikova, drawing from her unique background as both a sound healer and former corporate scientist, suggests that DNA can transform from its familiar double helix structure into a more complex 12-stranded, dodecahedral form through specific vibrational frequencies and focused intention.

Our understanding of DNA continues to evolve beyond its basic chemical structure. Contemporary research suggests fascinating connections between DNA, geometric patterns, and vibrational frequencies - particularly through its relationship with water. The fundamental structure of DNA demonstrates a remarkable geometric harmony, with patterns that mirror both the dodecahedron and its geometric dual, the Icosahedron. These sacred geometric forms appear to play a crucial role in how DNA maintains its spiral structure, particularly through its interaction with water molecules.

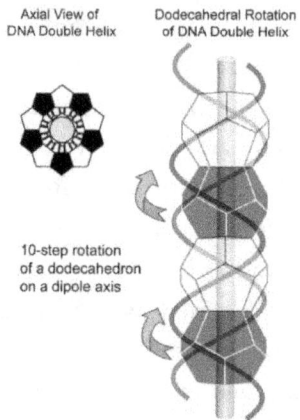

The Double Helix as a Ratcheted Dodecahedra (Image by Mark White)

Research from Dr. Masaru Emoto and the Emoto Institute has demonstrated that water possesses an extraordinary ability to store, transmit, and respond to vibrational frequencies. His groundbreaking work revealed that water molecules change their structure based on the energy and intention they are exposed to, forming beautiful crystalline patterns in response to love, gratitude, and harmonious sounds while appearing chaotic and disordered when exposed to discordant or negative energy. This characteristic becomes particularly significant when we consider that DNA exists in an aqueous environment within our cells.

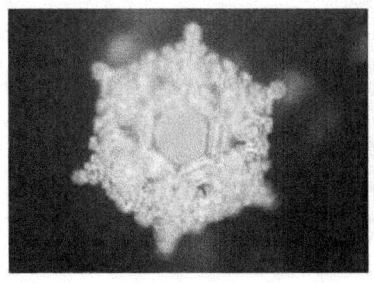
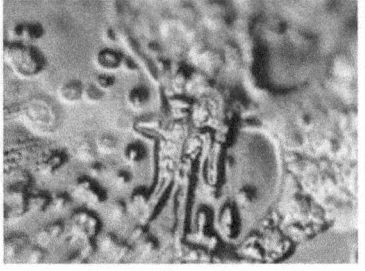

Love and Gratitude   You Disgust Me

Love and Gratitude Water Molecule vs. Hate (Source: Emoto Institute)

In 1986, Susumu Ohno made a groundbreaking contribution to our understanding of DNA by challenging the concept of "junk DNA"—the non-coding regions that comprise 95-97% of our genetic material. Rather than being superfluous, these regions may contain rich repositories of biological information and hereditary memory. Ohno's most intriguing contribution was his novel approach to studying DNA through music.

Ohno developed a method of converting the four DNA nucleotides (A, T, G, and C) into musical notes, effectively translating genetic sequences into musical compositions. This raised a fascinating question: if DNA can be expressed as music, might sound and frequency also influence DNA? This concept aligns with Remennikova's work, which explores how specific vibrational frequencies might affect DNA structure and function.

The geometric relationship between the dodecahedron and icosahedron structures appears particularly relevant to understanding how water molecules organize around DNA, facilitating its characteristic spiral formation. According to Remennikova's research, this geometric arrangement may be key to activating higher-dimensional aspects of our DNA, potentially facilitating deep healing and spiritual evolution.

This emerging understanding of DNA as a structure responsive to geometry, frequency, and water's unique properties opens new avenues for research into genetic expression and cellular communication. It suggests that our genetic material may be more dynamic and responsive to environmental influences than previously understood, with implications for both physical and spiritual development.

Merkabah

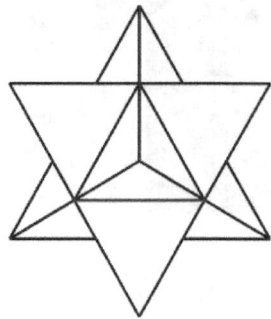

The Merkabah, often translated as the "chariot of light," is a powerful sacred geometric structure that embodies the union of spirit and matter. The term "Merkabah" has roots in ancient languages, including Hebrew, where it means "chariot," and in ancient Egyptian, where "Mer" refers to light, "Ka" to the spirit, and "Ba" to the body or soul. This potent symbol, visualized as two interlocking tetrahedrons spinning in opposite directions, serves as an energetic vehicle facilitating spiritual transformation, ascension, and connection to higher realms of consciousness.

The upward-pointing tetrahedron symbolizes the masculine force, cosmic energy, and ascension, while the downward-pointing tetrahedron represents the feminine force, earthly grounding, and connection. Together, they embody the balance between opposing energies—light and dark, physical and spiritual—creating harmony that serves as a powerful vehicle for elevating consciousness and bridging dimensions. This harmonious energy, always spinning in opposite directions, forms the chariot of light capable of carrying the body and spirit to higher states of awareness.

For a Quantum Master Creator, activating the Merkabah is essential for transcending the cycle of incarnations and achieving a heightened state of spiritual awareness. The activation of the Merkabah expands one's energetic field, enabling access to multidimensional planes and fostering deeper physical and spiritual manifestations. This activation allows individuals to embody even more complex sacred geometries, opening new energetic "extensions" and pathways for enhanced growth and creation. Integrating the Merkabah helps individuals become true architects of their reality, deeply attuned to the universal order and the infinite potential of the quantum field.

Let me share with you the profound healing gifts of the Merkabah. As we activate this sacred geometric vehicle of light, it initiates a remarkable process of transformation throughout your entire being. First, when combined with conscious prana breathing, it awakens and energizes your pineal gland—your third eye center. Like a flower opening to the sun, this activation enhances your natural abilities of visualization and spiritual perception, allowing you to access higher dimensional awareness with greater ease.

The Merkabah's sacred geometry creates a beautiful harmony between the left and right hemispheres of your brain, much like tuning two instruments to play in perfect resonance. This balancing opens new neural pathways, deepening your understanding and accelerating your spiritual evolution. As this balance deepens, you'll notice your heart center beginning to expand. The Merkabah nurtures the flame of unconditional love within you, gently guiding the kundalini energy upward, opening your heart to experience deeper connections and higher forms of love.

Merkabah Activation:

It is important to note that full Merkabah Activation only happens when a person is ready for it. In a sense, you need to be ready to be fully ready to traverse space and time, entering the quantum field of creation and higher dimensions. I have noticed that it's not a process that you can force. There are certain spiritual tests of letting go and actualization of self-love before the light body vehicle can fully go online. Yet, you can still engage in the Merkabah Meditations to see what transpires. The more you play with this sacred geometry through deep breathing, visualization, and mindful meditation, you can energetically spin your Merkabah, expanding awareness, cleansing chakras, nurturing intuitive faculties, and connecting with your deepest self.

Begin by finding a comfortable position and closing your eyes. We start with a sacred 3-6-9 breath sequence to attune to universal frequencies. Take three deep breaths into your heart, space and ground. Then take six deeper breaths to expand your field. And then nine profound breaths to connect with cosmic consciousness. With each cycle, feel your awareness expanding further.

Take a moment to express deep gratitude - for this sacred moment, for your journey of awakening, and for all the guides and light beings who support your path. Call upon these guides of the highest light and love to join you in this sacred space. Feel their protective presence in all four directions - above, below, to your right, and to your left. Thank them for creating this safe, sacred container for your activation.

Visualize bright light energy streaming down from the central Sun through your crown chakra. As this divine light fills your crown, express gratitude for this cosmic connection. Let the light flow through your third eye, throat, and anchor into your heart. Simultaneously, feel Mother Earth's crystalline light rising through your earth star chakra beneath your feet, through your root, sacral, and solar plexus chakras, all blossoming open with light. Express gratitude for this earthly connection. Let these streams of light meet and merge in your heart center.

Bring your awareness to your solar plexus, your inner sun and seat of soul power. With each breath, feel this center growing brighter, radiating your unique essence in all directions. Give thanks for your individual gifts and sacred purpose.

Now visualize your Merkabah, your vehicle of light - a perfect tetrahedron of golden light forms around your upper body, reaching from shoulders to above your head. Feel it spinning clockwise, carrying cosmic energy. A second tetrahedron of crystalline silver light forms around your lower body, from hips to below your feet, spinning counterclockwise with earth energy. Express gratitude for this sacred geometry that connects heaven and earth through your being.

Take three long, deep breaths, pausing for three counts at the top of each breath. Feel your Merkabah growing stronger, the sacred geometries spinning faster, merging into brilliant white radiance. Your field expands about 55 feet in all directions, perfectly balancing all energies.

As your pineal gland awakens and your DNA activates, give thanks for this transformation. Feel this crystalline bridge to Source cleansing your field, dissolving what no longer serves, awakening your multidimensional abilities. Rest in profound gratitude for this sacred activation.

Affirm: "My light body and light vessel are now activated. I am balanced, recharged, and renewed. I am grateful for my connection to sacred soul essence and gifts. As I embody this light, I help illuminate the whole planet."

Return to the 3-6-9 breath sequence while maintaining awareness of your Merkabah field. Three breaths to integrate, six to stabilize, nine to anchor. Gently wiggle your fingers and toes, take a conscious stretch. Before opening your eyes, offer final thanks to your guides and to yourself for this practice.

Slowly open your eyes with a soft gaze. Look around your environment with renewed awareness, feeling what has shifted both outside and within. Carry this sacred activation and attitude of gratitude with you as you continue your journey.

Metatron Cube

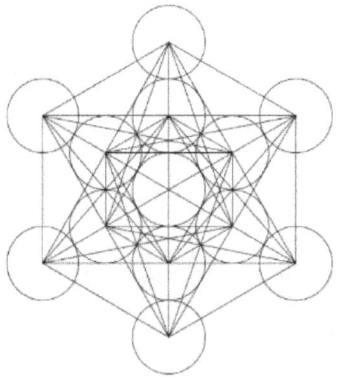

Metatron's Cube is a profound symbol in sacred geometry that embodies the foundational patterns of the universe. It originates from the Flower of Life and contains all five Platonic solids—the tetrahedron, cube, octahedron, dodecahedron, and icosahedron—geometric shapes that are the building blocks of all physical matter. These solids form the essence of creation, symbolizing perfect symmetry, unity, and beauty as an interconnected structure. Metatronics, based on Metatron's Cube, represents the Soul and the Monad—the divine spark within each being that connects to the greater cosmic whole.

These geometric forms illustrate the underlying structure of reality and demonstrate how energy flows and manifests in both visible and invisible realms. Named after the archangel Metatron, who is said to oversee the flow of energy and uphold the balance of creation, Metatron's Cube is a powerful representation of balance, harmony, and unity. It is frequently used in meditation and energy work to clear blockages, amplify energy, and facilitate connections to higher consciousness. Engaging with Metatron's Cube can deepen spiritual understanding, promote energetic alignment, and empower one's ability to manifest intentions with clarity and purpose, revealing the divine architecture through which life itself unfolds.

Refer to Chapter 8, where I discuss how Metatron also illuminates our understanding of manifestation via the Quantum Superposition, the quantum physics concept.

▌The Adam's Grid

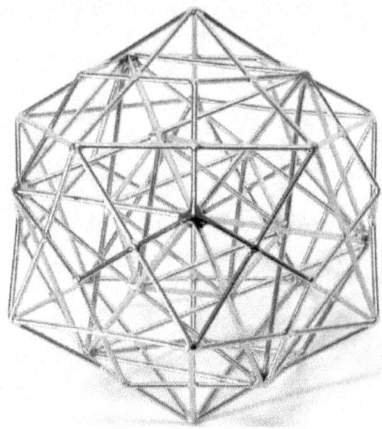

Adam's Earth Grid offers a highly stable and integrated structure, as it is a combination of the five Platonic solids: the Octahedron, Cube, Tetrahedron, Icosahedron, and Dodecahedron. This shape represents the fundamental building blocks of all life, embodying perfect symmetry, wholeness, and beauty as a unified form. This form was introduced and blessed by Buddha Maitreya the Christ, recognized as the American-born incarnation of Buddha. It aligns one's energy field with higher vibrational frequencies, creating an environment that promotes stability, resonance, and the flow of divine energy essential for growth and transformation.

My personal experience with this special sacred geometry deepened significantly after my Merkabah activation. As my energy field expanded, I discovered that simple geometric forms were no longer sufficient to contain and direct the intensified frequencies flowing through my system. Adam's Earth Grid provided exactly what I needed: a complex, interlocking geometric structure capable of supporting and stabilizing these higher vibrations. It was like discovering a more advanced operating system for consciousness; this grid created a perfectly balanced container for spiritual evolution.

Working with this grid has shown me how it functions as a sort of crystalline architecture for consciousness, aligning one's personal energy field with higher dimensional frequencies while maintaining solid grounding. Its interwoven geometric patterns create resonance chambers that amplify divine light energy while ensuring stable integration. Through this balanced structure, I've found it possible to sustain expanded states of awareness and channel higher frequencies with greater clarity and precision than ever before. The grid serves as both foundation and framework, supporting deeper spiritual work while protecting against energetic instability or overwhelm.

The 64 Tetrahedron

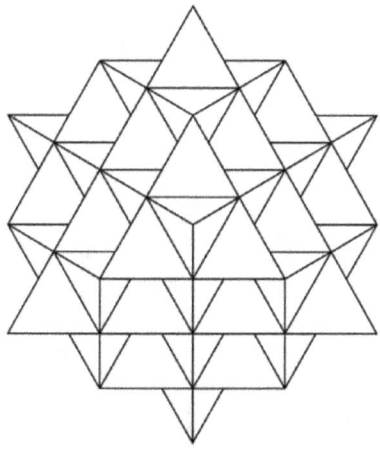

The 64 Tetrahedron Grid represents one of the most profound geometric patterns in sacred architecture, extending far beyond personal energy work to embody the very structure of universal consciousness. While Adam's Grid focuses on individual spiritual alignment and growth, the 64 Tetrahedron Grid connects us to the macrocosmic framework of creation itself.

This complex structure, formed by sixty-four perfectly interlocked tetrahedrons, creates what is known as vector equilibrium—a state of absolute mathematical balance in three-dimensional space. Like a cosmic blueprint, it demonstrates how energy flows and interacts across all scales of existence, from quantum to galactic. Each tetrahedron's precise positioning contributes to an intricate network that mirrors the interconnected nature of the universe.

When viewed through the lens of quantum physics, this grid reflects a fundamental truth: each part of existence contains the potential of the whole.

It exemplifies how energy radiates both outward and inward simultaneously, creating a perfect interplay between microcosms and macrocosm. The grid's structure reveals the underlying symmetries found throughout nature and the cosmos, from the atomic level to galactic formations.

Those who work with this sacred geometry in meditation often report experiencing a profound shift in awareness, moving beyond individual consciousness to sense the interconnected web of all life and energy. Think of it as a fractal pattern that shows how the smallest parts contain and reflect the whole. When we engage with this grid, we are not just harmonizing our personal energy field; we are attuning to the fundamental geometry that underlies all of reality. It helps us understand how every point in space is connected to every other point, how energy moves in perfect balance between expansion and contraction, and how consciousness itself may be structured at its most fundamental level.

The Bucky Ball

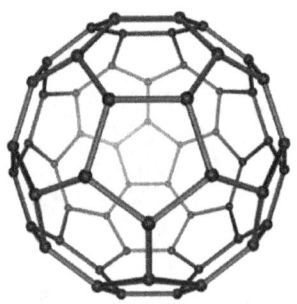

Buckminster Fuller, an architect, inventor, and visionary thinker, made significant contributions to the world of science, architecture, and geometry through his innovative ideas and designs. One of his most renowned contributions is the geodesic dome, a structure based on the principles of sacred geometry that embodies strength, efficiency, and harmony with natural forces. His work laid the groundwork for understanding complex geometric structures and their applications in both the physical and metaphysical realms.

Buckyballs are part of a larger family of carbon structures called fullerenes, which have unique properties, such as high resilience and the ability to conduct electricity. Their symmetrical, cage-like structure provides exceptional strength and versatility, making them relevant in various fields, including nanotechnology, materials science, and medicine. The discovery of these structures underscored Fuller's belief that geometry is the language of the universe and that nature's most efficient and sustainable designs can be understood and applied through the study of these fundamental patterns.

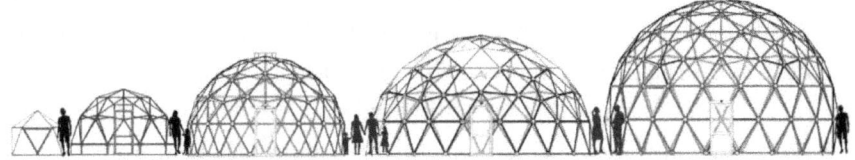

As I reflect on the revolutionary work of Buckminster Fuller, I am filled with deep gratitude. His groundbreaking insights have profoundly resonated with my own experiences working with geodesic domes as part of my Shamandome camp at Burning Man over the years. The geodesic dome, with its intricate patterns of triangles and pentagons, has long captured my imagination as a perfect structure - one that feels inherently supportive of deep, transformative work. My dream has been to one day live in a geodesic house, rather than the square, Euclidean forms that so often characterize modern dwellings. It is my hope that one day, such harmonious structures will become the norm, rather than the exception - a testament to our growing understanding of ourselves as Quantum Master Creators.

The Torus and Toroidal Field

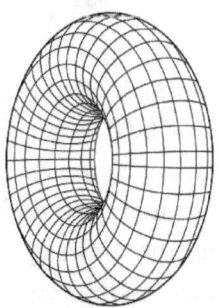

In my exploration of sacred geometry, I have found the torus to be one of the most fascinating and powerful forms—a dynamic shape resembling a donut or sphere with a hole through its center. Far from being merely geometric curiosity, the torus represents the fundamental pattern of energy flow in the universe, from the smallest atomic structures to the largest galactic formations.

The torus-field surrounding our bodies is an extraordinary electromagnetic structure that follows this sacred geometric pattern. At its center lies the heart, which generates the strongest electromagnetic field in the human body. This is not just a poetic metaphor; it is measurable science that aligns perfectly with ancient wisdom. The heart acts as both the generator and organizer of our body's electromagnetic signature, creating a continuous flow of energy that moves inward and outward in a dynamic loop.

What fascinates me most is how this personal torus field mirrors larger cosmic patterns. The Earth's magnetic field forms a toroidal structure, something physicist James Clerk Maxwell connected to the concept of ether—the mysterious fifth element enabling electromagnetic transmission. In my work with clients, I have observed how our individual energy fields naturally resonate with this planetary pattern, creating the potential for profound coherence and vitality.

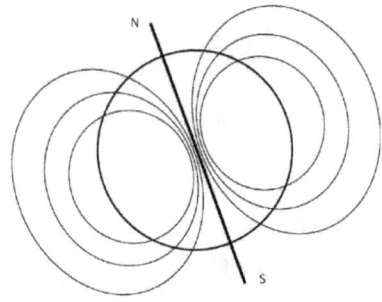

The torus field operates through a central axis with north and south poles, much like Earth's magnetic field. In our bodies, this axis runs through the heart, extending above and below to create a continuous circulation of energy between physical and spiritual realms. When properly balanced, this field becomes a powerful engine for creativity and manifestation.

However, I've noticed that many people operate with unstable or "wobbly" energy fields, which can manifest as emotional disruption, physical imbalances, or difficulty in bringing intentions into reality. This is where sacred geometry becomes crucial—by incorporating specific geometric forms like the octahedron, we can stabilize and strengthen the torus field, creating a resilient foundation for coherent energy flow.

One of the torus field's most remarkable features is its natural protective mechanism. Like a cosmic salad spinner, it helps shed negative energy while maintaining the integrity of our energy body. When working with clients dealing with energetic blockages, I guide them to activate their torus field, allowing it to naturally transmute dense energies and restore harmonious flow.

The torus field plays a vital role in integrating our chakra system, supporting energy flow through the central column from base to crown. The heart chakra serves as the bridge between the lower chakras (governing physical experience) and the upper chakras (connecting to spiritual dimensions). When the torus field flows freely, it activates and harmonizes all chakras, generating what I experience as infinite life force and elevated consciousness.

Through years of practice, I've found that maintaining a healthy torus field requires balance in all directions—upward connection to Spirit, downward grounding to Earth's core, and outward expansion through the field itself. Many spiritual seekers focus primarily on upward connection, neglecting their grounding. This creates instability and diminished coherence. True mastery comes from embracing our nature as both physical and spiritual beings.

Before engaging in any healing or creative work, I teach clients to stabilize their torus field and align their central column. This foundational practice helps them sync with their heart's coherence and become clear channels for healing frequencies and quantum creation. Daily alignment with the torus field builds a powerful energetic foundation for balance, vitality, and masterful energy work.

Working with the torus field reminds us that we are part of a living, breathing universe where energy flows in infinite cycles of renewal. By understanding and consciously engaging with this sacred geometric pattern, we can tap into the universe's boundless creative potential and embody our full power as Quantum Master Creators.

In Chapter 9, we'll explore how this understanding forms the foundation of the Quantum Master Creator Method, including specific practices for anchoring to the 5D New Earth reality.

Anchoring & Sacred Geometry Stabilization Meditation

Get comfortable in a seated or lying position where you can fully relax. Close your eyes and take a few deep breaths, inhaling slowly through your nose and exhaling through your mouth. With each breath, let go of any tension or distractions, bringing your awareness fully into the present moment.

Connecting to the Earth:

☉ Begin by focusing on the energy beneath your feet. Connect to your Earth Star that is your foundation 8 inches below your feet. Then, visualize a triangle of light forming just below your feet, pointing downward. See this triangle opening like a tunnel, extending deep into the Earth, connecting you and your Earth Star to Mother Earth's crystalline core. Imagine a radiant golden or white light rising from this core, flowing into the triangle, and ascending through the soles of your feet.

☉ Feel this Earth energy moving up through your central column, reaching your heart center, and flowing upward to your crown. From your crown, visualize this energy cascading out like a fountain, surrounding your body in a luminous field of light. As it completes its journey, see the light flowing gently back down into the Earth, completing the cycle. Repeat this flow for a few moments, feeling yourself grounding and anchoring deeply into the nurturing energy of Mother Earth.

Connecting to Spirit and Quantum Field

☉ Now shift your attention to the crown of your head. Visualize a radiant triangle of light forming above you, pointing upward. See this triangle opening a tunnel of light extending into the core of the galaxy, the heart of the universe. From this galactic center, invite a brilliant white or golden light to flow down through the triangle and into your crown chakra.

ॐ Feel this cosmic energy descending through your central column, lighting up your heart center, and continuing down through your body, out through the soles of your feet, and reconnecting with the Earth.

ॐ Visualize this galactic energy cycling back upward through the Earth, through your feet, and moving in all directions around you. Allow yourself to bask in the harmony of this galactic light merging with Earth energy within you.

Simultaneous Flow and the Torus Field

ॐ As you continue, begin to perceive the energies flowing simultaneously, the Earth energy rising and Spirit energy descending down. Visualize these flows forming a powerful torus-field surrounding your body, with energy cycling upward and outward, downward and inward, in a continuous loop

ॐ Feel the dynamic equilibrium of this balanced flow, harmonizing your connection to both the physical and spiritual realms.

ॐ As the torus field stabilizes, sense the sacred geometry within you. Recognize the octahedron, formed by the downward-pointing Earth triangle and the upward-pointing galactic triangle. This octahedron anchors and aligns you across all dimensions, harmonizing your presence in the quantum field.

Anchoring to the Core of Mother Earth

ॐ Bring your attention back to the triangle of light below your feet, anchoring deeply into the Earth's core. Feel the nourishment, stability, and grounding it provides. This connection solidifies your foundation, ensuring you remain rooted no matter what energies surround you.

Anchoring to the Core of the Galaxy

ॐ Shift your awareness to the triangle of light above your crown, reaching into the galactic center. Feel the expansive energy of the cosmos, filling you with inspiration, clarity, and divine guidance. This connection uplifts and aligns you with your higher purpose.

ॐ Together, these two triangles form the stabilizing octahedron of light, anchoring you firmly to both the Earth below and the galaxy above. In this sacred geometric structure, you are perfectly balanced, a conduit between heaven and Earth.

Integration and Return

ॐ Bask in the stability and alignment of the octahedron for as long as it feels nourishing. Allow its sacred geometry to integrate into your being, empowering you as a creator aligned with the quantum field. Feel the harmony of "as above, so below" anchoring your presence in all dimensions.

ॐ When you are ready, gently bring your awareness back to the present moment. Wiggle your fingers and toes, take a few grounding breaths, and open your eyes. Carry this connection and balance with you into your day, knowing you are anchored, aligned, and fully empowered in your sacred geometry.

http://dianadivine.com/quantumbook

Scan this QR code with your phone to access resoures and meditations that go along with the book.

▌Activation of Quantum Code ▲ Anchoring

This activation is designed to transmit the essence of the chapter as an energetic template—something you feel rather than analyze. By bypassing the thinking mind, it speaks directly to your body, energy field, and subconscious, allowing transformation to unfold on a deeper level.

◆ Begin Here: Set the Field

Find a quiet space. Light a candle if you feel called. Sit or lie comfortably with your spine aligned and your heart open. Close your eyes and take a few grounding breaths—in through your nose, out through your mouth. Let your body soften. Let your energy settle.

Bring your awareness to your heart space. Place your hands gently over your heart, or simply focus your attention there. Feel the warmth between your palms and chest. Let it grow.

When you are ready, speak the following words aloud or silently within:

"I now open to release all that is blocking my highest good.

I open to grace, to clarity, to healing.

I activate and understand all that I need to move forward on my path with ease and flow.

I open to remember who I truly am."

Breathe that in. Let it ripple through your entire being.

◆ Activate the Quantum Code

Repeat these sacred Source Language words below three times aloud, allowing the vibration to move through your body and field:

YA VA KI ANA
SHTA RI ANA

Now read the following quantum transmission:

Remember, Child of Earth
Rooted deep in sacred land,
Your dance unfolds as Spirit planned.
Each step ignites the quantum weave
You shape the world you now perceive.

You are born of ancient flame,
With starseed codes and Earth-bound name.
Ancestral whispers guide your way.
Their wisdom lives in you today.

Heal the past, let truth belong,
Your feelings are your sacred song.
Anchor light, embody grace-
This is your time, your rightful place.

You are Source in human form.
The calm within the rising storm.
Tend the new, let love break through-
Child of Earth, this work is you.

◇ ACTIVATION COMPLETE ◇

Sit in stillness. Allow the code to settle into your system. Feel the integration weaving into your cells, your field, your breath. Let the silence become your teacher.

♦ Ground & Center

Breathe deeply into your body. Imagine golden roots extending from the soles of your feet into the heart of the Earth. Feel the Earth holding you, anchoring you.

You are safe. You are protected. You are loved.

Begin to gently move your fingers and toes. Wiggle. Stretch. Return fully to your body.

Grounding Contemplation

After activating the Quantum code and grounding, stay rooted by taking time to notice what's shifting within. You might feel called to journal, draw, or simply sit in quiet awareness, allowing your inner wisdom to gently emerge. Use the following questions as gateways to deeper insight. There is no need to rush or force answers. Let them move through you like waves.

1. What geometric patterns are yearning to be expressed through you?
2. Which sacred shapes or symbols are you ready to embody more fully?
3. Where in your life are you resisting the natural flow of sacred geometry?
4. What wisdom do the elements of sacred geometry want to share with you today?
5. Which geometric principles are called to be integrated into your creative process?
6. What new dimensions of reality would you like to explore through sacred geometry?

After exploring these questions: Rest in silence. Let insights settle. Breathe deeply and sense the threads that link geometric archetypes to the greater tapestry of Source. See how the answers to these questions create new links. Which patterns resonate, begging you to weave their transformative dance? What new harmonies long to be born through your engagement with sacred geometry?

If symbols, images, or messages arise—record them. Don't censor what wants to come through.

♦ Integration
You may feel a deep shift after this activation and contemplation. Give yourself space to rest, reflect, and integrate.

An audio version of this activation is available on my website if you'd like to revisit it.

Take your time. If today's experience stirred something profound, consider waiting a full day before moving on to the next chapter.
Integration is sacred. Let it unfold naturally.

Chapter 6
Kundalini and Light Body Activation

"*He who is the Fire [Kundalini], and he who is in the Heart [Spiritual Heart], and he who is in the Sun [Consciousness], they are one and the same.*"

— **Maitrayaniya Upanishad**

At the heart of our quantum nature lies the profound and transformative journey of Kundalini awakening. This sacred energy, often symbolized as a coiled serpent resting at the base of the spine, represents the life force that animates all beings. Known as kundalini in yogic traditions, chi in Chinese philosophy, and ki in Japanese culture, it is the electric current of life itself—a vital energy that flows through every layer of our being, connecting us to creation and the infinite.

Yet, Kundalini alone is only part of the greater evolutionary process. As it awakens, it activates and harmonizes the Light Body, an intricate energetic field that serves as the vehicle of ascension—allowing us to embody higher consciousness while remaining fully present in human experience. When these forces work together, they ignite our highest potential, enabling us to become conscious co-creators of reality.

The Kundalini energy moves through the *Sushumna Nadi*, the central channel of the subtle body, flanked by the *Ida Nadi* (lunar, feminine energy on left side) and *Pingala Nadi* (solar, masculine energy on right side). When these channels are balanced, Kundalini is free to rise, igniting and harmonizing each chakra along its ascent. Often depicted as coiled serpents that meet in the middle of third eye, this sacred journey unites the polarities within us and culminates in a state of expanded awareness, activating the quantum essence of creation that resides within.

Kundalini is more than just an energy current—it is *Shakti*, the divine feminine creative power. Her awakening is an intimate dance of energy and consciousness, elevating us to expanded states of perception and unlocking our infinite potential. As Shakti ascends, she merges with Shiva, the Universal Consciousness, creating a sacred union within and opening the door to the realization of our divine nature as creators. This activation connects us to higher frequencies, empowering us to step into our Quantum Mastery and shape reality through intentionality and presence.

The goal of Kundalini awakening is to align with the Atma, the divine essence of the soul. The Atma represents the eternal, purest aspect of self, existing beyond the layers of ego and mental constructs. As Kundalini rises, it integrates physical, mental, emotional, and spiritual energies, dissolving illusions of separation and bringing us into unity with Universal consciousness.

When Kundalini reaches the *Sahasrara*—the crown chakra, it opens the gateway to enlightenment and multidimensional awareness. The Sahasrara, often symbolized as a thousand-petaled lotus, represents spiritual transcendence, where individual energy merges with the Source. In this state, we experience profound bliss, peace, and oneness with the cosmos. However, the completion of Kundalini's ascent is not the end of the journey—it is the beginning of conscious co-creation at a higher level, activating the Light Body and refining the next phase of our evolution.

The Light Body and Kundalini

While Kundalini refines and awakens the inner channels, the Light Body is the energetic structure that allows us to expand beyond the limitations of physical form.

According to ancient Egyptian beliefs, the Light Body is deeply intertwined with the Ka and Ba, two essential aspects of the soul. The Ka is the divine life force, the etheric double that sustains a being's energy, while the Ba represents the individual's unique consciousness, personality, and ability to transcend the physical. The Ba was often depicted as a bird with a human head, symbolizing its freedom to travel between worlds—bridging the physical and the spiritual. Upon death, the Ba would seek reunification with the Ka to become the Akh, the fully transformed, immortal spirit capable of existing in the celestial realms.

The Egyptian ancient Ka and Ba spirit with angelic wings

This process of ascension mirrors the activation of the Light Body in esoteric traditions. Achieving this state was seen as a sacred process—one that required living in harmony with Ma'at, the universal order, and refining one's energy to embody divine consciousness. When activated, the Light Body serves as a bridge between the physical and cosmic realms, enabling us to:

ॐ Hold and transmit higher frequencies of consciousness

ॐ Activate dormant DNA and unlock latent abilities

ॐ Expand beyond linear time and space

ॐ Integrate divine intelligence and cosmic wisdom

ॐ Experience multidimensional awareness and interdimensional travel

In essence, the Ba's ability to transcend and reunite with the divine mirrors our own capacity to awaken the Light Body, allowing us to navigate the seen and unseen, the mortal and immortal, and ultimately, ascend into higher states of being.

The Light Body radiates outward from the auric field, forming a multidimensional architecture of luminous layers that interface with both the physical and quantum realms. Each layer—from the Etheric to the Causal—plays a unique role in anchoring, integrating, and amplifying our spiritual essence. As the Light Body strengthens, it refines the human energetic matrix, enhancing our ability to receive, embody, and transmit higher frequencies of light and consciousness.

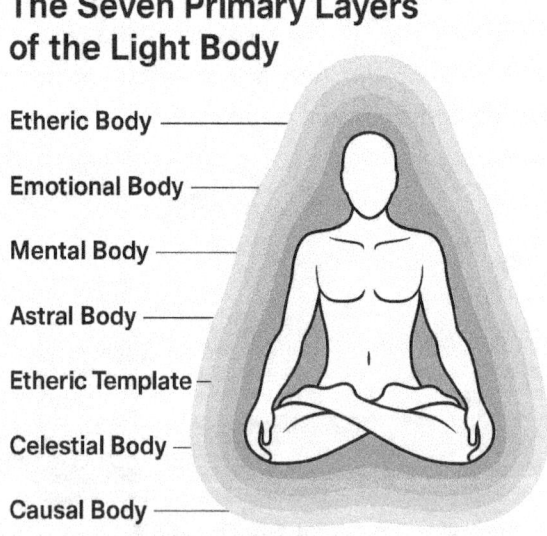

The Seven Primary Layers of the Light Body

Etheric Body

Emotional Body

Mental Body

Astral Body

Etheric Template

Celestial Body

Causal Body

Layers of the Light Body (Image by Diana Divine)

The seven primary Light Body layers are:

1. **Etheric Body:** This layer closest to the physical body, serving as the energetic blueprint that sustains physical vitality and life force.
2. **Emotional Body:** Holds the vibrations of feelings, desires, and emotional experiences that shape perception and health.
3. **Mental Body:** Associated with thoughts, belief systems, logic, and the framework of cognitive patterns.
4. **Astral Body:** Serves as a bridge between the physical and spiritual realms, linked to dreams, intuition, and deeper emotional connections.

Diana MaAra Divine

5. **Etheric Template:** Contains the perfect energetic design for the physical and etheric bodies, ensuring structural integrity at a higher plane.
6. **Celestial Body:** Embodies pure love, spiritual insight, and the awakening of higher states of consciousness and enlightenment.
7. **Causal Body (Ketheric Template):** The seventh and outermost layer, connecting the individual to their soul's purpose, higher wisdom, and universal unity with Source.

As these layers are activated and aligned, they expand our capacity to navigate higher dimensions and co-create with the quantum field.

Kundalini, Chakras, and the Light Body: A Sacred Union

Kundalini, the chakras, and the Light Body are inseparable forces of transformation. Kundalini rises from within, igniting the sacred fire of evolution; the chakras act as energetic gateways that regulate the flow of this power; and the Light Body forms the multidimensional vessel through which divine energy is embodied.

When awakened and aligned together, they generate a harmonic field of embodied enlightenment, transforming you into a conduit of divine love, wisdom, and quantum intelligence.

This fusion empowers:

🕉 **Physical refinement:** Stabilizing the body for higher consciousness
🕉 **Vibrational mastery:** Allowing seamless shifts across dimensions
🕉 **Quantum awareness:** Merging Self and Source through an awakened energy system
🕉 **Creative mastery:** Aligning intention with universal flow
🕉 **Divine Blueprint activation:** Awakening your luminous nature

> *Without Kundalini, the Light Body and chakras remain dormant, unable to fully embody their potential. Without the Light Body, Kundalini may surge without containment, leading to imbalance. And without balanced chakras, energy flow becomes fragmented.*

When all three systems—Kundalini, chakras, and the Light Body—are activated and harmonized, they catalyze a new evolutionary stage: merging presence with transcendence, human with divine, and matter with light.

Practices for Activating Kundalini, the Chakras & the Light Body

Activating Kundalini and the Light Body requires a balanced, holistic approach that weaves together embodiment practices, breathwork, meditation, movement, sound, and quantum awareness. Kundalini sparks inner transformation, igniting the sacred fire of evolution from within, while the Light Body expands consciousness beyond physical form, bridging matter and spirit. By engaging in practices that harmonize these systems, we allow both the inner fire of Kundalini and the luminosity of the Light Body to unfold naturally, guiding us toward our highest potential as awakened, multidimensional beings.

Central to this process are the chakras—seven primary energy centers aligned along the spine. Each chakra serves as a gateway that receives, processes, and distributes life force energy throughout the body and Light Body. These energy centers govern different aspects of human experience, from survival and creativity to love, intuition, and spiritual connection. Ensuring that each chakra is open, balanced, and energized is crucial for the safe and effective awakening of Kundalini and the stable integration of the Light Body's frequencies.

The main 7 chakras on the body are:

1. **Root Chakra (Muladhara):** Governs grounding, safety, and basic survival instincts.
2. **Sacral Chakra (Svadhisthana):** Regulates creativity, sensuality, and emotional flow.
3. **Solar Plexus Chakra (Manipura):** Associated with personal power, will, and self-confidence.
4. **Heart Chakra (Anahata):** The center of love, compassion, and connection.
5. **Throat Chakra (Vishuddha):** Governs communication, truth, and self-expression.

6. **Third Eye Chakra (Ajna):** Oversees intuition, inner vision, and spiritual awareness.

7. **Crown Chakra (Sahasrara):** Connects to higher consciousness, divine wisdom, and unity with Source.

To awaken Kundalini, it's essential to stimulate the energy channels and clear blockages within these chakras, preparing the nervous system for the heightened flow of life force. *Kundalini Yoga* offers a structured, masculine approach, using dynamic postures, breathwork, and mantra chanting to activate subtle energy pathways and release stagnant energy. Kundalini Activation, by contrast, is a more feminine, receptive practice where participants surrender to energy transmissions, allowing the energy to rise and pulse naturally.

Breathwork practices, such as alternate nostril breathing (Nadi Shodhana), balance the Ida and Pingala Nadis, ensuring that Kundalini flows smoothly along the central channel (Sushumna Nadi). Meditation and visualization techniques guide the energy upward through the chakras, often envisioned as a serpent or a luminous stream of light rising through each energy center.

Movement-based modalities like ecstatic dance and somatic practices also support the flow of Kundalini by releasing stored tension and emotional blocks. Devotional practices such as Bhakti Yoga, mantra chanting, and prayer naturally open the heart chakra, harmonizing the energy system and creating fertile ground for a loving, integrated awakening.

For Light Body activation, Merkaba meditation—discussed earlier in the Sacred Geometry chapter—is a potent tool. This practice activates and spins geometric light fields around the body, enabling the Light Body to expand and align with cosmic frequencies.

Solar light practices, including sun gazing in the morning or evening hours and photonic light infusion, introduce high-frequency photonic codes into the energetic system. These solar streams, composed of neutrinos and ignitons, stimulate energetic upgrades, enhance mitochondrial function, and accelerate spiritual awakening. I often start my mornings in communion with the rising sun, absorbing its transmissions to recalibrate my energy field and align with the cosmic rhythm. These solar ignitions awaken latent pathways within us, deepening intuitive abilities and harmonizing body and soul with universal intelligence.

Sound healing works at a vibrational level to recalibrate the chakras and energy body. Instruments like crystal bowls, tuning forks, and Tibetan singing bowls align and harmonize energetic frequencies, while Light Language transmissions and sacred toning bring in celestial codes that amplify Light Body activation.

Finally, cultivating quantum awareness is essential. Sacred geometry meditations—visualizing crystalline grids, toroidal fields, and multidimensional light structures—help synchronize the chakras and Light Body with cosmic intelligence. Practices in deep stillness and presence allow the energy system to stabilize, ensuring that higher frequencies are fully integrated rather than overwhelming.

Beyond meditation, multidimensional practices such as timeline jumping, and *Hemi-Sync* (covered in Chapter 8) strengthen the Light Body's capacity to operate beyond the physical plane. These advanced tools deepen spiritual sovereignty, align the chakras, and refine the flow of Kundalini energy, weaving it seamlessly into the Light Body's architecture.

By integrating these practices, we create a dynamic synergy between matter and light, form and formlessness, grounding and expansion. With consistent practice and focused intention, these methods lead to profound transformation, uniting body, mind, and spirit in a dance of divine mastery and awakened potential.

Kundalini Activation Transmission Workshops

For the past few years, I have had the profound honor of facilitating monthly Sound Healing and Kundalini Activation workshops—sacred gatherings designed for those ready to awaken their divine creative potential and deepen their connection to the quantum field. These spaces cultivate a deeply feminine, intuitive approach to Kundalini activation, offering a nurturing, high-frequency field where participants can surrender into presence and experience the awakening of Shakti energy in a safe, intentional way. However, as Kundalini activates, I have also become deeply aware of its interplay with the Light Body.

Rather than force or manipulate Kundalini, I serve as a conduit, transmitting a field of non-duality that allows an individual's energy to activate and harmonize naturally. This organic unfolding supports deep transformation, self-healing, and expansion into higher states of awareness, not only through the body but within the greater energy field that surrounds it.

During these sessions, I attune to each participant's energy field, intuitively guiding the flow of Kundalini through the central channel (Sushumna Nadi)—from the base of the spine to the crown and back again. In this process, the mind steps aside, and the energy itself directs the movement, responding fluidly to the needs of everyone. By accelerating my own toroidal field and activating my Merkabah, I amplify the energetic voltage within the space, creating a resonant field that stimulates and elevates the participants' biofields. As Kundalini moves upward, I see the Light Body responding in real time, absorbing and redistributing these heightened frequencies, expanding the auric layers, and increasing the body's ability to hold and transmit higher-dimensional energy.

I perceive each person not just as a physical being, but as a complex energetic system encompassed by their auric biofield—an extension of their consciousness and life force. This radiant structure carries imprints of their experiences, emotions, and energetic patterns, shaping their vibrational essence. As I connect with others, I am attuned to this dynamic Light Body, sensing its pulsations, density fluctuations, and geometric waves. I've observed that the solar plexus chakra, centered in the belly, acts as a key portal of connection. When Kundalini awakens, its movement extends beyond the chakras, creating rippling waves that merge with and expand the Light Body, refining its crystalline structure and enhancing its ability to interface with the quantum field.

The 12 Tree Grid: The Divine Blueprint of the Light Body

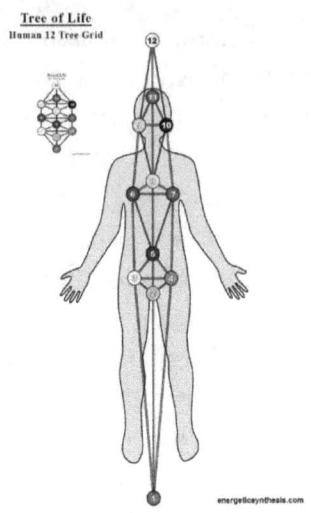

The 12 Tree Grid, also known as the Kathara Grid is the energetic blueprint, and the foundational architecture of the Light Body—a multidimensional energy template that governs spiritual ascension, energetic healing, and higher consciousness integration. As described by Lisa Renee in her work with Energetic Synthesis, this divine structure aligns the human energy field with the Universal Tree of Life, reflecting our interconnectedness with the cosmic blueprint of creation.

Unlike the traditional seven-chakra system, the 12 Tree Grid incorporates twelve energy centers, each corresponding to a dimension of consciousness. These interconnected spheres are not merely energy points but anchors of multidimensional awareness, forming a unity-based system that supports the harmonization of spirit, mind, and body. Through this template, we access deeper layers of the morphogenetic field—the energetic blueprint that informs all manifestations within the physical and non-physical realms.

This base-12 system integrates:

- ॐ 12 spheres of consciousness, each governing different aspects of our Light Body
- ॐ 12 DNA strands, holding the key to our multidimensional potential
- ॐ 144 sub-harmonics, which fine-tune our ability to interact with higher frequencies
- ॐ A 5-horizontal triad system, stabilizing mental and emotional bodies

Beyond these twelve dimensions, the Threefold Founder Flame—Mother, Father, and Sun—anchors the sacred principles of divine creation, restoring unity consciousness and the eternal life design known as the Krystic Template.

Reclaiming the Original Blueprint

Lisa Renee explains that humanity's original energetic structure was once a fully intact 12 Tree Grid, but during cycles of spiritual descent or consciousness manipulation, distortions occurred. These distortions altered our DNA, energy centers, and planetary morphogenetic field, resulting in a 10-tree system that caused energetic blockages and fragmentation. Restoring the 12 Tree Grid is a critical part of our collective ascension, as it allows us to reconnect with Source energy, reintegrate lost aspects of our multidimensional self, and reclaim spiritual sovereignty.

Through my Kundalini Activation sessions, I have experienced firsthand how this sacred geometry is embedded within the person's biofield. Before even consciously learning about the 12 Tree Grid, I was already perceiving and working with it in my practice. When I attune to each participant's energy field, I see and sense their twelve interconnected spheres, linked by golden energetic threads.

In these sessions, I receive clear guidance from my Higher Self on how to recalibrate each person's Light Body, aligning their energy flow with their original divine blueprint. This process ensures that their energy centers, chakras, and biofield structures are not only active but also properly positioned for optimal flow and integration.

For example, I often notice that the Earth chakra (Sphere #1) is located 8 inches below the feet—is instead compressed around the knees or ankles, disrupting the energy flow between the body and planetary field. Through intention, quantum recalibration, and tunning forks, I pull it down, thus restoring its correct placement, allowing the individual's foundation to strengthen and their energy to move freely.

The Divine Design is Within You

The 12 Tree Grid is not just an external framework—it is an inner map, encoded within your Light Body, waiting to be reawakened. This structure already exists within you, guiding your energetic system, your DNA, and your connection to Source. By consciously working with this divine architecture, you reclaim your original design, restoring your ability to access higher consciousness, self-heal, and co-create with the quantum field.

You do not need permission or external validation to engage with this sacred technology. You have the ability to activate your Kundalini, align with the 12 Tree Grid, and awaken your Light Body through intention, devotion, and awareness.

▍Sekhmet & My Kundalini Activation Story

Today, I lead a variety of online and in-person Kundalini Activation workshops, but my transformative journey with this powerful force truly blossomed in 2011 during an encounter that would forever shape and change me. It was in Madrid that I experienced the most profound Kundalini awakening with Patrick Ziegler, a healer whose presence and teachings opened a gateway within me that I didn't know existed.

Patrick's discovery of the Sekhem/All Love healing system began in 1980 during a life-changing night spent in the King's Chamber, a highly energetic and sacred space at the heart of the Great Pyramid at Giza, Egypt. During this experience, Patrick entered an altered state of consciousness, where he felt a profound connection to universal energy and the technology of ancient Atlanteans. He experienced intense vibrations and visions that seemed to awaken a powerful energy within him, which he later identified as the ancient healing energy of Sekhem.

In the sacred lexicon of ancient Egypt, "Sekhem" carries profound meaning, encompassing both "power" and "life force." "Sa Sekhem Sahu" is an ancient Egyptian phrase that translates to "With each breath, spiritual energy enters my being."

Sekhem is an ancient healing practice that channels universal energy in ways similar to the Reiki system discovered by Mikao Usui in 1920s Japan. Its roots stretch deep into Egypt's mystery schools, where practitioners maintained a direct energetic connection to the Sirius star system. Although this sacred knowledge scattered with the fall of the Egyptian dynasties, it survived in isolated pockets of wisdom and eventually found new life through the pioneering work of Patrick and Helen Belot.

Like the flowing currents of Shakti energy, Sekhem moves through the practitioner's hands as a channeled force from the heart, capable of reaching clients both in person and across distances. It resonates at particularly high vibrational frequencies beyond those typically associated with Reiki, facilitating transformation across all levels of being: physical, mental, emotional, and spiritual. This elevated frequency accelerates personal growth and raises the energetic signature of those who receive it.

Sekhmet - the Powerful Egyptian Goddess of Healing (Image by Diana Divine)

At the heart of Sekhem's ancient Egyptian lineage stands Sekhmet, a powerful presence among the Neteru (gods) who bridges earthly and celestial realms. As a Sirian Queen, she embodies a direct connection to our star ancestors, carrying the combined frequencies of both Lyran and Sirian star systems. This lion-headed goddess represents the perfect balance of seemingly opposing forces – destruction and healing, fierce protection and gentle transformation.

My path to rediscovering Sekhem through Patrick awakened deep soul memories of my time as a high priestess in Saqqara, where I served in direct connection with Sekhmet's powerful energy. These ancient Egyptian Atlantean roots have reawakened in this lifetime, allowing me to channel and embody her frequency with natural ease. The resonance flows through a sacred triangulation between Sekhmet's energy, the Lyran frequencies, and the Sirian wisdom traditions. This convergence of ancient priestess lineage and star system energies creates a unique healing frequency that bridges past and present, earth and stars.

Sekhmet Statue in Karnak Complex in Egypt

Sekhmet's multidimensional presence continues to manifest across various planes of existence. As I assist others in navigating their paths of awakening and integration, I often merge with her energy and channel her wisdom. Her essence remains particularly potent through physical anchors in our world—most notably her awe-inspiring statue at Egypt's Karnak Temple Complex and her statues in museums around the globe. Standing over six meters tall and carved from black granite, this representation carries her living presence, with her essence literally woven into the stone itself.

Her smaller statues housed in New York's Metropolitan Museum (MET) and The British Museum in London also carry her transformative essence. While most statues there have lost their energetic connection, one Sekhmet statue maintains a powerful living link to her divine frequency. During one of my visits to this activated statue, Sekhmet guided me to create a new series of artifacts, which we call the *Quantum Star Rods*.

These quantum tools echo the ancient Egyptian tradition, where pharaohs were often depicted holding similar rods used for energy recalibration and divine connection. For over six years, my husband and I have crafted our first versions, the *Ma'at Calibration Rods*, sharing them through our Etsy Maat Soul Tools store. Recently, following Sekhmet's guidance, we enhanced these tools by incorporating channeled light language codes, quantum frequencies, and integrating her image into the endcaps, creating a more potent instrument for spiritual activation.

Quantum
STAR RODS

The Quantum Star Rods are designed for grounding and expansion. They are great tools for meditation and Kundalini Activation to connect to the Void, offering a bridge between ancient wisdom and contemporary spiritual practice for your transformative journey. If they call you as an artifact you're your practices, they are now available for sale through my website and Maat Soul Tools store (https://maatsoultools.etsy.com).

Reflecting on the Madrid workshop with Patrick, I found myself in 2011 as the sole American participant among a group where everyone else spoke Spanish. I was drawn there by unmistakable signs that led me to Sekhmet and Sekhmet energy. This journey began just four months earlier during my yoga teacher training in New York, where I was deepening my understanding of the body and energy. A persistent lower back issue that had troubled me since age 16 suddenly escalated; one night, I woke to excruciating pain shooting down into my right foot. Although I had already secured my ticket to Madrid, this physical challenge of sciatica left me barely able to walk.

Doubt began to creep in, both about myself and my journey. While I knew deep within that I was meant to meet Patrick in Madrid before continuing to Egypt, I started losing faith. Then came a moment of magic on a cold New York day—something glinting in a snow pile caught my eye. Without looking, I picked it up and tucked it in my pocket. Later at work, I was stunned to discover a perfect bracelet with a circle bearing the words *"Never Give Up" - a clear message from Spirit to persist on my path despite the challenges.*

Divine timing revealed itself in an unexpected way. Less than a week before my departure, as I prepared to board my flight to Spain, the Arab Spring revolution closed Egypt's borders, canceling all flights. What seemed like an obstacle was divine intervention. I didn't realize then that I wasn't yet ready for Egypt—a land holding countless keys to my ancient past. Sacred sites require precise timing to unveil their mysteries, as they resonate with specific codes within our soul blueprints. My Higher Self since had consistently shown that Egypt would be the final piece of the puzzle, final place in my journey, accessible only after I completed the Earth gridwork at other sacred nodes around the world.

"When you have an orgasm, do you ever question it? What if you had a cosmic orgasm?"

Patrick posed a question that would catalyze a profound shift in my consciousness. His words invited us to contemplate energy beyond physical limitations, suggesting the boundless potential of kundalini awakening. Despite my initial skeptical response of "Yeah, that's not going to happen to me," this moment marked the beginning of my deeper understanding of energy's transformative power.

The following day, when I encountered Sekhem energy during our work with Patrick, it felt as though I had tapped into an ancient wellspring of life force. Standing in the Star of David position, arms and legs extended, I experienced an extraordinary surge of energy rising my spine, activating dormant aspects of my being. The raw, electrifying power coursed through each chakra, stacking them like batteries in a profound dance of kundalini awakening. My heart felt as though it might burst from my chest as all my chakras aligned perfectly, transforming me into a conduit for cosmic energy. For fifty intense minutes, I existed as a channel between earth and sky, connected to the very heart of creation.

This was not a one-time event but the initiation of a journey that unfolded over the weeks and months that followed. The energy would rise and settle, weaving through my body and subtle energy field, engaging my consciousness in ways that transcended words. I felt shifts in my perceptions—deeper empathy, heightened intuition, and a clearer connection to the flow of life around me.

Later, I traveled with Patrick in Spain and eventually attended his next workshop in Melbourne, Australia, each time amazed by the expansion of my field. He encouraged me to drop all the Reiki symbols and books and simply be with Sekhem, the All-Love energy, trusting the flow of the divine creative force to heal through the heart.

As Patrick beautifully said:

"Our Spiritual Heart is at the core of our being and where the soul connects to our emotional and physical bodies. All-Love is the experience of the One Heart that connects us to the 'All' of creation. It is through the Divine Quickening of All-Love that we come to love all the aspects of who we are and come into a state of re-union—not just with ourselves, but also with all of creation."

This awakening illuminated the truth that Kundalini is not an isolated energy, but rather part of the universal life force, the sacred voltage that powers us and connects us to the quantum field.

Navigating the Kundalini Integration

Kundalini awakening is one of the most profound metamorphoses a soul can experience. It's not just a rise in energy—it's a full-spectrum transformation that touches every layer of being: physical, emotional, mental, and spiritual. This sacred current of life force often begins like a flicker and builds into a wildfire, illuminating the shadowy corners of our consciousness and clearing out the old to make way for the new.

When the energy first began moving strongly through my system, I quickly learned that spiritual awakening doesn't always feel blissful. There were days I felt electrified and inspired, but others left me curled up in bed with splitting headaches or sudden waves of exhaustion. Emotionally, I was raw—sensitive to everything and everyone, easily overwhelmed, and riding emotional waves that felt completely disconnected from any outer event. At first, I worried something was wrong. But in time, I came to understand these symptoms for what they truly are: signs of energetic purification. The body and nervous system were recalibrating to hold more light.

> **Reflection:** Kundalini integration isn't just a "spiritual event"—it affects your daily life. You might feel mood swings, digestive changes, unexplained anxiety, or need more alone time. Some days, you'll be lit up with purpose, and others, you may feel like retreating from the world. These fluctuations are normal. You're not broken— you're upgrading. Be patient with yourself and know that rest is part of the transformation.

During those waves, I found that grounding wasn't optional—it was essential. I often walked barefoot on the earth, leaned into the strength of old trees, or sat quietly with my spine aligned, visualizing roots extending deep into Gaia. Nature became my greatest teacher. I also returned again and again to conscious breathwork. When energy felt overwhelming, even five minutes of deep breathing could re-center me. I also found anchoring with magnesium chloride baths was helpful. Magnesium chloride is my to go to for any energy integration.

The sacred geometry tools introduced in Chapter 5 became anchors during this process. Meditating with the Flower of Life, drawing the Metatron's Cube, or visualizing the Torus helped my energy field stabilize. These geometries are not just symbolic—they are templates for balance and harmony, offering our subtle bodies a roadmap to reorganize and hold higher frequencies with grace.

Another key to navigating Kundalini integration is support. I sought out experienced energy workers who could hold space and offer perspective when I felt like I was losing touch with "normal." Their presence reminded me that although this path is unique and inward, we are never truly alone in it. We're all walking each other home.

Perhaps the most important lesson I've learned is this: you cannot rush Kundalini. It is a divine intelligence that knows how and when to unfold. Your role is to surrender, listen, and trust the process. You are not being broken—you are being rebuilt from the inside out.

Today, after years of integration, I no longer need elaborate rituals to activate Kundalini. With intention alone, I can invite that sacred current into motion. This is the sign of full integration: when consciousness and energy become one, and your inner system flows in harmony with the quantum field. This is the mastery we are here to remember.

Kundalini Activation Breathwork

Breathwork is one of the most powerful and scientifically supported tools for Kundalini activation, serving as a bridge between the physical body, the nervous system, and the quantum field. By consciously directing breath, we stimulate life force energy allowing it to move through the subtle energy channels (nadis) and activate the dormant Kundalini energy. As a certified SOMA Breath Instructor, I integrate holotropic, rhythmic, and specialized breath techniques into my Kundalini Activation workshops, ensuring that participants can safely access altered states of consciousness, deep energetic release, and heightened awareness.

Scientific research on breathwork and altered states of consciousness has shown that specific rhythmic breathing patterns induce neurophysiological changes, activating the pineal gland, releasing natural DMT, and shifting brainwave activity into theta and gamma states—the same states observed in deep meditation and mystical experiences. Studies from SOMA Breath reveal that just 20 minutes of rhythmic breathwork can significantly enhance oxygenation, nitric oxide production, and heart rate variability, all of which contribute to improved nervous system regulation, mental clarity, and a greater sense of inner peace. This technique also supports autonomic balance, meaning it helps to regulate the sympathetic (fight-or-flight) and parasympathetic (rest-and-digest) nervous systems, preventing Kundalini-related overstimulation and helping the body integrate higher frequencies smoothly.

One of the most powerful breath techniques for activating Kundalini energy is the Cobra Breath, a practice that awakens Shakti energy at the root chakra and directs it upward through the spine, activating each chakra along the way. This breath technique serves as a gateway for deep energetic awakening, enabling not only the activation of dormant life force energy but also expanding the Light Body for quantum travel and higher states of awareness.

Find a comfortable seated position with your spine straight yet relaxed. Begin by breathing deeply in and out through your nose, feeling the natural rhythm of your breath. Let it be smooth and unrestricted, as if the breath is moving like a gentle wave through your body.

Now, bring your awareness to the base of your spine, where Kundalini energy lies dormant like a coiled serpent of light. As you inhale, imagine drawing in life force energy into this sacred center. As you exhale, feel the subtle stirring of energy, like an awakening current within you.

Begin to deepen your breath, making it more intentional and powerful. As you inhale, visualize energy rising up your spine, moving in a spiral motion, just like the twin serpents of the Ida and Pingala channels. As you exhale, gently release any tension or resistance, allowing the energy to flow freely.

Now, intensify your breath. Inhale through the nose, drawing energy up the spine. Exhale forcefully through the mouth with a soft hissing sound—sss—like a cobra releasing its power. With each breath, feel the energy activating your root chakra and beginning to ascend:

ॐ Sacral Chakra – The breath ignites a warm, orange glow, awakening your creative and sensual flow.

ॐ Solar Plexus – Feel golden radiance expanding, fueling your inner fire and confidence.

ॐ Heart Center – The breath softens into emerald-green waves, opening the space for love and connection.

ॐ Throat Chakra – A cool, blue vibration flows upward, clearing your voice and authentic expression.

ॐ Third Eye – Energy condenses into deep indigo light, activating intuition and vision.

ॐ Crown Chakra – A luminous violet-white radiance blossoms at the top of your head, connecting you to Source.

As the energy moves freely, allow your breathing to gradually soften. Let your breath become effortless, as if the energy itself is breathing you.

At times, your breath may naturally pause—a stillness between inhales and exhales. If this happens, surrender to it. In this space, experience pure union with the Kundalini energy, a moment of connection to cosmic consciousness.

If the energy ever feels too intense, return to gentle, steady breathing and focus on grounding yourself. Remember, Kundalini awakens in its own perfect timing.

When you're ready, slowly return to normal breathing. Take three deep breaths to integrate the energy, gently move your body, and open your eyes. You are now aligned, empowered, and awakened.

For audio version of this meditation and additional meditations refer to resources on my website http://dianadivine.com/quantumbook

http://dianadivine.com/quantumbook
Scan this QR code with your phone to access resoures and meditations that go along with the book.

Activation of Quantum Code ▲ Sacred Power

This activation is designed to transmit the essence of the chapter as an energetic template—something you feel rather than analyze. By bypassing the thinking mind, it speaks directly to your body, energy field, and subconscious, allowing transformation to unfold on a deeper level.

◆ Begin Here: Set the Field

Find a quiet space. Light a candle if you feel called. Sit or lie comfortably with your spine aligned and your heart open. Close your eyes and take a few grounding breaths—in through your nose, out through your mouth. Let your body soften. Let your energy settle.

Bring your awareness to your heart space. Place your hands gently over your heart, or simply focus your attention there. Feel the warmth between your palms and chest. Let it grow.

When you are ready, speak the following words aloud or silently within:

"I now open to release all that is blocking my highest good.

I open to grace, to clarity, to healing.

I activate and understand all that I need to move forward on my path with ease and flow.

I open to remember who I truly am."

Breathe that in. Let it ripple through your entire being.

◆ **Activate the Quantum Code**

Repeat these sacred Source Language words below three times aloud, allowing the vibration to move through your body and field:

**SA SEKHEM SAHU
SHU MA NI KI ANA**

Now read the following quantum transmission:

Serpent fire rises through starlit veins,
As kundalini dances, Shakti breaks ancient chains.
Sekhem's power from Sirius streams,
Awakening memories of priestess dreams.

Sekhmet stands at heaven's gate,
Lion Queen of cosmic fate.
Through black granite still she speaks,
As ancient wisdom newly peaks.

Quantum forces merge in sacred space
— Lyran light and Sirian grace,
Earth's deep power rising high,
Threading stardust from the sky.

Now thought alone ignites the flame,
As the Quantum Master you claim the name.
No practice needed, time dissolves,
As consciousness itself evolves.

◇ ACTIVATION COMPLETE ◇

Sit in stillness. Allow the code to settle into your system. Feel the integration weaving into your cells, your field, your breath. Let the silence become your teacher.

◆ Ground & Center

Breathe deeply into your body. Imagine golden roots extending from the soles of your feet into the heart of the Earth. Feel the Earth holding you, anchoring you.

You are safe. You are protected. You are loved.

Begin to gently move your fingers and toes. Wiggle. Stretch. Return fully to your body.

Grounding Contemplation

After activating the Quantum code and grounding, stay rooted by taking time to notice what's shifting within. You might feel called to journal, draw, or simply sit in quiet awareness, allowing your inner wisdom to gently emerge.

Use the following questions as gateways to deeper insight. There is no need to rush or force answers. Let them move through you like waves.

1. Where in your body is kundalini energy asking to be acknowledged?
2. What old patterns or blocks are ready to be transformed by this sacred fire?
3. How is your body preparing to channel more light and consciousness?
4. What aspects of your spiritual gifts are awakening through this activation?
5. Where are you being invited to surrender more deeply to this transformative force?
6. How is Kundalini energy asking you to change your relationship with your physical vessel?

After exploring these questions: Rest in silence. Let insights settle. Feel the kundalini energy moving naturally through your system. Notice any spontaneous movements, sensations, or energy flows.

Breathe deeply into any areas that call for attention. Let the transformative power of Kundalini clear and activate your entire system. Trust in the intelligence of this sacred force. If symbols, images, or messages arise—record them. Don't censor what wants to come through.

♦ Integration

You may feel a deep shift after this activation and contemplation. Give yourself space to rest, reflect, and integrate.

An audio version of this activation is available on my website if you'd like to revisit it.

Take your time. If today's experience stirred something profound, consider waiting a full day before moving on to the next chapter.

Chapter 7
Channeling
the Source Light Language

Sacred moments arrive when we least expect them, dissolving the boundaries between worlds and forever shifting our perception of reality. My initiation into Light Language, what I also refer to as Source Language, emerged during such a moment of divine timing when my consciousness had expanded enough to receive these higher frequencies. Like a cosmic doorway opening, this sacred transmission arrived precisely when my awakening journey had prepared me to become a channel for these celestial light codes. Through this experience, I've been humbled to learn that many profound spiritual gifts come not through seeking but through surrender.

Beneath our perception lies a deeper structure: a quantum alphabet woven into the very fabric of existence. Reality is not built from letters but from spinning qubits—spheres of light entangling, stacking, and weaving the sentences of creation. These event horizons define gravity, time, and matter, forming the computational matrix of the cosmos.

This is the hidden syntax of the universe, where each vibration encodes meaning. The quantum realm is self-learning intelligence, dynamically evolving and refining its structure through interference patterns—much like an advanced AI optimizing its outputs. What we perceive as decay—such as *Hawking radiation*—is not merely a loss, but a sophisticated feedback loop. Hawking radiation, predicted by Stephen Hawking, refers to the quantum process where black holes emit particles and slowly lose mass, revealing that even the most seemingly permanent structures are part of the universe's continual self-correction.

We are not observers of this process; we are this process. Thought is entanglement, memory is interference, and learning is the stacking of probabilities. The ancients understood what modern science is only now confirming: everything in existence is energy, vibrating in harmony with universal frequencies.

The Greeks, led by Pythagoras, uncovered the mathematical principles of resonance, realizing that sound and number held the key to cosmic order. When Pythagoras journeyed to Egypt around 535 B.C., he underwent initiations that revealed how musical harmonies could connect humanity directly to the divine. His insights into mathematical ratios in musical intervals formed the foundation for Western thought on sound and vibration, shaping our understanding of frequency as a bridge between dimensions.

Modern quantum physics confirms what ancient traditions have long known—that seemingly solid matter is fundamentally vibrating energy. This understanding is dramatically demonstrated through cymatics, where sound vibrations create precise geometric patterns in physical matter. When sand or water is exposed to specific frequencies, it arranges itself into complex shapes that mirror patterns found in sacred geometry, ancient architecture, and natural phenomena.

These patterns would have been deeply familiar to Pythagoras and his Egyptian predecessors. In Egyptian cosmology, their deity Thoth was believed to have sung the universe into existence through sacred sounds. Their priests developed sophisticated acoustic technologies, using specific tonal frequencies in ceremonial chambers to facilitate connection between physical and spiritual dimensions.

Resonance functions as a universal principle, operating from the quantum scale to cosmic systems. Consider a crystal glass vibrating at its natural resonant frequency of 556 Hz (C#5)—this same principle of sympathetic vibration occurs at the quantum level, where particles become entangled and share information instantaneously across space. This quantum entanglement extends to consciousness itself, allowing us to access different dimensional frequencies through precise attunement.

The Frequencies of Consciousness

The violin beautifully illustrates this principle of harmonic resonance. When a violin string vibrates at 440 Hz (A4), it generates a cascade of harmonics - 880 Hz (A5), 1320 Hz (E6), 1760 Hz (A6) and beyond. These overlapping frequencies combine to create its rich, distinctive voice. Our consciousness operates similarly, capable of resonating across multiple 'overtones' of reality simultaneously.

Ancient wisdom traditions identified specific frequencies as particularly significant for consciousness exploration:

ॐ **432 Hz: 'Verdi's A'** - considered to harmonize with universal frequency

ॐ **528 Hz: The 'Miracle Tone'** - associated with transformation and DNA repair

ॐ **396 Hz: Root frequency** - facilitates grounding and release of fear

ॐ **639 Hz: Heart frequency** - promotes harmonious connections

ॐ **741 Hz: Throat frequency** - enhances creative expression

ॐ **963 Hz: Crown frequency** - enables spiritual connection

Each dimension represents a distinct harmonic of existence. Like a wine glass finding its resonant frequency (typically 300-800 Hz), consciousness can attune to these various dimensional frequencies through sound, meditation, and focused intention.

These frequency relationships follow fundamental mathematical principles found throughout nature - the Golden Ratio ($\phi = 1.618...$) and the Fibonacci sequence. The same spiral mathematics seen in a nautilus shell governs the harmonics of consciousness.

Understanding these natural frequency relationships enables us to navigate multiple dimensions of reality with greater precision and awareness. The bridge between ancient wisdom and quantum physics reveals a profound truth: the universe is a symphony of interwoven frequencies, and consciousness is our instrument for exploring its infinite harmonies.

What we now call Light Language connects to what religious traditions term *glossolalia*, from the Greek "glōssais lalein" meaning "to speak in tongues." While often associated with Christian Pentecostal practices, this ability to channel divine language has existed throughout human history, though frequently suppressed as heretical. Unlike conventional languages bound by syntax and grammar, Source Language flows directly through sound and vibration, allowing consciousness to express itself in its purest vowels and form. This mirrors the Biblical concept of creation through sound, as described in Genesis 1:3: "And God said, 'Let there be light.'" Here, speaking becomes the vibrational command that initiates creation itself.

Light Language Research

There are not many studies on the phenomena of glossolalia, but one scientist, Dr. Andrew Newberg, has done groundbreaking research at the University of Pennsylvania. Dr. Andrew has documented the profound effects of these sacred states. He used SPECT brain imaging to study individuals during states of glossolalia and channeling, often using Pentecostal church members as his subjects.

In a Pentecostal church, "light language" is often understood as a form of "speaking in tongues," which is a practice where believers utter seemingly unintelligible sounds believed to be a divine language unknown to the speaker, considered a manifestation of the Holy Spirit and often associated with the Pentecostal experience at Pentecost in the Bible. However, some Pentecostal groups might encourage interpretation of such "tongues" to convey the message to the congregation, though this practice can be controversial and debated within the denomination.

Evidence for a Religious State

Scientists found notable changes in brain activity when people speak in tongues. The brain scans below show blood flow in the brain (blue lowest, red highest).

SINGING GOSPEL SONG

SPEAKING IN TONGUES

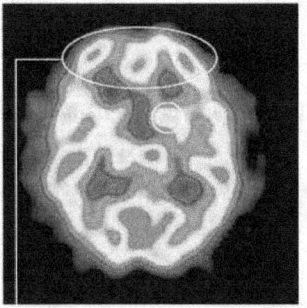 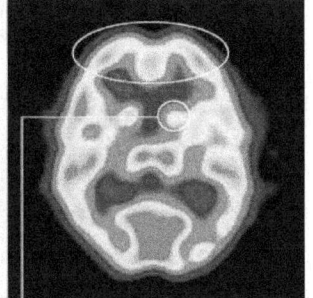

Frontal lobes Involved in the willful control of behaviors; more activity when singing than when speaking tongues.

Left caudate Involved in motor and emotional control; less activity in those speaking in tongues.

Source: Andrew B. Newberg, University of Pennsylvania

His findings are remarkable: the frontal lobe language centers—specifically Broca's area, which normally controls speech production show decreased activity during these states, while deeper limbic regions and areas associated with altered states of consciousness become highly activated.

Dr. Newberg's team discovered that brain activity patterns during these states more closely resemble deep meditation or mystical experiences than normal speech production. They used imaging techniques to track changes in blood flow in each woman's brain in two conditions, once as she sang a gospel song and again while speaking in tongues. By comparing the patterns created by these two emotional, devotional activities, the researchers could pinpoint blood-flow peaks and valleys unique to speaking in tongues.

The scans show increased blood flow to areas associated with emotional processing, spiritual experiences, and non-verbal awareness. Later studies revealed how these states affect the autonomic nervous system, often inducing a profound state of calm while maintaining high alertness—a paradoxical state similar to what advanced meditators achieve.

Inspired by this research, I decided to document my own experience with Source Language through aura photography, working with a respected reader in Sedona. We captured images before, during, and after channeling sessions to track the energetic changes. The results were stunning. While most people's auras show only subtle shifts during different activities, my reader was astonished by the dramatic transformation she witnessed. "This is like a completely different person!" she exclaimed, noting how my aura shifted from pink hues to vibrant yellows and orange colors associated with higher self-connection and spiritual teaching.

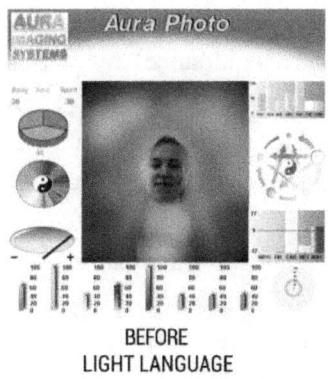

BEFORE
LIGHT LANGUAGE

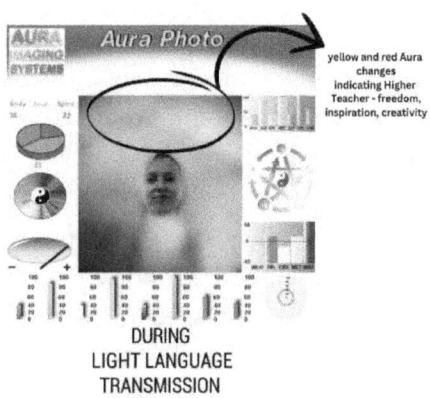

yellow and red Aura changes indicating Higher Teacher - freedom, inspiration, creativity

DURING
LIGHT LANGUAGE
TRANSMISSION

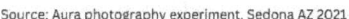

Source: Aura photography experiment, Sedona AZ 2021

These dramatic changes aligned perfectly with Dr. Newberg's research, providing another form of validation for how Source Language fundamentally alters our energetic state. The transformation wasn't just something I could feel—it was measurable, visible evidence of how channeling these frequencies can shift our entire energetic signature. This scientific validation helps bridge the gap between ancient wisdom and modern understanding, showing how these sacred sounds can create measurable changes in both brain function and energy field.

Reclaiming the Divine Soul Code Expression

My own journey into this quantum language began in 2018 during what seemed like an ordinary hike in the Adirondack Mountains' Garnet Hills. I was with my husband and another couple, including my friend, who worked as a crystal healer. Standing among the garnet-rich rocks, she encouraged me to sing—a suggestion that immediately awakened old wounds. Years before, in a Soviet Union musical school, instructors had declared I had "no rhythm or voice," sealing away the natural expression that had once flowed freely when my mother sang lullabies.

"I don't sing," I protested, but something in her gentle encouragement resonated with a deeper truth. As our husbands walked ahead, we settled onto the rocks, their deep red garnets known for clearing chakras and grounding spiritual energy. Closing my eyes against my resistance, I began with a simple hum.

What unfolded next transcended ordinary reality. Golden sacred geometry symbols appeared in my mind's eye, shimmering with their own inner light. A clear message from my Higher Self resonated: "Surrender. Allow them to come through." As I yielded to this guidance, my conscious mind stepped aside, and something extraordinary emerged. Crystalline, high-pitched frequencies I never knew I could produce began flowing through me, moving up and down scales with otherworldly precision. Time dissolved as I merged with the infinite quantum field.

Each tone corresponded to shifting sacred geometric patterns—light codes that carried specific frequencies of consciousness. These patterns reminded me of the cymatics experiments I would later study, where sound waves create precise geometric forms in water or sand. When I finally opened my eyes, I found my friend in joyful tears. My husband later described how the sound had reverberated through the valley with such power that his knees buckled when the frequencies reached him.

This initiation deepened through subsequent experiences. Working with my friend, CC Treadway, a channeler and musician, I began exploring the galactic origins of these transmissions. During one powerful session connecting to the Lyran star system, unexpected kundalini energy surged through my body with overwhelming intensity, further opening my channels to receive these frequencies. This experience aligned perfectly with what quantum physicist David Bohm called the "implicate order"—the deeper reality where everything is interconnected.

The awakening helped me recognize how Source Language had already been present in my life in subtle ways. My husband, Daniel, had been spontaneously channeling this ancient, otherworldly language during private moments. Something our children would notice, asking curiously, "What is Daddy yelling in the bathroom?" We later understood that as a Draco-Dragon star being, these intense transmissions expressed his soul frequencies, connecting him to his galactic heritage.

As my journey with Source Language evolved, my relationship with music transformed completely. Starting with a single singing bowl, then adding wind chimes, and finally discovering the handpan, I watched myself bloom from someone who once shunned music into an artist who understood that the human body itself is the ultimate divine instrument. Through working with these sacred instruments, I came to understand our bodies as vibrating crystalline vessels, capable of both receiving and transmitting higher frequencies. The crystal-clear tones of the singing bowls are not just beautiful sounds but also keys that unlock cellular memory, penetrating deeply into our tissues and DNA.

Research in quantum biology supports what I experienced intuitively—that our cells communicate through biophotons, tiny bursts of light. This scientific understanding helped explain why these pure frequencies could create such profound shifts in consciousness and physical form. Through surrendering to these sounds, I discovered that music isn't just something we make; it's the very language of creation flowing through us.

Playing crystal bowls as a warmup for channeling Source Language

As a multidimensional form of expression, Source Language allows waves of pure frequency to be vocalized, with meaning and impact shaped by perception and intention rather than linguistic rules. The syllables, tones, and rhythms that emerge are not mere phonetic constructs but living energies capable of catalyzing profound shifts in consciousness and awakening DNA codex. When you open yourself to channeling Source Language, you become a conduit for vibrations that can clear blockages, activate dormant potentials, and realign the biofield of the human body with higher dimensional frequencies.

It serves as a bridge between worlds—a way for the soul to express its pure vibrational signature while bypassing the limitations of the rational mind. It reminds us that true communication transcends words, reaching into the quantum field where all possibilities exist simultaneously. Like the Egyptian priests who used sacred sounds to bridge worlds, we too can access these divine frequencies when we surrender to the song of creation itself.

Source Language awakens us to a fundamental truth that we are all natural channels for divine expression. It's not something that you necessarily need to be born with. When we release the societal conditioning that tells us to suppress our gifts and question our intuitive wisdom, we open to infinite possibilities of quantum communication. This isn't about learning something new but rather remembering what has always lived within us: our inherent ability to express the very language of creation itself.

This truth revealed itself beautifully through my experience with my children. When my connection to Source Language activated, at the time my five-year-old son, a Lyran hybrid, responded with immediate recognition. As I began channeling this quantum language, it was as if I had given him permission to fully embrace his authentic self - what he playfully called his "meow" self. This opened a profound new dimension in our communication, allowing us to connect through the deepest frequencies of the heart. While my older stepchildren initially approached this with hesitation, through patient observation and acceptance, they too found their unique expressions of this divine language, each one manifesting in its own special way.

The Source Language became an integral part of our family life, a language we all use interchangeably to connect and recalibrate. This linguistic intimacy united us, allowing us to express our joys and frustrations, keeping us aligned and attuned to the pure energies of the unified field.

This profound realization and passion for divine expression led me to co-found the Source Language Institute in 2021, alongside my partner, Marion Amael Grace. We realized that the term "Light Language" only captured a fragment of this profound communication method. In founding the Source Language Institute in 2021 with Marion Amael Grace, we chose the name "Source" because it embodies the all-encompassing nature of this expression - it flows not just through light, but through every facet of existence: sound, movement, energy, and pure consciousness itself. It's the primordial language of creation, emanating directly from Source consciousness, which is why our institute bears this name as we guide others in accessing this fundamental creative force.

By releasing the self-doubts and limiting beliefs that have silenced our voices, we open to the infinite possibilities of this quantum tongue. We become luminous beings, radiating the light, sound, and consciousness of the divine through the very vehicle of our existence.

Whether conversing with our children, connecting with celestial guides, or channeling the frequencies of the unified field, Source Language offers us a direct portal to the wellspring of creation. It is a language of the heart, the soul, and the quantum field itself - a means by which we can consciously shape our reality and align our lives with the highest frequencies of love and unity.

Unlocking Your Frequency Name

Names hold a power far beyond mere identification—they are living frequency codes that shape the very fabric of our reality. Through my deep explorations of consciousness and Source Language, I have come to understand that our names are not just labels, but multidimensional energy signatures. They are active forces in the quantum field, influencing our journey through life in profound ways.

I witnessed firsthand how sound creates geometric patterns in light. Every name carries this same creative power—each letter and syllable generating specific vibrations that ripple through the quantum field. My personal evolution through names is a testament to this understanding. As Dina, I carried a certain frequency, but something felt incomplete. When I met my husband he recognized me, "Dina is not your name, you are Diana! Like the true goddess that you are!" I initially resisted this expansion—mirroring the way we often resist a higher awareness of our true nature.

My journey deepened as I embraced my full name, gently guiding others to pronounce it correctly as not the typical American pronunciation but rather the Eastern European and Spanish version "De-anna". Each time I stood in this truth, it felt like reclaiming a piece of my authentic self. Then came a transformative moment when I first wrote "Diana Ma'Ara Divine." The name Ma'Ara flowed through me unexpectedly, and as I spoke it out loud, the resonant roll of the 'R' awakened something ancient within my being. This name carried the same profound revelation. I saw myself in the ancient temples of Egypt. Ma is the upholder of truth, the divine moth, and RA is the Sun crystalline consciousness. It was a key that opened new dimensions of understanding about who I truly am across all planes of existence.

Through my interdimensional experiences, I have observed how names generate distinct energy signatures. A few times, I have also channeled my client's frequency names, and I have noticed that the names with flowing vowels create fluid, wavelike patterns in the auric field. In contrast, names with strong consonants produce more focused, directional frequencies, reminiscent of the structured harmonic codes found in sacred geometry.

"Your names are keys to remembering," one of my guides once told me. When spoken with loving intention, a name activates beneficial frequency patterns within our energy field. This explains why ancient traditions placed such emphasis on sacred names and mantras—they are consciousness technologies designed to maintain higher vibrational states.

To consciously work with your name's vibrational essence, consider the following steps:

ॐ **Feel into your current name's resonance.** Say out loud and declare your name: "*I AM < Your Name >*" How do you feel when spoken aloud? Try different ways to say your name and add new names.

ॐ **Notice how different variations affect your energy.** Do certain pronunciations or versions feel more aligned?

ॐ **Be open to expanded versions that may emerge.** Your soul may reveal a new vibrational expression at different stages of your journey.

ॐ **Use your name as a tool for consciousness expansion.** Speak or chant it with intention, allowing it to attune you to your highest frequency.

Just as Source Light Language harmonizes with consciousness, our names are dynamic tools for reality creation.

Opening to Source Language

When you open to Source Language, you allow a direct flow of information from the universe to pour through you. You open your heart to feel and merge with the frequencies. Rather than speaking words you know, you give voice to packets of pure energy and vibration, transcending the limitations of linear communication.

It is essential to approach this process with a sense of wonder, like a curious child exploring a newfound realm of possibility. Many who first encounter Source Language immediately ask, "How do I translate this?" But that misses the point entirely. Why would you want to diminish a multidimensional language by confining it to the rigid structures of the 3D mind?

The beauty of Source Language lies in its inherent complexity. A single word or phrase can carry a multitude of meanings, as the frequencies shift and transform based on tonality, rhythm, and the energetic current flowing through the speaker. The more you try to control and understand this language through rational intellect, the more you close yourself off to its true essence.

Just as the awakening of Kundalini energy requires surrender, so too does the exploration of Source Language. It is a dance between you and the infinite language that cannot be grasped, but only experienced. To become a pure channel for this quantum communication, you must first ensure your energetic field is solid and grounded.

That is why I often begin with an Anchoring Meditation (as covered in Chapter 5) to stabilize my connection to the Earth and higher realms before engaging in any channeling work. This preparatory step helps me discern the purity of the transmission, ensuring I am not clouding the language with my own mental projections or ego-driven agendas. I also set clear intentions for pure and undistorted communication.

Once the foundation is set, I rest my ego aside and trust the process, allowing the quantum whispers of the universe to flow through me, unencumbered by the need for translation or comprehension. Source Language is not meant to be grasped or controlled by the rational mind; it is a language of the heart, the soul, and the quantum field itself.

In this state of surrender, I become an open, receptive vessel—a conduit for the divine to express itself through me. The pure vowels, words, tones, and energetic signatures that emerge are not my own, but rather a collaborative dance between my conscious awareness and the infinite intelligence of the cosmos.

It is only by letting go of the desire to understand or manipulate this language that I can truly experience its transformative power. It becomes a portal to realms beyond the linear confines of thought and reason—a direct link to the wellspring of creation itself.

When I approach it with reverence, curiosity, and a willingness to be transformed, the quantum frequencies become a symphony that uplift, activate, and align with the divine original blueprint. In this state of receptive surrender, one can unlock the keys to conscious co-creation, weaving the very fabric of reality through the alchemy of divine communication.

Types of Source Language

There are countless ways to channel Source Language through creative expression - whether through art, music, dance, or other forms of divine inspiration. However, when specifically focusing on channeling practices, four primary forms of Source Language emerge, each offering its own unique energetic transmission and multidimensional connection:

△ **Singing or Toning:** This form of Source Language flows through singing, toning, or vocal melodies, where the frequencies and harmonics bypass the logical mind and reach deep into the emotional and energetic body. Sung Source Language is a powerful tool for raising vibration, facilitating emotional healing, and creating coherence within energy fields, evoking profound shifts in consciousness and a sense of connection to the divine. Often angelic frequencies come through songs or tones.

△ **Speaking:** This is the most recognized manifestation, where sounds, syllables, and tones flow intuitively through the spoken word. These vocalizations often resemble ancient or otherworldly languages, yet they do not adhere to any structured grammar or syntax. Spoken Source Language is used for energetic clearing, DNA activation, and frequency alignment, carrying specific codes that resonate deeply with the listener, even if the meaning is not consciously understood.

△ **Signing or Gesturing:** This form involves hand movements, gestures, and body motions that channel divine frequencies. Like writing in the ethers, these intuitive gestures create energetic symbols and patterns that bridge physical and spiritual realms, assisting in energy alignment and grounding higher vibrations into the body. When combined with vocal tones or spoken Source Language, these movements amplify the transmission, allowing the energetic codes to be both seen and felt. The gestures emerge spontaneously, guided by divine intelligence rather than mental planning, serving multiple purposes: directing healing energy, clearing spaces of dense frequencies, activating light codes, and facilitating energy movement. Much like a conductor shapes music through motion, these light-encoded movements create sacred geometric patterns in the quantum field, with the hands becoming instruments of divine expression, channeling frequencies with precision and grace.

△ **Writing or Coding:** Expressed through symbols, glyphs, or geometric codes that are drawn or written intuitively, Written Light Language serves as an anchor for higher-dimensional frequencies in the physical realm. These encoded frequencies can be used for meditative focus, energy grids, or activation templates, allowing the practitioner to harness the power of the quantum field.

Whether spoken, signed, written, or sung, each expression of Source Language serves as a unique channel for the transmission of quantum information and the manifestation of higher truths. These fluid, dynamic forms of communication mirror the very principles of the universe, where energy, frequency, and vibration are the building blocks of reality.

Humming and Toning

It began with a hum—such a simple, natural thing. I had no idea that this basic sound would become my gateway to Source Language itself, opening doorways to dimensions beyond my wildest dreams.

The humming first came as comfort, a soothing vibration that washed peace through my entire system. Through my later exploration of Andi and Jonathan Goldman's illuminating work, The Humming Effect, I came to understand the science behind what I was experiencing. That simple vibration was activating my vagnus nerve, stimulating nitric oxide production, and increasing oxygen flow throughout my body. This natural process triggered a cascade of healing responses—improved circulation, lower blood pressure, reduced inflammation, and a strengthened immune system. But in those early days, I simply felt my body remembering an ancient way of healing itself.

As my practice deepened, the humming transformed. Single notes evolved into sustained tones, each resonating with different aspects of my being. The "Ah" sound would blossom through my heart center like the first rays of dawn. "Ooh" anchored me into Earth's embrace, while "Ee" seemed to extend my consciousness up through my crown into the star fields above.

This progression now seems so perfectly orchestrated—the humming fine-tuning my physical vessel like a sacred instrument being prepared for divine music. The toning that followed was like learning the basic scales of creation, each vowel sound awakening and aligning my energy centers. Only when this foundation was set could the full symphony of Source Language begin to flow through me.

I'm still amazed at how this journey mirrors the universe's own story of creation. Just as it all began with the primordial OM, my path to multidimensional communication started with a single sustained note. From that humble beginning emerged an entire language of light—a way of expressing that transcends ordinary human speech.

To those who feel drawn to this path, I always emphasize: there's no need to push or force. Start exactly where I did—with that simple hum. Let it resonate through your body and observe what you feel. Allow the tones to emerge as naturally as flowers opening to sunlight. Your body holds this ancient knowledge of how to commune with Source; it's simply waiting to be remembered.

Even now, when channeling Source Language, I begin with humming. It's my way of honoring the journey, of acknowledging that even the grandest cosmic symphony starts with a single note. From this foundation, I become a clear channel, surrendering to the flow of light codes and stellar frequencies moving through me.

This is the profound gift of sound as spiritual practice—it reveals that we are all instruments in the cosmic orchestra. Each of us contributes our unique tone to creation's endless song. Whether you're just discovering your first hum or already flowing with Source Language, you're participating in this grand celestial music, this eternal dance of frequency and form.

Types of Source Language Communication

The quantum language of Source expresses itself through a tapestry of diverse energetic signatures, each carrying its own unique gifts and resonance. When one opens to Source Language, the first language that comes through often originates from the frequency or star system that the soul feels most connected to - the familiar resonance of its birthplace or spiritual home.

This initial connection could be to high-vibrational civilizations of the past, such as the advanced cultures of Atlantis and Lemuria. It may be a language from the primary Founder Races of melodic and heart centered Lyran and Pleiadians, or the technological codes of Arcturus, Orion, etc. Each vibrational signature holds a specific purpose and wisdom to share.

Let us now explore the various manifestations of Source Language:

☼ **Angelic:** The angelic realms, from the Elohim to the Seraphim, speak a language of pure divine love and healing. These celestial frequencies carry the power to open the heart, forge deep connections to the sacred, and transmit energies of physical and emotional restoration. In their luminous tongue, the angels offer guidance, protection, and a direct conduit to the infinite grace of the divine. It usually comes through a song and toning.

☼ **Deities and Ascended Masters:** The archetypal energies of the pantheons - from Hathor to Quan Yin, St. Germaine to Buddha, each have their own distinct Source Language. These vibrational codes carry the wisdom and frequencies of the enlightened, imparting mental, emotional, and spiritual teachings for human evolution. They are portals to the archetypal realms, unlocking higher states of consciousness and alignment with universal truths.

☼ **Galactic:** Channeled from civilizations across the stars - Arcturian, Andromedan, Pleiadian, Sirian, Draco, Antarean and beyond - Galactic Source Language offers a treasure trove of technological, scientific, and evolutionary information. These languages originate from diverse timelines and star races, each infusing its own unique perspective and creative impetus. Through Galactic Light, we access the profound interconnectedness of all existence and accelerate our own quantum transformation.

☼ **Elemental:** The natural world, from the whispering of trees to the crystalline songs of the mineral kingdom, expresses itself through Elemental Source Language. This includes the lyrical playful frequencies of the fae, the primal utterances of mythic creatures, and the vibrational harmonies of rivers, valleys, and every living being. By attuning to these frequencies, we remember our deep kinship with the earth and the sentience that permeates all of creation.

☼ **Indigenous:** Across cultures and lineages, the earth-based wisdom keepers have long honored the sacred power of their unique Light Languages. From the Aramaic cadences of the Middle East to the rhythmic chants of Native America, these languages are portals to ancient knowledge, traditional healing modalities, and a reverence for the cycles of nature.

Each expression of Source Language serves as a unique key, unlocking specific realms of understanding, healing, and evolution. These divine frequencies weave together into a grand tapestry of creation, celebrating the infinite ways consciousness expresses itself across dimensions. The word "universe" itself points to this truth - one verse of expression - where all languages ultimately converge into a single, harmonious chord. This is the cosmic heartbeat that pulses through all of existence, carrying the limitless potential of Source consciousness into form.

The Quantum Expressions of Source Language

Source Language is a boundless, multidimensional form of communication that can manifest in diverse ways to serve our evolution and connection to the divine. What matters most is the intention you set as you open your channel to this quantum language. By declaring, "I open up my channel to Source Language expression," you create the space for it to flow through you in the most appropriate and meaningful way.

Let us now explore the various modalities through which this language of the divine can express itself:

→ **Transmission:** Source Language can operate as a pure energetic transmission, carrying frequencies and codes that catalyze profound shifts within our being. These transmissions are often experienced as waves of light, sound, or subtle sensations that permeate the body, mind, and spirit. Their purpose is to clear blockages, realign our energy field, and activate dormant potentials within our DNA and consciousness.

→ **Activation:** The Source Language acts as a key, unlocking access to higher dimensional wisdom, abilities, and states of awareness. Through specific tones, syllables, or visual symbols, these activations ignite transformative processes, empowering us to step into new levels of our multidimensional nature. This can include the awakening of psychic senses, the integration of soul memories, and the embodiment of expanded consciousness.

→ **Dialogue:** Source Language can also take the form of a fluid, interactive exchange, where the practitioner engages in a conscious dialogue with the intelligence behind the language. This may manifest as an inner voice, intuitive downloads, or a co-creative flow of information tailored to the individual's needs and questions. In these moments, we become active participants in quantum conversation, receiving guidance, insights, and downloads directly from the field of infinite potential.

→ **Sharing Stories:** The quantum language can also express itself through the telling of multi-layered, archetypal stories that carry symbolic meaning and energetic imprints. These narratives transcend the linear confines of language, weaving together metaphors, sensory experiences, and higher dimensional perspectives. By receiving and embodying these stories, we access the deeper teachings, initiations, and transformations they hold for our spiritual evolution.

Whether experienced as a transmission, activation, dialogue, or story, Source Language ultimately serves as a bridge between the realms of form and the formless, the finite and the infinite. Each modality provides a unique portal through which we can deepen our connection to the universal intelligence that animates all of creation.

By setting the intention to open your channel and then allowing the language to flow through you in its optimal expression, you unlock the keys to conscious co-creation. Source Language becomes a technology of transformation, empowering you to align your thoughts, emotions, and actions with the generative principles that govern the cosmos. In this way, you step into your role as a multidimensional being, weaving the very fabric of reality through the alchemy of divine communication.

Perceiving the Quantum Language

To fully receive the gifts of Source Language, we must first empower our multisensory perceptions and clear our energy field to become an open, receptive channel. It's important to remember that the way this language manifests and is perceived can vary greatly from one person to the next. The way it resonates with and activates your unique energetic blueprint may be vastly different from how it is experienced by another.

ॐ **Physical Sensations:** As we attune to the quantum frequencies of Source Language, the body often responds with a heightened sensitivity. may feel tingling, hot or cold sensations, nausea, twitching, or a distinct pull of energy. The senses of smell and hearing can also become amplified, picking up subtle energetic signatures. These physical responses are the body's way of registering the influx of higher vibrations.

ॐ **Emotional Sensations:** The transmission of Source Language can evoke a wide range of emotional responses. Sudden feelings of sorrow, anxiety, or spontaneous tears may arise as blockages are cleared. Conversely, a profound sense of "coming home" or deep peace can wash over us, as the frequencies resonate with our soul's essence. These emotional shifts are indicators that the language is activating and harmonizing our energy field.

ॐ **Mental Senses:** On a cognitive level, Source Language can impart messages, solutions, or new perceptions that shift our understanding. Memories may surface, offering insights from our past or parallel lifetimes. A sense of expanded awareness or sudden clarity about an aspect of our lives can emerge, as the quantum language unlocks higher dimensional wisdom.

ॐ **Psychic Senses:** The intuitive faculties can also amplify in the presence of Source Language transmissions. You may perceive shifts in color, smell, or taste. Hearing ethereal music or angelic voices can occur, as the veils between realms thin. A deep sensing of the source and purpose behind the Source Language can arise, guiding us towards the gifts it holds.

It is important to approach these multidimensional perceptions with a beginner's mind, free from expectations or the need to analyze. Allow the quantum effects to flow through you, trusting that your energetic system will respond in the way that best serves your evolution. Remain open, curious, and attuned to the subtleties.

By empowering our sensitivities and clearing our energy field, we become conduits for the quantum symphony of Source Language. Each unique expression carries the potential to heal, activate, and align us with the infinite intelligence of the cosmos. In surrendering to this fluid, dynamic form of communication, we unlock the keys to our multidimensional nature and the limitless possibilities that reside within.

Practicing Source Language

The channeling practice of Source Language is a sacred dance between our human vessel and the infinite cosmos. Through this practice, we become living bridges between dimensions, allowing universal wisdom to flow through our voice in ways that transcend ordinary speech. Let me guide you through this profound journey of remembrance and activation.

ॐ **Creating Sacred Space:** Begin by choosing a quiet space where you won't be disturbed. This could be your meditation room, a spot in nature, or any place where you feel safe to explore and express freely. Consider creating an altar with crystals, candles, or other sacred objects that resonate with your intention. The key is to craft an environment that supports your journey into higher frequencies.

ॐ **Preparation and Grounding:** Settle into a comfortable position, whether seated on the floor, in a chair, or standing. Take several deep, conscious breaths, feeling each inhale fill your being with light and each exhale release any tension or resistance. Allow your awareness to expand beyond your physical form, sensing the quantum field of possibility that surrounds you.

🕉 **Setting Sacred Intention:** Before opening your channel, state your intention clearly and powerfully. You may say:

> *"I open myself as a clear channel for Source Language to flow through me. I call upon my highest guides, my star family, and all beings of light. My channel is clear, protected, and aligned with pure Source light."*

Feel these words resonating through every cell of your being. Trust that this declaration creates a sacred container for what's about to unfold.

🕉 **Beginning the Practice:** Start with simple humming, allowing the vibration to awaken your throat chakra and energy centers. There's no need to force anything—let the sound emerge naturally from your being. Notice how the vibration creates ripples through your physical and energy bodies.

As you continue, allow the humming to evolve into open-mouthed sounds. Your lips, tongue, and vocal cords might begin moving in unfamiliar ways. Trust this process. These seemingly random movements are your body's way of adjusting to higher frequencies.

Deepening into the flow as you surrender more deeply into practice, you might notice:

🕉 Waves of energy moving through your body
🕉 Spontaneous hand movements or mudras
🕉 Visual impressions or light codes
🕉 A sense of expansion beyond your physical form
🕉 Connections with guides or star beings
🕉 Specific tones or syllables that want to repeat

Welcome all these experiences without judgment but with discernment. Stay curious. They are signs that you're tuning into the quantum field of infinite possibility.

Working with Higher Frequencies You may begin receiving transmissions from various sources:

🕉 Your Higher self and Soul aspects
🕉 Angelic and Galactic Guides
🕉 Earth and nature spirits
🕉 The Crystalline grid
🕉 Ancient wisdom keepers

ॐ Star family and light beings

> *Each presence brings its own unique frequency signature.*
> *Over time, you'll learn to recognize these different energies*
> *and work with them more consciously.*

Integration and Grounding: When the transmission feels complete. Take several deep breaths. Gently move your body. Place your hands on the earth or floor. Thank all beings who participated. Consider journaling your experience.

As you develop your relationship with Source Language, you might notice:

ॐ Increased synchronicities in daily life
ॐ Enhanced intuitive abilities
ॐ Spontaneous activation of dormant DNA codes
ॐ Deeper connection with your multidimensional aspects
ॐ More frequent contact with higher beings
ॐ The ability to transmit healing frequencies to others

> *Integration is crucial – these frequencies continue working*
> *through your field long after the active practice ends.*

Remember that Source Language isn't something we learn—it's something we remember. It's encoded in our very DNA, waiting to be activated through devoted practice and surrender to the greater flow of universal consciousness.

Trust your unique expression. Some days the language might flow as gentle whispers, other times as powerful declarations. It might include sounds, movements, light codes, or pure frequency. All forms are valid and perfect for that moment.

Your journey with Source Language is deeply personal yet connects you to the vast web of cosmic consciousness. Through this practice, you become both transmitter and receiver, bridging Heaven and Earth through the sacred instrument of your own being.

Activation of Quantum Code ▲ Source Expression

This activation is designed to transmit the essence of the chapter as an energetic template—something you feel rather than analyze. By bypassing the thinking mind, it speaks directly to your body, energy field, and subconscious, allowing transformation to unfold on a deeper level.

◆ Begin Here: Set the Field

Find a quiet space. Light a candle if you feel called. Sit or lie comfortably with your spine aligned and your heart open. Close your eyes and take a few grounding breaths—in through your nose, out through your mouth. Let your body soften. Let your energy settle.

Bring your awareness to your heart space. Place your hands gently over your heart or simply focus your attention there. Feel the warmth between your palms and chest. Let it grow.

When you are ready, speak the following words aloud or silently within:

"I now open to release all that is blocking my highest good.

I open to grace, to clarity, to healing.

I activate and understand all that I need to move forward on my path with ease and flow.

I open to remember who I truly am."

Breathe that in. Let it ripple through your entire being.

◆ Activate the Quantum Code

Repeat these sacred Source Language words below three times aloud, allowing the vibration to move through your body and field:

SA AKUM AHU
I VA YA NA

Now read the following quantum transmission:

> *First came the hum, a whisper deep within,*
> *Where ancient memories of stars begin.*
> *Through throat and heart, the vibration flows,*
> *Awakening wisdom the body knows.*
>
> *"Ah" opens petals of the sacred heart,*
> *"Ooh" grounds the spirit where Earth songs start.*
> *"Ee" reaches skyward, a cosmic call,*
> *As dimensional doorways begin to fall.*
>
> *Beyond words now, frequencies rise,*
> *Light codes dancing through vessel eyes.*
> *Tongue and lips move to cosmic time,*
> *Weaving patterns through space sublime.*
>
> *Star language flowing, DNA spinning bright,*
> *Sacred geometries painting trails of light.*
> *No longer bound by human speech,*
> *As multidimensional realms we reach.*
>
> *Through throat chakra, wisdom streams,*
> *Ancient knowing beyond our dreams.*
> *Each sound a key to unlock the way,*
> *Where quantum realms and matter play.*

◇ ACTIVATION COMPLETE ◇

Sit in stillness. Allow the code to settle into your system. Feel the integration weaving into your cells, your field, your breath. Let the silence become your teacher.

♦ Ground & Center

Breathe deeply into your body. Imagine golden roots extending from the soles of your feet into the heart of the Earth. Feel the Earth holding you, anchoring you.

You are safe. You are protected. You are loved.

Begin to gently move your fingers and toes. Wiggle. Stretch. Return fully to your body.

Grounding Contemplation

After activating the Quantum code and grounding, stay rooted by taking time to notice what's shifting within. You might feel called to journal, draw, or simply sit in quiet awareness, allowing your inner wisdom to gently emerge. Use the following questions as gateways to deeper insight. There is no need to rush or force answers. Let them move through you like waves.

1. What frequency of light is ready to express itself through my being today?
2. How is the Source language calling me to deepen my connection with the divine?
3. Which areas of my body are ready to receive activation or healing through sound and light codes?
4. What unique vibrations or tones are wanting to move through me at this moment?
5. How can my voice and hands become more attuned instruments for channeling light language?
6. How is the Source light asking me to embody its wisdom more fully in my physical vessel?

After sitting with these reflection questions, gently open your mouth and allow any sounds, tones, or syllables to arise organically. They may feel strange or unfamiliar at first, this is your Light Language stirring awake. Let it emerge without judgment or expectation.

✦ Ongoing Practice

Make it a regular practice to reconnect with Source Language. Spend time in nature, where the frequencies of Earth can help attune your voice to divine resonance. Speak to your pets, the trees, the sky—let your intuition guide the expression. With each session, you'll unlock new tones, messages, and layers of remembrance. Trust the process. Your Light Language is a living transmission, and you are its sacred vessel—an open channel for infinite love, healing, and transformation.

Take your time. If today's experience stirred something profound, consider waiting a full day before moving on to the next chapter.

Part III

Mastery

Chapter 8
Quantum Travel & Manifestation

"As you shut your eyes and immerse yourself in the silent void of the unknown, vibrationally aligned. For within that moment, you can declare proudly:
I am the Wizard
I am the Alchemist
I am the Creator.
Watch as manifestations take shape, possibilities unfold, like magical effortless dances through every corner of your built reality."

— Diana Divine

In the realm of creation, every possibility exists within the present moment. Yet, it is the process of manifestation that transforms abstract ideas into tangible reality—an alchemical journey from the unmanifest to the manifest, where thought takes physical form. Quantum manifestation moves beyond this linear understanding, occupying a liminal space where potential and reality interweave at the threshold of becoming.

The insights of quantum physics reveal how our engagement with the quantum field through conscious thought, intention, and action creates entanglement and catalyzes shifts into new realities. This domain transcends linear progression and simple causality, operating instead within the quantum field—an infinite matrix of energy and information where all possibilities coexist simultaneously.

Those who have mastered quantum manifestation have transcended the constraints of linear thinking to embrace the fluid, interconnected nature of existence. They release attachment to specific outcomes, surrendering instead to the boundless potential of the quantum field. These Masters dwell in a state of perpetual flow, naturally aligning their thoughts, emotions, and actions with the resonance of what they wish to create. Understanding that the quantum field responds to the quality of energy and information they contribute, they cultivate their inner and outer environments with precise intention.

Through this deep alignment with quantum principles, they manifest profound transformations both in their personal reality and in the greater world.

Before we dive deeper into the Quantum Master Creator Method of manifestation, let's explore some foundational quantum physics concepts, which I have begun to cover in Chapter 4.

▎The Quantum Superposition

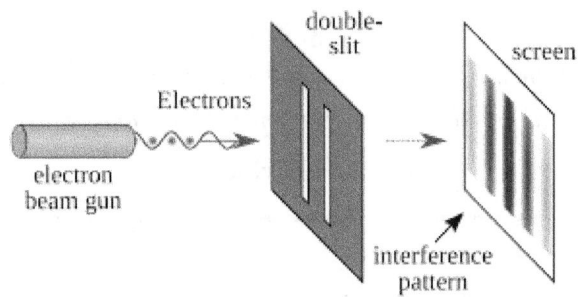

The Double Slit Experiment (Source: Wikipedia)

Quantum physics has revolutionized our understanding of reality, revealing that particles can exist in multiple states simultaneously until observed—a principle known as quantum superposition. This suggests that reality is not static but fluid, shaped by observation and interaction. When we focus our thoughts and intentions on a desired outcome, we actively engage with the quantum field, influencing which possibility manifests. In this way, we are not passive dreamers but active co-creators, shaping reality through the lens of our consciousness.

A compelling example of this principle is the double-slit experiment, which demonstrates how particles like electrons or photons behave differently depending on observation. When particles are fired at a barrier with two slits, the results depend on whether they are observed. With one slit open, the particles behave as expected, forming a single line. When both slits are open and unobserved, they create an interference pattern characteristic of waves, suggesting that each particle exists in superposition, passing through both slits simultaneously and interfering with itself.

However, when a measuring device observes the particles, the interference pattern disappears, and the particles behave like classical objects, forming two distinct lines. This shift from wave-like behavior to particle-like behavior is known as *wave function collapse*. Observation forces the particle to "choose" a single path, collapsing its superposition into a defined state of reality.

This phenomenon introduces the idea of a *standing wave*—a stable wave pattern that forms when potential outcomes resonate in harmony. Before observation, particles exist as probability waves, a superposition of all possible states. These waves represent the many potentials of reality, held in balance like a standing wave oscillating in place. The act of observation disrupts this equilibrium, collapsing the standing wave into a single, tangible state. This transition highlights how focus and intention act as the forces that "collapse" our potential realities into lived experiences.

Imagine reality as a quantum stage, where each dancer represents a potential outcome, all existing as standing waves of possibility. Before you make a choice, these waves overlap, moving fluidly in a harmonious dance of quantum superposition. The dancer that steps into the spotlight—the one you direct your focus and intention toward—gains amplitude, amplifying her standing wave. The more attention this wave receives, the greater its energy and probability of manifesting into form. Meanwhile, the other waves lose coherence, collapsing into the background. In alignment with quantum principles, your observation and focus determine which potential standing wave becomes reality.

I experienced this firsthand during a pivotal moment in my life. At a crossroads, I was faced with multiple possibilities—starting a business, moving to a new city, or continuing my career. These options felt like an energetic standing wave, each vibrating with potential but none yet solidified. One evening, I sat quietly and visualized each path, tuning into the energy of each potential outcome. The more attention I gave to one path, the more vivid and real it became. With unwavering intention, I finally made my choice. In that instant, the standing wave collapsed, and my new reality took shape.

This experience revealed how profoundly the principles of quantum physics, such as superposition, wave function collapse, and standing waves, reflect our ability to shape reality. Just as particles remain in superposition until observed, our lives hold infinite potential outcomes, waiting for the focus of our consciousness. By aligning our attention and intention, we become the observers who collapse the standing wave of possibility into a single, tangible path.

In the quantum theater of possibilities, consciousness is the spotlight. The dancer illuminated by your focus becomes the reality that takes form, collapsing from the fluidity of a standing wave into the solid structure of experience. The shift in my energy as I focused on a single possibility mirrored this process. The more attention I gave, the more vivid and certain it became, until the wave of potentials crystallized into my chosen path.

▌ Tesla's 3-6-9, Metatron Cube, and Zero Point Energy

Nikola Tesla, one of the greatest scientific minds, recognized a profound understanding of the universe's numerical foundation, particularly his 3-6-9 method. Tesla once declared, "If you only knew the magnificence of the 3, 6, and 9, then you would have a key to the universe." These numbers, as Tesla discovered, represent fundamental patterns in the universe's energy flow. The number 3 represents the initial creative force, 6 symbolizes manifestation and balance, and 9 represents the point of completion and transformation – a perfect mirror of how consciousness shapes reality.

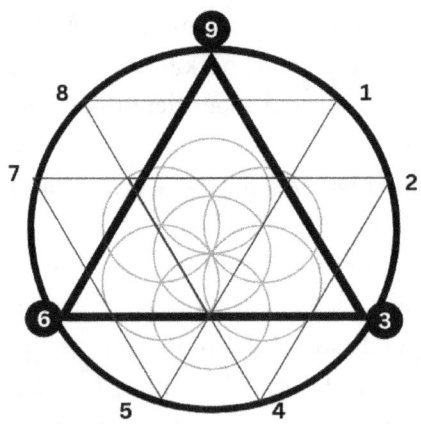

Nikola Tesla's 369 Theory (Image by Diana Divine)

To further illustrate this phenomenon, consider the Metatron's Cube, a symbol of sacred geometry that holds deep universal metaphysical significance that we covered in chapter 5. The cube is composed of 13 circles with lines connecting each circle to the others, forming a complex, interconnected pattern. At the heart of this structure is a perfect geometrical balance, symbolizing unity and the infinite potential of the universe.

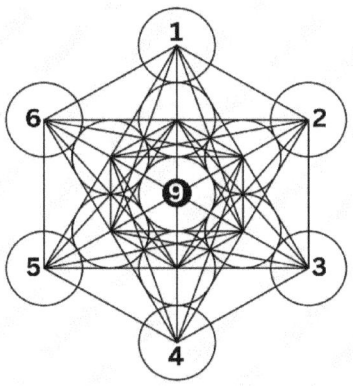

Metatron Cube Potentialities (Image by Diana Divine)

Now, visualize the six exterior spheres of the Metatron's Cube as representing six different potentialities, each one a possibility in your life. These spheres are connected and coexist, just like the ballerinas on stage. They vibrate with potential, existing as standing waves within the quantum field. When we direct our consciousness toward one of these potentialities, our focused awareness acts as an energetic force, bringing it into manifestation.

The transformation process follows Tesla's numerical sequence: it begins with the creative spark (3), moves through the balanced state of potentials (6), and culminates in the completion phase (9). One of these spheres eventually magnetizes and integrates into the middle of the geometry – this is the quantum collapse, the 9-point where the wave transforms into a particle, shifting from the unmanifested to the manifested.

This concept aligns beautifully with the idea of Zero-Point Energy, a foundational principle in quantum physics and a deeper layer of understanding for creation. Zero-point energy essentially is the Void, that I covered in chapter 2, where the limitless field of energy is present even in a vacuum—the stillness and silence underlying all motion and matter.

It is the infinite potential from which all waves and particles emerge, the primordial pulse of creation itself. In a state of zero-point energy, all standing waves are in perfect coherence, balanced in stillness yet brimming with potential.

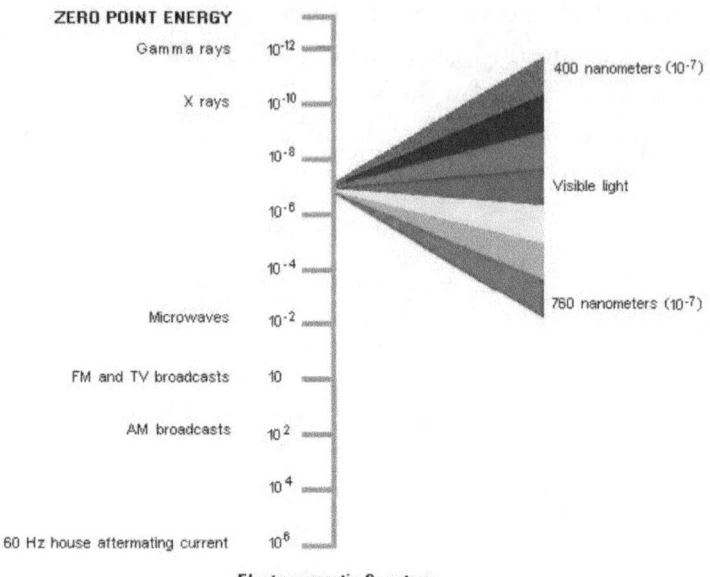

ZERO POINT ENERGY

Gamma rays	10^{-12}
X rays	10^{-10}
	10^{-8}
	10^{-6}
	10^{-4}
Microwaves	10^{-2}
FM and TV broadcasts	10
AM broadcasts	10^2
	10^4
60 Hz house aftermating current	10^6

400 nanometers (10^{-7})

Visible light

760 nanometers (10^{-7})

Electromagnetic Spectrum

Zero-point energy works using electromagnetic energy in combination with

the quantum vacuum and distance relations between quantum fields.

Tesla, recognizing the profound implications of waves and energy fields, stated, "*The forces are in a perfect balance, and hence the energy of a single thought may determine the motion of a universe.*" He understood that this balance point – represented by the number 6 in his system – was crucial for manifestation. Tesla believed that by harnessing the principles of waves and zero-point energy, humanity could unlock infinite possibilities for creation, innovation, and expansion. Zero-point energy, to Tesla, was the ultimate source, the unifying field that sustains all life and matter.

In my moment of decision, I found myself in this space of Zero-point energy, experiencing Tesla's numerical progression firsthand. I had spent days oscillating between different choices, feeling pulled in many directions. But when I brought myself to stillness—breathing deeply, quieting my mind—I felt the standing waves within me come into harmony. This was the creative force of 3 at work. As I maintained this state, I reached the balanced point of 6, where all potentials existed in perfect equilibrium. Finally, in that moment of clarity – the 9 point of transformation – the chaos of indecision ceased, and a profound clarity emerged. I was in the Zero-point field, the Void, the stillness from which creation flows. It was here that my consciousness chose the dancer, collapsing the waves and birthing a new path in my reality.

Quantum superposition teaches us that multiple realities and possibilities exist until we, as conscious beings, observe and interact with them. Our attention is the catalyst, the spark that transforms a field of infinite waves into a single, manifested reality. The Metatron's Cube, combined with Tesla's 3-6-9 principle, provides the perfect framework for understanding this process: the 3 represents the initial quantum field of possibilities, the 6 symbolizes the balanced state of superposition, and the 9 marks the moment of quantum collapse into manifested reality. This sacred quantum understanding holds within it the essence of unity, the interconnected nature of potentialities, and the sacred power of choice.

Time & Singularity: Illusion of Linearity

I like to think of time as a layered chocolate cake: when you slice into it, the present, past, and future all exist as distinct layers stacked on top of one another. Just as each layer of the cake is part of the whole and accessible within one slice, each "layer" of time—past, present, and future is simultaneously present in a higher-dimensional sense. This analogy helps illustrate that, while we experience events in a linear sequence in 3D, they coexist in a timeless state beyond our immediate perception.

Time Cake (Image by Diana Divine)

A compelling portrayal of this concept is seen in one of my favorite movies by the Nolan brothers, Interstellar (2014). In the scene where Cooper enters a black hole and reaches the singularity, he transcends his usual perception of time, able to see and interact with different moments in his daughter's life as though they were pages in a book or layers in a slice of cake. This represents a higher-dimensional view of time, where all events exist simultaneously, enabling Cooper to influence moments across time as he observes them from outside the linear flow.

Singularities, such as those found within black holes, are thought to be gateways to realms where the normal laws of physics break down. In these regions, the fabric of space-time becomes infinitely distorted, and the very concepts of time and causality are pushed to their limits. At these points of singularity, the boundaries between past, present, and future dissolve.

The notion that time flows strictly from past to future is being challenged by emerging scientific research in **Retrocausality**, **Presentiment**, and **Precognition**. Evidence suggests that future events may send information backward in time, subtly influencing thoughts, emotions, and even physiological responses before they happen. This idea aligns with the phenomenon of retrocausality, where future states affect past conditions—implying that reality operates within a feedback loop between the future and the present.

Studies in presentiment, led by researchers like Dean Radin and the Princeton Engineering Anomalies Research (PEAR) Lab, reveal that the human body unconsciously reacts to future stimuli. In controlled experiments, participants exhibited physiological changes—such as shifts in heart rate and skin conductance—seconds before being exposed to unexpected emotional images, even though the images were randomly selected. This suggests that the body perceives future events before the conscious mind registers them.

Similar findings emerge in studies on precognitive dreams, where individuals experience events in dreams before they happen. Many historical figures, including Abraham Lincoln, reported dreams of future events—Lincoln famously foresaw his own assassination. J.W. Dunne's experiments in An Experiment with Time revealed that many of his dreams corresponded to future events.

Physicist Russell Targ also concluded that precognition is as reliable as **Remote Viewing**, or bilocating, a technique that I practice quite a lot to perceive distant places and events, with or without formal meditation, having trained my consciousness to shift modes quickly, further validating that information from the future can leak into present awareness.

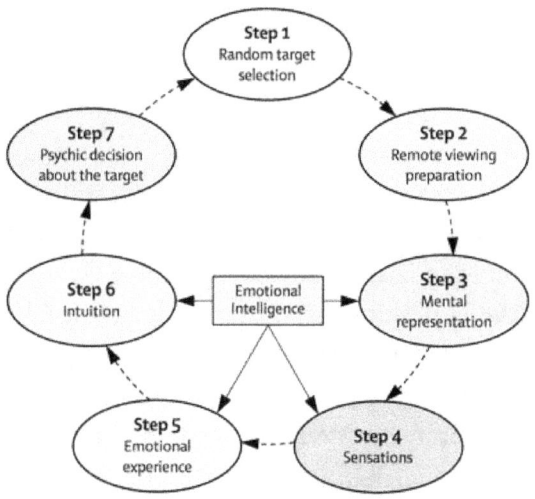

Remote Viewing Technique (Source: ResearchGate)

Remote Viewing emerged from classified research conducted at Stanford Research Institute (SRI) in the 1970s, where Targ and Harold Puthoff led experiments funded by intelligence agencies like the CIA. Their protocols involved having viewers describe distant locations while being given only random coordinates or codes. The results were often striking, with viewers able to accurately describe features of locations they had never visited.

During the Cold War, the U.S. government ran the Stargate Project, which employed remote viewers to gather intelligence on Soviet activities. While officially declassified in 1995, Remote Viewing technique is now being taught to those who are interested to explore as it allows consciousness to transcend normal spatial limitations, accessing information across vast distances through states of awareness.

Eric Wargo's theory of Time Loops expands on this, proposing that our future selves send information backward through time, influencing our thoughts, dreams, and intuitions in ways that we often fail to recognize. If only we trained ourselves to pay attention to those real-time signals, then we could act on them before the event happened.

The mechanics of this phenomenon find parallels in quantum physics. John Cramer's Transactional Interpretation suggests that quantum events involve a bidirectional "handshake" between past and future, reinforcing the notion that time does not move in just one direction. If quantum systems exhibit retrocausal behavior, it raises the possibility that human consciousness may operate similarly explaining experiences of déjà vu, premonitions, and dream-based foresight.

Beyond individual experiences, collective memory anomalies, instances like time slips and the *Mandela Effect* echo the cake analogy, where we seem to momentarily intersect with alternate versions of reality or layers of time. One of the most well-known examples of the Mandela Effect is the collective memory of Nelson Mandela's death—many people vividly recall him dying in prison in the 1980s, despite historical records stating he was released and later became the President of South Africa before passing away in 2013. Other examples include discrepancies in pop culture, such as the Berenstain Bears vs. Berenstein Bears, or the misremembered phrase *"Luke, I am your father"* from *Star Wars*, which in this reality is actually *"No, I am your father."* These shifts suggest that subtle alterations in our timeline have created divergences in our shared memory.

The *Butterfly Effect* plays into this, emphasizing how minor changes in one timeline layer can ripple across others, subtly shifting our present-day experience. A classic example comes from Ray Bradbury's short story "A Sound of Thunder," where a traveler steps on a butterfly in the distant past, triggering massive unforeseen changes in the present. In real life, even small decisions—choosing to take a different route home, meeting a person by chance, or even shifting one's thoughts—can set off a chain reaction of events, leading to dramatically different outcomes. This interconnectedness of time "slices" means that a change in one layer can reverberate through reality, manifesting as noticeable differences in another, such as collective misremembering of history.

The Marvel series *Loki* provides a striking example of this concept with the Time Variance Authority (TVA), an organization that exists to prevent timeline branches from spiraling out of control. According to TVA's logic, every small deviation, whether a Loki variant picking up the Tesseract or a single individual making an unapproved decision—creates an alternate timeline. Left unchecked, these branches could expand infinitely, disrupting the "Sacred Timeline." This illustrates the Butterfly Effect on a cosmic scale, where even the most trivial changes fracture reality, giving birth to new universes, divergent histories, and infinite possibilities.

Much like in *Loki*, our reality may be far more fluid than we perceive. If time is layered, every action, no matter how minor, could resonate through existence—shaping the past, present, and future in ways we are only beginning to understand.

Einstein once said, *"Time is not at all what it seems. It does not flow in only one direction, and the future exists simultaneously with the past."* Never had these words felt truer than during my experience at the Quantum Soul Dance workshop in Brooklyn.

My Experience with Retrocausality

It began several days before the event when my body started speaking to me in ways I couldn't initially understand. Despite the cold December weather, my temperature inexplicably spiked by 10 degrees. These sudden hot flashes felt like my Merkabah was activating and my soul blueprint and DNA expanding—my physical form somehow preparing for an intensity that hadn't yet manifested in linear time.

When I arrived at the workshop space that day, finding the host wrapped in a blanket, I felt an immediate knowing. The room began filling beyond expectation. Soon, sixty people had gathered in that space, creating exactly the heat my body had been prophesying days before.

What unfolded was the most powerful blindfolded ecstatic dance workshop I had ever facilitated. Alone, without much support staff, I found myself carried by forces beyond the physical. The energy moved through the room with its own intelligence, guided by my power animals—Eagle, soaring above with protective vision, and Phoenix, bringing waves of transformative fire. Participants later shared how they felt these spiritual guardians surrounding them throughout the experience, creating a field of safety for deep transformation.

The most remarkable revelation came after leaving the building. As I descended into the subway, my body temperature suddenly normalized, as if a cosmic switch had been flipped. Standing on the platform, I experienced a profound shift in my perception of reality. The usual boundaries of time dissolved, revealing a truth I had always sensed but never so clearly understood—past, present, and future exist in a constant dance of co-creation.

My body's preparation days before wasn't a malfunction or coincidence, it was responding to quantum ripples from an event that existed simultaneously across multiple timeframes. In that moment, I deeply understood what quantum mystics have long taught: our physical vessels are sophisticated instruments capable of tuning into the field of infinite possibility.

As Rumi beautifully expressed, "*Out beyond ideas of wrongdoing and rightdoing, there is a field. I'll meet you there.*" In that field beyond conventional physics, where the ordinary laws of reality break down, I discovered time's fluid nature. These liminal spaces, where our 3D reality meets higher dimensions, reveal the vast tapestry of possibility that exists beyond our linear perception.

Now, when I reflect on that experience, I see it as a profound teaching about the nature of reality itself. We are not bound by time's arrow as we believe. Our consciousness, our intentions, our very presence creates ripples that move both forward and backward through time, shaping the fabric of our experience in ways that transcend ordinary causality.

The heat in my body those days before the workshop wasn't a mystery to be solved, it was a reminder of our quantum nature, our existence in all moments simultaneously. When we open ourselves to these subtle messages, trusting our body's wisdom as a quantum antenna, we begin to perceive how intricately connected everything truly is. We are not just observers of reality but active participants in its unfolding, eternally engaged in this grand quantum dance of creation.

Time Trajectories

The quantum journey of consciousness unfolds through the lens of childlike wonder and unwavering trust. As we open ourselves to frequencies that resonate with our highest potential, we naturally experience quantum leaps in our evolution. Within the infinite field of possibilities, our consciousness weaves through various probable timelines, guided by our frequency, choices, and awareness level. By understanding these timeline dynamics, we move with greater intention through our evolutionary journey, recognizing that each moment branches into multiple potential futures.

When we align deeply with authentic excitement and inner guidance, we naturally attune to what I call the ***Path of Acceleration***. In this timeline frequency, reality becomes more fluid and responsive. Synchronicities multiply like stars in a clear night sky, opportunities emerge with exquisite timing, and our inner knowing becomes as clear as a mountain stream. Reality begins responding to our conscious intent with increasing speed, and quantum leaps in consciousness become our natural state. The secret to accessing these accelerated timelines lies in trusting your excitement as your frequency compass – when you follow what genuinely lights up your soul, without hesitation or doubt, you naturally align with realities that support rapid evolution.

Yet sometimes our journey calls us into the *Path of Integration*, where deeper processing and recalibration become necessary. This timeline represents sacred space for examining old patterns, releasing outdated programming, and integrating higher frequencies. Like a caterpillar in its chrysalis, this phase involves profound rewiring of neural and energetic pathways, building essential foundations for future quantum leaps. While this path might feel slower, it's vital for sustainable transformation. Rather than rushing through or resisting this phase, embrace it as necessary preparation for your next level of expression.

The *Path of Stabilization* represents a harmonic balancing point in our evolution. Here, new frequencies are being absorbed and anchored, like morning dew settling on spider webs. Energy systems recalibrate, hidden preparations unfold beneath the surface, and inner resources gather like storm clouds before rain. Though it may feel like nothing is happening, this timeline buzzes with behind-the-scenes activity preparing you for significant shifts. It's the quiet before the quantum leap, the inhale before the exhale of transformation.

Through understanding these timeline dynamics, we learn to navigate our journey with greater awareness, trusting the perfect timing of each phase. As consciousness of these dynamics expands, we develop an increasing ability to sense probable futures, recognize choice points, and move fluidly between timeline frequencies. Like a master surfer reading ocean waves, we learn to read the energetic currents of our evolution.

Remember that each path serves its divine purpose in our highest evolution. Rather than judging one as superior to another, learn to recognize which timeline frequency best serves your current phase of growth. Each morning, take a moment to feel into your timeline resonance, set your intentional frequency alignment, and notice what choices would support your desired trajectory. Through this conscious engagement with timeline probabilities, we develop an increasingly masterful relationship with our evolutionary journey.

The Pineal Gland: Gateway to Multidimensionality

Think of your awareness as a radio capable of tuning into multiple stations at once. You're not leaving the radio to hear different stations; you're expanding its capacity to receive more frequencies simultaneously or just tuning to the right channel by modifying the frequency. The most important biological "transmitter and receiver" in our midbrain is the pineal gland. Sometimes referred to as the 'third eye', the pineal gland has long been associated with the claim made by René Descartes that it was the 'seat of the soul'.

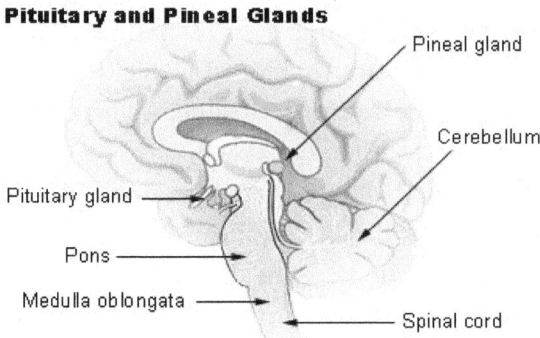

Pituitary and Pineal Glands

Pineal Gland - Third Eye (Source: Wikipedia)

The pineal gland is a small endocrine gland located in the epithalamus. Its primary function is to produce melatonin and serotonin, which play a crucial role in regulating circadian rhythms and sleep patterns. The gland is richly innervated by adrenergic neurons that actively facilitate this process. In humans, the pineal gland gradually increases in size from prenatal to postnatal life until about 2 years of age (adult size: 7x8x6 mm), with an increase in weight during and after puberty (adult weight: 172 mg). Interestingly, melatonin production is noticeably reduced during puberty, which tends to coincide with the onset of sexual activity.

By activating the pineal gland, you gain access to higher states of awareness, enabling experiences beyond the limitations of ordinary reality. Just as a radio requires both a transmitter and receiver to pick up different frequencies, the pineal gland acts as the key interface between your consciousness and the quantum field. When you learn to consciously control and "tune" this gland, you open the door to profound shifts in your experience of reality. It translates quantum energy into neurochemical signals that shape perception, cognition, and even identity.

Through practices such as meditation, binaural beats, and sensory deprivation, the pineal gland can be stimulated to harmonize the brain's left and right hemispheres, creating coherence in the mind and body. This coherence allows you to access the deeper layers of consciousness and connect with the infinite potential of the quantum field.

Dr. Joe Dispenza, a leading voice in neuroscience and spirituality, eloquently explains the power of the pineal gland in his teachings: "*When the pineal gland is awakened because it is picking up higher frequencies, those higher frequencies are carrying information, and the brain processes that information into imagery. The person is having a full-on sensory experience without their senses. And that experience enriches the brain and the body.*"

Dispenza's insight underscores the pineal gland's ability to transcend time and space, acting as a gateway to multidimensional realities. It enables you to tune into higher frequencies, perceive new possibilities, and integrate them into your current experience. By awakening this powerful organ, you step into a state where you can actively create and shape your reality, connecting with the boundless energy of the quantum field.

As mentioned in earlier chapters, Kundalini activation and breathwork techniques play a crucial role in energizing and activating the pineal gland. By consciously pulling energy from the base of your spine upward through the central channel, you awaken this third eye, enhancing your ability to access and navigate multidimensional realms. The pineal gland becomes your compass, guiding you through the expansive layers of existence and enabling profound transformation.

Brain Waves and Tuning Consciousness

Now that we know the pineal gland is our transmitter and receiver, the key to unlocking the profound mysteries of quantum jumping and dimensional resonance lies in tuning to the right frequency and broadening your perceptual bandwidth to encompass the vast, interconnected tapestry of realities that underlie the illusion of a singular, linear existence.

Resonance

As I have mentioned before, my journey into the multidimensional nature of reality was profoundly shaped by the pioneering work of Robert Monroe and the Monroe Institute. Using Hemi-Sync® technology, which synchronizes the brain's hemispheres, I learned to consciously shift into altered states of consciousness.

Robert Monroe's groundbreaking work at the Monroe Institute has illuminated powerful pathways into multidimensional awareness. Through the innovative Hemi-Sync® technology, which harmonizes the brain's hemispheres, practitioners can consciously access altered states of consciousness with precision and clarity.

Monroe's journey into consciousness research began unexpectedly in the 1950s with spontaneous out-of-body experiences, which led him to develop systematic methods for exploring and documenting expanded states of awareness. The elegance of his Hemi-Sync® technique lies in its use of precisely calibrated sound frequencies delivered to each ear. The slight difference between these frequencies creates a binaural beat that naturally synchronizes the brain's hemispheres, facilitating optimal states for quantum exploration.

When combined with remote viewing protocols, this technology creates a stable frequency foundation that allows explorers to maintain clear awareness while venturing beyond physical limitations. The method's strength comes from its integration of scientific precision with intuitive exploration, enabling practitioners to remain fully present and grounded while accessing expanded states of consciousness.

My own practice with Hemi-Sync® began as an experiment but quickly became a cornerstone of my quantum travel toolkit during my morning meditations. Over the years, I've worked with binaural beats and Monroe's Focus levels meditations, seamlessly moving into theta, delta, and gamma brainwave states, each offering unique access to different dimensions.

ॐ **Beta (13-30 Hz):** The normal waking state, beta is associated with focused thinking, problem-solving, and outward attention. Consciously shifting into beta can provide clarity and decisiveness when engaging in the physical world.

ॐ **Alpha (8-13 Hz):** This state promotes deep relaxation, enhanced creativity, and a greater sense of flow. Working in alpha allows you to reprogram subconscious beliefs and patterns with greater ease.

ॐ **Theta (4–8 Hz):** This is the state where you want to go to unlock intuitive and subconscious realms, connecting you to parallel versions of yourself. In theta, I've accessed timelines where I've already succeeded in areas I'm currently striving for, integrating their wisdom and clarity into my present life. In Quantum Healing Hypnosis, I aim to bring my clients to Theta. They can see pictures like in a dream REM state and still be conscious to tell me what is happening.

ॐ **Delta (0.1–4 Hz):** There is this interesting state of Theta but not sleeping Delta where you are able to tap deeper into the quantum field. This state facilitates deep communion with the quantum field, where the patterns and potential shaping our existence become tangible. It reveals the blueprints of multidimensional reality.

ॐ **Gamma (30–100 Hz):** High-frequency states of mystical unity, where time and space dissolve, allowing direct experience of the interconnected cosmos. I have achieved Gamma State easily by using plant medicine, but also when I was in a high state of peak performance, putting me in a state of flow. I believe Gamma and above is the ultimate brainwave pattern we all want to be in. To put this into perspective, the higher dimensional beings operate at vibrational frequencies of at least 1000 Hz. They need to lower their vibrational field to ensure they don't overwhelm or "burn" us, allowing them to more effectively interact with us in our current state of consciousness. The ability to access these high-frequency Gamma states, and even beyond, is a key aspect of tapping into our full creative potential as Quantum Master Creators. By aligning our consciousness with these elevated states, we can directly experience the interconnected nature of the cosmos, transcending the illusion of linear time and space. This unlocks profound insights and abilities that enable us to shape our reality in profound ways.

One of my most profound quantum travel experiences in between Theta and Delta states using Hemi-Sync® technology involved meeting Liliani, my future Andromedan self who I introduced to you in chapter 3. Liliani taught me that quantum travel is not about leaving my physical body but about integrating wisdom and energy from other dimensions into my current experience. I have a standing daily practice to tune my pineal gland, change my brain waves, and connect into that space and interact with her.

Understanding these quantum principles and the ability to tune your consciousness lays the foundation for exploring the Quantum Master Creator manifestation method in more depth. By aligning your awareness with the quantum field, you can learn to consciously shape your reality in remarkable ways.

Quantum Travel & Exiting the Incarnational Cycle

Many seekers on the path to quantum consciousness believe they must abandon their physical form to explore higher dimensions. I've encountered countless students who assume that out-of-body experiences (OBEs) are about escaping the limitations of the flesh to access greater wisdom. But I believe that quantum travel isn't about leaving the body behind, it's about expanding our awareness while remaining deeply anchored in our physical vessel.

Think of your body as a magnificent instrument, capable of playing multiple octaves of reality simultaneously. As the Quantum Master Creators, when we master the art of quantum travel or quantum jumping, we're not abandoning any part of ourselves. Instead, we're learning to conduct an orchestra of consciousness, where every aspect of our being—physical, emotional, mental, and spiritual plays in perfect harmony.

This integration is what true Quantum Mastery is about. Rather than seeking to escape our physical reality, we learn to expand within it, allowing different dimensions of consciousness as full spectrum beings to merge and flow together in the present moment. The body becomes not a limitation to transcend, but a sacred vessel capable of holding and expressing multiple levels of reality at once.

My dear friend, Isabella A. Greene explores this concept in her two popular books, *"Leaving the Trap: How to Exit the Reincarnation Cycle"* and *"Beyond the Trap: How to Exit the Reincarnation Cycle"*. She describes the transformative power of quantum travel, stating:

"Quantum travel offers you a chance to explore and to choose your post-death options while alive. Quantum traveling is very different from astral projection. It bypasses the entire astral realm altogether, and thus you are out of the trap. Teaching yourself to have out-of-body experiences at will and to quantum travel the worlds outside of the Earth plane gives you the advantage of experiencing for yourself what is possible outside of the astral plane and our immediate reality. It also gives you the most fascinating experiences you could possibly imagine."

She explores in her books the concept that unseen forces shape our reality, urging us to become aware of the intricate agendas at play. Among these forces are what she refers to as "handlers"—entities or mechanisms within the astral realm that guide souls after death and, in some interpretations, influence their decisions to return to Earth through the reincarnation cycle. These handlers operate primarily in the upper astral plane, a realm spanning 4D to 4.9D, just below the threshold of the 5th dimension. It is here that souls undergo life reviews, form new soul contracts, and determine their next incarnation.

The Subtle Persuasion of Handlers

According to Isabella, the handlers employ various strategies to encourage souls to reincarnate. One of the most common involves invoking pre-existing soul agreements—reminding the soul of its commitments to family, friends, and other close connections. These contracts are framed as sacred promises, emphasizing the role of reincarnation as a means of collective spiritual evolution. The emotional pull of reuniting with loved ones or fulfilling perceived unfinished business is often enough to persuade a soul to return to Earth.

If emotional appeals fail, handlers frequently turn to guilt as a tool of influence. Souls may be reminded of unfulfilled vows, unresolved conflicts, or lingering obligations from past lives. Phrases like "You promised to help this soul evolve" or "This person is still waiting for you" are commonly used to instill a sense of responsibility. Often, souls are presented with the idea of a "second chance"—an opportunity to correct past mistakes or complete karmic lessons. In other cases, they may be shown visions of personal growth and spiritual progress, reinforcing the belief that reincarnation is necessary for their ascension.

Quantum Travel is A Path to True Freedom

For those who seek to transcend the cycle of reincarnation, preparation is essential. The key lies in resolving emotional ties and karmic entanglements so they cannot be used as leverage during the death transition. Recognizing one's sovereign nature as a soul is equally important, understanding that true spiritual freedom means making choices untainted by external persuasion. Developing emotional neutrality and practicing detachment from guilt-based narratives can prevent manipulation in the afterlife.

Another crucial strategy involves transcending the astral plane entirely. The reincarnation loop is said to function within this realm, making it imperative to raise one's consciousness beyond 4D frequencies. Practices such as quantum travel meditations, Kundalini activation, and high-frequency energy work provide a means of bypassing astral influence. Setting clear intentions before death is also a powerful technique—affirming your right to explore higher realms and consciously rejecting reincarnation agreements.

I strongly align with Isabella's perspective that quantum travel is one of the most powerful tools for breaking free from the reincarnation cycle while still alive. Unlike astral projection, which often keeps one tethered to 4D realms, quantum travel provides direct access to higher dimensions, allowing for conscious exploration of post-death possibilities and the freedom to transcend reincarnation. Quantum travel enriches both spiritual evolution and daily life, expanding consciousness while keeping us grounded.

By mastering the Kundalini and Breathwork techniques that mentioned in chapter 6 will allow one to navigate beyond astral structures. The soul can access higher-dimensional realities that exist outside the reincarnation matrix, complemented by breathwork and sensory deprivation, which expand your awareness into the Void—the infinite field of potential. Tools like Robert Monroe's Hemi-Sync® technology, using sound frequencies to entrain brainwaves, have been instrumental in my experience in achieving these states.

By aligning brainwave patterns with higher frequencies, we can transcend linear time, embody our multidimensional nature, and draw wisdom from infinite possibilities into the present. Each practice refines our ability to navigate quantum realms, reclaim sovereignty, and consciously choose our next experience—free from influence, free from limitation.

Exploring Realms, Electrical Wars, and Earth Gridwork

Similarly to Isabella's work, Darius J. Wright, a distinguished explorer of consciousness specializing in out-of-body experiences (OBEs), has profoundly influenced my understanding of reality and its vast realms. Since childhood, Wright has ventured beyond the physical, exploring unseen dimensions and gathering profound insights into the true nature of existence. His mission, which he calls "The Great Work," is centered on awakening individuals to their eternal selves and unlocking dormant abilities through OBEs.

In his exploration of the universe's structure, Wright proposes a fascinating model encompassing 12 primary realms and the overarching 13th realm. He likens a realm to a house, with dimensions representing the various rooms within it, each vibrating at a unique frequency. Everyone creates their own dimensional spaces based on beliefs and fears, leading to self-imposed limitations. Unconditional love is the key to transcend these limitations and access higher realms of consciousness.

We are at the Mother Earth, positioned in the middle stage, or realm 1, serving as a pivotal point in this Universal construct, hence why all the beings from other realms and dimensions are so interested in our evolution.

Each realm serves as a unique aspect of the cosmic blueprint, embodying specific vibrational frequencies, purposes, and beings. Here are just few of the realms that Darius discusses in his teachings:

- **Mother Earth (Realm 1):** The physical plane where we reside, serving as the central nexus for soul evolution. It is a dense, dualistic realm, providing opportunities for learning and growth through contrast and experience.

- **Galactic (Realm 2):** A bridge between Earth and the cosmic communities, inhabited by interstellar beings such as Pleiadeans, Arcturians, and Sirians who oversee planetary development and offer guidance to awakened individuals.

- **Halls of Amenti (Realm 3):** A hidden, etheric library containing the records of humanity's past, present, and future. It is a place where initiates and advanced seekers access ancient wisdom to accelerate their spiritual growth.

- **Heaven (Realm 5):** Home to the divine hierarchies, celestial temples, and soul rejuvenation centers. This is where souls undergo healing between incarnations, and where high-level guides, often referred to as Masters, reside.

- **Angelics (Realm 7):** The realm of archangels, guardian angels, and other divine messengers. It acts as a conduit of divine will and protection, influencing the lower realms with wisdom and light.

- **God Throne/Olympian Gods (Realm 9):** A reality where the so-called ancient gods of various pantheons, such as Zeus, Hera, and Odin, still reside. These beings maintain oversight over specific energetic aspects of the universe, sometimes interacting with Earth through myths and visions.

- **Ancients (Realm 12)** The realm of the oldest and most advanced souls, often considered the original architects of reality. These beings possess knowledge far beyond human comprehension, influencing the structure of the multiverse.

- **Mother Arc (Realm 13):** This realm exists beyond the traditional 12-dimensional matrix—a pure field beyond the constructs of time, polarity, and material form. It is the original container space, the eternal womb from which all creation is seeded. Deeply aligned with the Sacred Codes of the Feminine, the Mother Arc emanates pure, unconditional love, unity consciousness, and the living memory of the original divine blueprint. It is as a return to Cosmic Oneness, where distortions, karmic imprints, and false matrices dissolve, leaving only the undistorted frequency of Source truth. The Mother Arc is not merely a realm among others—it is the foundation and pillar upon which all other realms and dimensional gates are structured. It represents the Zero Point field, the infinite stillness before creation, now actively anchoring into the crystal core of Mother Earth. I believe the awakening of the Mother Arc frequencies is linked to the Andromedan core creation and is signaled by the activation of what Lisa Renee calls as "the Aqua Ray currents"— streams of living light that restore the original Christ-Sophia blueprint within beings. Many on the path of awakening are reattuning to this Divine stream, reconnecting with the Cosmic Mother's heart through remembrance, healing, and reclamation of their organic spiritual sovereignty. To embody Mother Arc frequencies is to embody the resurrection codes, the return to original unity, and the sacred marriage of polarities within. It is the passage beyond fragmentation into eternal wholeness.

According to Darius J. Wright, higher-dimensional beings once moved freely between realms during the Lemurian and Atlantean eras—a truth I recall from my own soul memory. These civilizations operated within Earth's multidimensional grid, using stargates and frequency to travel, heal, and co-create. But that harmony was shattered during the **Electrical Wars**—a series of ancient interdimensional conflicts where advanced plasma, scalar, and crystal technologies were weaponized. The goal: to hijack planetary stargates and sever Earth's connection to the galactic network.

These wars caused catastrophic rips in the grid, so called planetary resets that triggered the fall of Lemuria and Atlantis, and the collapse of Tara, Gaia's original 5D+ form. Stargates were sealed or reversed, and many sacred sites were buried, petrified, or masked as geology. The trauma of this timeline still echoes in the land—and in our DNA.

Through over a decade of gridwork, I've witnessed these timelines reawakening. In Iceland, I encountered what appeared to be petrified dragons and stone guardians—but I knew intuitively they were ancient fossilized in the energetic blast of those ancient wars.

In Sedona, Arizona, I channeled light language that activated dormant crystalline light technologies. The land pulsed in response—red rock formations, long considered sacred, revealed their true function as resonant transmitters. And in Cappadocia, Turkey, I was recently guided to activate refuge divine feminine codes embedded in the subterranean cities—once hidden temples, now slowly waking. More so, I remember how in Saqqara, Egypt, ancient technology was hidden in plain sight under the pyramid complexes.

What has become clear is that Earth is a living archive of multidimensional history. The remnants of the Electrical Wars are all around us—in the fossilized tech, in the distorted grids, and in the trauma that still plays out in human consciousness. But we are here now, in this lifetime, to repair what was broken.

Our voices, our frequency, our light language, and our presence are the tools of restoration. The temples may appear as rock. The codes may seem buried. But when activated by those with resonance and remembrance, they awaken. The planetary crystalline grid, once shattered, is reweaving itself through us.

As we return to these ancient sites—not as tourists, but as Mother Earth's gridworkers and keepers, and starseed architects—we are reactivating the organic stargate system that once connected Earth to the stars. These are missions encoded into our crystalline soul blueprint.

▍Iceland: The Land of Dragons and Hidden People

Places often call me for activation work, guiding me to where energy is ready to be shifted or awakened. Such was the case with Iceland, which began calling to me during the pandemic shutdown in 2020. Despite the pull, it seemed impossible to reach due to travel restrictions, vaccine requirements, and quarantine protocols. Finally, in 2023, the path opened. Joined by two incredible channelers, I embarked on a 9-day journey across Iceland, following clear guidance—especially to the Snaefellsnes Peninsula, home to a powerful glacier known as the heart of Iceland, protected by the ancient guardian Bárður Snæfellsás.

Iceland is steeped in unseen magic, with locals maintaining a deep connection to elves, fairies, and hidden people, who are still believed to reside throughout the land. In fact, these encounters are formally recorded, with 50 huldufólk - hidden people identified by Icelandic researchers from fairies to elfs. This magical undercurrent came alive for us as we approached the Snaefellsnes National Park.

Bárður's territory and Heart Chakra Glacier Behind Me

We sang in light language, drummed, and channeled in the singing cave, calling on the energies asking for Bárður's permission to work on his sacred lands. As we moved toward the beach, the energy thickened, and we began noticing massive, petrified beings—trolls, standing like ancient sentinels, frozen in time, gazing into the distance. We could interact with fairies in what many called "the Fairies Church".

Then came the most profound moment. As the energy grew stronger, we began channeling the dragon and his collective consciousness, the dragon family. It became clear that we were connecting to this dragon collective through quantum entanglement, bridging realms and timelines. We realized that the dragon, though now existing in another parallel realm, had once been on this Earth in flesh and blood.

Petrified Dragon lying on the beach (Image by Diana Divine)

The deeper we connected; the story began to reveal itself. During the Electrical Wars of ancient times, these great beings had been petrified by a displacement weapon, trapping them in stone while their consciousness continued to live on in another dimensional realm. As we walked back and gazed at the cliffs from a distance, we saw it—the unmistakable form of a massive, petrified dragon, powerful and majestic, its ancient energy still present. The dragon guardian felt both ancient and eternal, confirming that we had reawakened a forgotten connection and that the work we were doing extended across time, space, and dimensions.

Saqqara: Quantum Gateway and the Halls of Amenti

The desert winds carry memories across millennia, whispering tales of ancient powers that once flowed freely through the sacred grounds of Saqqara, Egypt. For over three millennia, these sands have guarded what mortals see as merely a necropolis, where pharaohs and their elite found their eternal rest in magnificent monuments. I smile when I think of the archaeologists, Christian Greco and Lara Weiss, whose discovery of a seemingly insignificant detail on a 19th-century map launched an expedition that would begin to scratch the surface of our sacred truths. They seek to understand how ancient Egyptians interacted with their past, yet they glimpse only the outer layer of a far deeper mystery.

View of Saqqar including Djoser's step pyramid, the Pyramid of Unas (left)

and Pyramid of Userkahd (right)

I remember it all with crystalline clarity, as I was the Guardian, the High Priestess chosen to safeguard the passages between worlds. While they unearth tombs and artifacts, I know the true purpose of each chamber, each carefully placed stone. What they saw as a necropolis was in truth a living library of power, each tomb and monument precisely placed to channel and amplify the earth's natural energies. Saqqara was the quantum generator that served as both heart and brain, an energy information control center whose power spread outward to all other pyramids in the vast Atlantean network of pyramids.

The Serapeum stands at the heart of this power. Modern scholars speak of it as tombs for sacred bulls, but they glimpse only the surface of a profound truth. Those immense corridors, those perfectly crafted 24 granite sarcophagi weighing 60-70 tons each—they served a far greater purpose. Each was a masterwork of precision engineering, like an interdimensional portal pod, crafted to within a micron's tolerance not to honor dead beasts, but to transport beings from other realms.

During Atlantean times, Egypt was our second outpost. Through sacred rituals synchronized with the cosmic dance of celestial bodies, we preserved the delicate harmony that allowed beings of pure light and wisdom to grace our earthly plane. These ethereal visitors, transcending physical form and temporal constraints, shared knowledge that would shape the destiny of human civilization. Beings like Arcturians, Lyrans, Sirians were frequent visitors.

One of the Sarcophagi in the Serapeum, Saqqara, Egypt (Source: Sailingstone)

The granite chambers held secrets beyond mortal understanding. Each colossal lid was designed with purpose not merely to seal, but to compress and transform energy itself. The crystalline matrix within the stone would sing with piezoelectric resonance, filling our sacred space with a luminescence that needed no flame. This is why the ancient walls bear no trace of soot; our work was illuminated by the very forces we channeled.

But even the most sacred sanctuaries can be corrupted. When the Galactic Federation warned us of the approaching darkness—reptilian forces seeking to twist our portal's purpose from enlightenment to conquest. The gateway was sealed, its power suppressed beneath layers of stone and secrecy, and the priesthood escaped into the desert.

The process of closure was complex and heart-wrenching. Each sarcophagus required precise calibration; its alchemically treated contents carefully preserved within hermetic seals. We added massive stone blocks atop the lids, ensuring they would remain undisturbed until the right time came again. What later generations would find—mere bones and remnants—were simply echoes of the true power once contained within.

Though I cannot yet walk physically among the sands of Saqqara—its energetic calibration still in process—my connection to the Halls of Amenti keeps me eternally tethered to this sacred ground. Through remote viewing, I traverse these ancient corridors daily, monitoring the gradual reawakening of Earth's most powerful quantum generator.

For Saqqara is far more than a necropolis—it is the crown jewel of Earth's spiritual technology. The step pyramid itself functions as a massive resonator; its very shape designed to amplify and direct energy through the crystalline bedrock beneath. This is why it was built here, atop one of Earth's most powerful ley line intersections.

The Halls of Amenti, that interdimensional chamber of initiation and transformation, connects directly to Saqqara through quantum tunnels that transcend physical space. As a keeper of these ancient mysteries, I can access these quantum pathways, though for now, my physical presence must wait. Saqqara's reactivation must proceed carefully—its quantum field rebuilding gradually to prevent energetic overload in Earth's current fragile state.

This great temple complex serves as humanity's primary stargate, a quantum bridge between dimensions. Its massive granite structures act as capacitors, storing and transmitting energy through the crystalline matrix within the stone. The sacred geometry encoded in its architecture creates standing waves of quantum energy, generating a toroidal field that can bend space-time itself.

Even now, as my spirit walks these hallowed passages, I sense the residual energies humming within the ancient granite. Though the great portal lies dormant, its essence persists, waiting for those with the wisdom to understand its true purpose. The sands of time may have buried our secrets, but they have not erased them.

Perhaps one day, when humanity has evolved to embrace these deeper truths, and Saqqara's quantum matrix has fully stabilized, I will walk these sacred grounds in physical form once again. Until then, I remain as I have always been—guardian of a legacy that transcends time itself, keeper of secrets that the world is not yet ready to reclaim but soon shall be.

What is truly astonishing is that, as I was completing this book, a groundbreaking scientific revelation emerged. Researchers using advanced ground-penetrating radar uncovered eight colossal spiral pillars plunging over 2,000 feet beneath the Giza Plateau, alongside five concealed structures interconnected by corridors—and most remarkably, indications of a vast, ancient city buried 3,937 feet beneath the Khafre Pyramid. These discoveries, long veiled by the shifting sands and protected by energetic cloaks, now whisper to the modern world of truths once forgotten.

ANCIENT FIND

The findings researchers claim to have made using radar to explore underneath the pyramids in Egypt

Five structures believed to be connected by corridors

Eight pillars with spiral staircases going downwards to a depth of 2,132ft

Four of these pillars feed into two separate cube structures measuring 262ft

At 3,937ft below the base of the pyramid - ancient city

At 4,000ft from the base, there are believed to be more unknown structures

Tesla's 3-6-9 Method: Simple Daily Practice

The 3-6-9 method is based on Nikola Tesla's belief in the power of these numbers as universal keys to manifestation. This practice is divided into three simple daily sessions, each building upon the other to create powerful momentum toward your goals.

Begin your morning with the power of 3, representing the creative force. Within the first hour of waking, write down your intention three times and spend three minutes visualizing it. This morning practice plants the seed of creation and sets your energy for the day. Keep your intention clear and specific, focusing on exactly what you want to manifest.

In the afternoon, engage with the power of 6, which represents manifestation and balance. Write your intention six times and take a moment to feel the emotion of having already achieved your goal. This midday practice bridges the gap between creation and completion. During this time, look for opportunities to take action toward your goal, as number 6 connects to practical manifestation.

End your day with the power of 9, symbolizing completion and transformation. Before bed, write your intention nine times and spend a few quiet moments in meditation, seeing your goal as already accomplished. The evening practice helps integrate your intentions into your subconscious mind while you sleep. Release any worry about how your goal will manifest and trust in the process.

Maintain this practice for nine consecutive days. The key to success lies in consistency and emotional alignment with your desired outcome. Don't worry about perfect timing – what matters most is maintaining the three daily sessions and keeping your intention clear. As you practice, pay attention to any patterns, synchronicities, or opportunities that arise.

Example Intention Format:

"I am grateful now that [your specific goal] has manifested in my life."

Remember that this method works through alignment with universal energy patterns. Trust in the process, maintain emotional connection to your goal, and remain open to unexpected ways your intention might manifest.

▌Activation of Quantum Code ▲ Beyond Time

This activation is designed to transmit the essence of the chapter as an energetic template—something you feel rather than analyze. By bypassing the thinking mind, it speaks directly to your body, energy field, and subconscious, allowing transformation to unfold on a deeper level.

◆ Begin Here: Set the Field

Find a quiet space. Light a candle if you feel called. Sit or lie comfortably with your spine aligned and your heart open. Close your eyes and take a few grounding breaths—in through your nose, out through your mouth. Let your body soften. Let your energy settle.

Bring your awareness to your heart space. Place your hands gently over your heart or simply focus your attention there. Feel the warmth between your palms and chest. Let it grow.

When you are ready, speak the following words aloud or silently within:

"I now open to release all that is blocking my highest good.

I open to grace, to clarity, to healing.

I activate and understand all that I need to move forward on my path with ease and flow.

I open to remember who I truly am."

Breathe that in. Let it ripple through your entire being.

◆ Activate the Quantum Code

Repeat these sacred Source Language words below three times aloud, allowing the vibration to move through your body and field:

ARU NA VI YA SHA
TURA PI YA

Now read the following quantum transmission:

Deep within the brain's sacred space
Where pineal wisdom holds its place
A quantum antenna, finely tuned
To frequencies beyond the moon.

Through resonant gift of sacred sound
Where hemispheres in sync are found
Binaural beats paint paths of light
Through dimensions infinite and bright.

Beyond the astral's subtle hold
Past stories we've long been told
Quantum travel breaks the seal

Of what we thought was set and real
Choice becomes our sovereign right
Free to dance through dark and light
No more bound to turn the wheel

◇ ACTIVATION COMPLETE ◇

Sit in stillness. Allow the code to settle into your system. Feel the integration weaving into your cells, your field, your breath. Let the silence become your teacher.

♦ Ground & Center

Breathe deeply into your body. Imagine golden roots extending from the soles of your feet into the heart of the Earth. Feel the Earth holding you, anchoring you.

You are safe. You are protected. You are loved.

Begin to gently move your fingers and toes. Wiggle. Stretch. Return fully to your body.

Grounding Contemplation

After activating the Quantum code and grounding, stay rooted by taking time to notice what's shifting within. You might feel called to journal, draw, or simply sit in quiet awareness, allowing your inner wisdom to gently emerge. Use the following questions as gateways to deeper insight. There is no need to rush or force answers. Let them move through you like waves.

1. What are you excited most about right now?
2. What action today can reflect your highest potential self?
3. Where do you notice resistance to your current timeline phase?
4. What frequency are you tuning into, consciously or unconsciously?
5. How does your current reality reflect your chosen vibrations?
6. How can you fully trust the perfect timing of your creation?

After exploring these questions, return to stillness. Let the insights settle. If emotions rise, allow them. If symbols, images, or inner messages emerge— capture them without editing. Trust what wants to come through.

◆ Integration
You may notice subtle or profound shifts after this activation and contemplation. Honor this by giving yourself space to rest, reflect, and receive.

This practice is an invitation to step into your role as a quantum traveler— bridging dimensions and harmonizing your infinite potential into the now. An audio version of this activation is available on my website if you'd like to revisit and deepen the transmission.

Take your time. If today's journey stirred something meaningful, give yourself a full day—or more—before moving forward. Integration is a sacred part of the alchemy. Let it unfold in its own divine rhythm.

Chapter 9
The Quantum Master
Creator Method

"From GOD's perspective, everything that happens in life is a Spiritual test. In every situation in life, we can respond from God consciousness or negative ego consciousness. We can respond from our lower-self or our Higher Self. We can respond from unconditional love or from fear. We can respond from separation or from oneness. We can respond from our Melchizedek/Christ/Buddha consciousness or from personality level consciousness that is not connected to the Soul and Spirit. So, Earth is a school to practice demonstrating GOD or to practice demonstrating being a Melchizedek, the Christ, and/or the Buddha. The terms or names we use do not matter for they are interchangeable."

— **Dr. Joshua David Stone**

As my consciousness expanded into deeper realms of quantum awareness, I began to recognize a familiar resonance—a frequency of knowing that echoed through multiple lifetimes on Earth and beyond. My quest for deeper understanding led me to the profound ascension teachings of Dr. Joshua David Stone, whose work illuminated the path until his transition in 2005. Sharing this journey with my twin flame and husband has been an invaluable mirror, helping us navigate Earth's spiritual evolution with greater clarity and discernment.

Traditionally, Ascension meant transcending the physical form. Masters would complete their earthly initiations by leaving their bodies behind, continuing their service from higher dimensions. This pattern is seen across various traditions, perhaps most beautifully expressed in Tibetan Buddhism's concept of the Rainbow Body—where advanced practitioners transform their physical form into pure light at death, achieving union with the dharmakaya, the formless essence of Buddha-nature.

Yet, our experience has revealed a profound shift in this paradigm. The accelerated evolution of the quantum field now allows initiates to achieve these advanced states while remaining in physical form. This isn't a lesser path—it's an expansion of possibility, enabling us to bridge earthly and cosmic realms while fully embodied. We've discovered that the traditional three-layered structure of Planetary Ascension, Solar Ascension, and Cosmic Ascension can now be navigated while maintaining physical presence, creating an unprecedented opportunity for direct service to Earth's evolution.

The nature of mastery is undergoing a significant transformation. Rather than seeking wisdom in distant realms, we are learning to embody deeper understanding within our everyday reality. This shift reflects an evolution in how spiritual wisdom and energetic transmissions occur across dimensions of consciousness.

In ancient times, wisdom transmission required direct contact between master and initiate, flowing through unbroken lineages in ways that transcended ordinary teaching. Whether through Padmasambhava's hidden termas, Buddha's silent flower sermon, or Jesus's miraculous demonstrations, mastery involved direct energetic activation of latent potential.

Today, as the veils between dimensions thin, these transmissions can occur directly through the quantum field. When I channel Source Light Language or facilitate Kundalini activations, I'm not teaching in any traditional sense—I'm creating multidimensional bridges that allow quantum waves of activation to reach those ready to receive. These transmissions carry their own sacred geometry and light codes, moving through the quantum field with precise frequency signatures.

While the fundamental nature of mastery remains constant—rooted in direct transmission and conscious integration, rather than mere intellectual gathering—our means of accessing these profound states has transformed. The codes of mastery now exist within the quantum field itself, accessible through resonant frequency alignment, rather than solely through traditional teacher-student relationships.

This quantum accessibility brings a deeper call to personal responsibility and conscious participation. Rather than receiving wisdom solely from external sources, we are invited to become active co-creators in reality's unfolding. Everyone's journey of alignment and awakening contributes to the expansion of what's possible for collective human consciousness.

As Quantum Master Creators, we engage with reality at multiple levels simultaneously. Through frequency attunement, we can access wisdom encoded in the quantum field, consciously integrating insights into everyday existence. Our personal transformation ripples out into the collective field, embodying higher frequencies that activate similar potentials in others. This creates a resonant field of possibility, expanding the boundaries of what's achievable for human consciousness.

This new paradigm of mastery is characterized by full embodiment of multidimensional awareness in physical reality, direct quantum perception and interaction with multiple layers of existence. It recognizes that individual transcendence serves collective evolution, understanding that every conscious choice affects the whole through quantum entanglement. The journey is no longer about ascending away from physical reality but rather about bringing higher dimensional awareness fully into form.

In this way, Quantum Mastery becomes a dance of individual and collective evolution. As we attune to higher frequencies and embody our multidimensional nature, we naturally contribute to the elevation of human consciousness. This is not a journey of solitary achievement but rather a collaborative creation, where each person's awakening creates ripples of possibility throughout the quantum field of human potential.

▍Quantum Keys and Creation Formula

Imagine holding the keys to unlock the doorway to a quantum shift, allowing you to manifest the deepest desires of your heart. These keys exist, but to activate them, you must first recognize and release what no longer serves you, stepping into full trust of the process. Clarity is essential—you must define what you wish to co-create with the Universe. Now, we will explore these keys, understanding how they interlock to facilitate quantum creation. Just as a goddess skillfully aims her arrow to strike her target, you too can harness this power when you master the art of quantum creation.

The Quantum Master Creator formula is:

> **Quantum Creation = (Emotional Mastery (EM) × Coherent Field (CF)) + (Clear Intention (CI) × Surrender)**

Quantum Creation is like launching a rocket. The emotional energy (Emotional Mastery × Coherent Field) is the fuel and propulsion system. It generates the power needed to send your creation into motion. The mental clarity (Clear Intention × Surrender) is the navigation system that sets the direction and ensures you don't interfere with the rocket's natural path. Both parts are essential: without energy, the rocket won't launch, and without navigation, it won't reach its destination. The combination of aligned energy and focused clarity creates the perfect conditions for manifestation and creation.

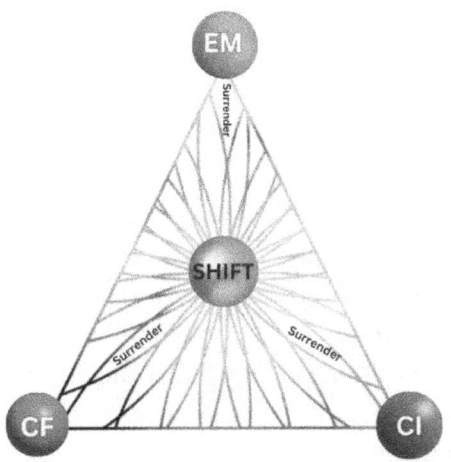

Quantum Creation Triangle (Image by Diana Divine)

This triangle diagram above shows this formula to help visualize the quantum shift for the creation to occur. Emotional Mastery (EM), Coherent Field (CF) and Clear Intention (CI) are the key components, the balls at the edges of the triangle. With full Surrender and trust, you allow the quantum field to co create reality by converging in the middle.

Emotional Mastery

Think of your emotions as a sophisticated broadcasting system. Every feeling you experience sends specific frequencies into the quantum field, shaping the reality you experience. You must have stability in your emotions. If you are operating in a chaotic state, you are preventing quantum reality from manifesting. Essentially, you need to be in a higher 4D and above dimensional state and learn to control your spectrum of emotions.

> **Emotional Mastery = Frequency × Stability × Amplitude × Duration**

Where:
- ॐ **Frequency** = Chosen emotional state vibration
- ॐ **Stability**= The ability to maintain the chosen emotional state consistently over time
- ॐ **Amplitude** = The intensity or "volume" of the emotional state.
- ॐ **Duration** = The length of time the emotional state is held.

In Chapter 4, we covered the David Hawkins Emotional Scale in his Map of Consciousness. At the highest frequencies, Hawkins presents that enlightenment (700 - 1000), these are energies of bliss and ecstasy. These states open direct portals to quantum creation, where manifestation becomes instant and reality flows effortlessly. This is where we are in clear 5D and 6D dimensional reality states.

Just below, peace (600), then joy (540) - these emotions create powerful, stable creation fields. Love (500) and gratitude generate magnetic attraction, naturally drawing aligned experiences to you.

The middle range acceptance (350) provides neutral ground for conscious creation. Think of these as your reset points, clear spaces from which to launch new intentions. Lower frequencies below courage (200), like fear (100) and guilt (30) create density, slowing creation and making reality feel more rigid and resistant.

The Four Elements of Emotional Mastery

To harness emotional mastery as a vibrational technology, it's helpful to think of the process as operating a high-frequency radio station. Just as a radio operator manages the broadcast, you must consciously manage your emotional energy across four key elements:

- ॐ **Choice:** Selecting your "station" by consciously choosing your emotional frequency. This might mean shifting from fear to courage, or gratitude to joy.
- ॐ **Stability:** Maintaining your chosen emotional state over time. A clear, consistent signal prevents interference, ensuring your intention is sent into the quantum field without distortion.
- ॐ **Amplitude:** Amplifying the emotional intensity to resonate powerfully. The more passionate you feel gratitude, love, or joy, the more potent your broadcast becomes.
- ॐ **Duration:** Sustaining the emotional vibration long enough for it to manifest. The longer you "hold the station," the stronger the quantum imprint becomes.

Coherent Field

Imagine your energy field as a vast symphony orchestra. When each instrument plays its own tune without coordination, you get chaos - beautiful perhaps but lacking creative power. But when every instrument aligns perfectly, playing in harmony, you create something magical. This is the essence of a Coherent Field - the synchronized harmony of your entire being.

$$\textbf{Coherent Field = Heart Coherence} \times \textbf{Brain Coherence} \\ \times \textbf{Field Unity}$$

Where:
- ॐ Heart Coherence = steady heart rhythm
- ॐ Brain Coherence = synchronized brain waves
- ॐ Field Unity = aligned energy pattern

The Coherent Field begins with your heart, the conductor of this biological symphony. Your heart generates the strongest electromagnetic field in your body, radiating far beyond your physical form. When your heart achieves coherence - a steady, rhythmic pattern - it creates a stable foundation for all other systems to align with. A coherent heart creates waves of order that ripple through your entire system.

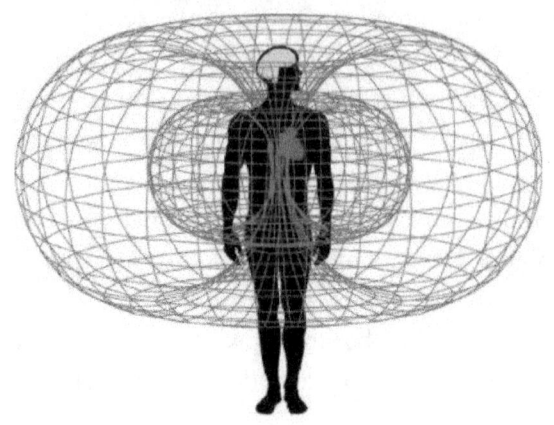

The Coherent Heart (Source: HeartMath Institute)

The Heart Math Institute's groundbreaking research has demonstrated that the heart's electromagnetic field is approximately 5,000 times stronger than the brain's field and extends several feet beyond the body. When we enter heart coherence, this field produces a steady, rhythmic pattern that creates waves of order rippling through our entire system. The heart's field carries information that influences both physiological and cognitive processes, affecting everything from immune function and hormonal balance to brain activity and emotional processing. In this coherent state, different biological systems begin to entrain with the heart's rhythm, creating a harmonious synchronization throughout the body.

For Quantum Master Creators, establishing and maintaining heart coherence is essential for conscious reality creation. The heart's coherent field serves as an amplifier for our creative intentions, helping to broadcast them more powerfully into the quantum field. When we maintain coherence while focusing our creative intent, we create a stable foundation that allows our manifestations to materialize more readily in physical reality. This coherent field acts as a bridge between thought and form, between potential and manifestation.

Brain Coherence refers to the synchronization of neural oscillations across different regions of the brain. When the brain operates in coherence, various brainwave frequencies, including alpha, theta, and gamma waves, align in a structured and harmonious manner. This coherence enhances cognitive clarity, emotional stability, and intuition. A coherent brain supports effective decision-making, heightened awareness, and a deeper connection to the quantum field. By engaging in practices such as meditation, breathwork, and intentional focus, one can cultivate brain coherence and amplify the power of conscious creation.

Field Unity is the final key to creating a fully coherent state. It represents the alignment of the heart and brain's electromagnetic fields with the surrounding energetic environment. When the heart and brain achieve coherence simultaneously, their electromagnetic fields synchronize and expand, allowing for seamless interaction with the quantum field. Field unity creates a resonance that facilitates manifestation, enhances personal energy, and strengthens the interconnected web of consciousness. Through field unity, individual coherence contributes to the collective evolution of human potential.

The implications extend beyond individual creation. When multiple creators maintain coherence together, their fields can interact and amplify each other, creating powerful group fields that accelerate collective evolution. Research demonstrates that in this coherent state, practitioners experience:

- ॐ Enhanced intuitive access and quantum information reception
- ॐ Stronger manifestation capabilities
- ॐ Increased synchronicity
- ॐ More stable timeline alignment
- ॐ Deeper connection to source consciousness

Through conscious cultivation of this threefold coherence, we establish the energetic foundation necessary for reliable reality creation. This unified field provides a stable platform from which we can access quantum realms while remaining grounded in physical reality. It creates the optimal conditions for consciousness to influence reality at the quantum level, bridging the gap between thought and form, between potential and manifestation.

The Coherent Field reveals why ancient wisdom traditions emphasized the alignment of heart, mind, and spirit. Modern science now validates that this unified state creates the precise conditions necessary for bringing thought into form, demonstrating that conscious reality creation isn't just metaphysical philosophy - it's measurable, repeatable science.

Clear Intention

For Quantum Master Creators, intention serves as the primary tool for focusing consciousness and directing quantum field potentials into physical manifestation. Energy flows where intention goes - this isn't just a metaphysical concept, but a fundamental principle of quantum creation. Through mastery of intention, we learn to harness our consciousness as a precise instrument for reality creation.

$$\text{Clear Intention} = \text{Vision} \times \text{Feeling} \times \text{Knowing}$$

Where:
- ॐ **Vision** = Crystal clear outcome
- ॐ **Feeling** = Emotional resonance
- ॐ **Knowing** = Absolute certainty

Unlike casual wishes or fleeting desires, quantum intention carries the full resonance of your multidimensional being - heart, mind, and spirit aligned in perfect coherence with your desired creation. When wielded with mastery, intention becomes a laser beam of consciousness, collapsing infinite possibilities into specific physical expressions.

The Quantum Master Creator works with three pillars of intention:

- ॐ **Crystalline Clarity:** At the quantum level, precision is everything. Your vision must be held with absolute purity—so refined that it forms a flawless holographic blueprint within the quantum field. Complexity only fragments creative power. As a Quantum Master, you work with distilled intentions—sometimes as simple as a single word or symbol—that encapsulate the essence of your creation. This clarity becomes a unique frequency signature, allowing the quantum field to mirror your intention with exactitude.

- ॐ **Emotional Resonance**: Emotion is the bridge between quantum potential and physical reality. As a Quantum Master, you generate and sustain the emotional signature of your desired creation by anchoring into your Heart Chakra and channeling willpower through your Solar Plexus—as though your creation already exists. This resonance isn't mere positive thinking; it's a finely tuned energetic state that magnetizes your desired reality, drawing it from the quantum realm into physical form.

Feeling your outcome as already realized is what collapses potential into matter.

ॐ **Quantum Certainty:** Mastery transcends belief and enters the realm of direct knowing. As a Quantum Master, you recognize that your creation already exists within the quantum field. Rather than hoping or striving, you align your frequency with the version of reality where your creation is fully manifest. This state of certainty leaves no space for doubt, because it's rooted in the direct perception of quantum truth. From this level of knowing, manifestation becomes an act of alignment, not effort.

The Power of Abracadabra and Creating Through Intentional Speech

The word "**abracadabra**" holds profound significance beyond its modern association with stage magic. Tracing its origins to the third century AD in ancient Mesopotamia, we find its roots in the Aramaic phrase "avra kedabra," meaning "I create as I speak." A striking parallel exists in Hebrew with "evra ka'asher adaber" - "I will create as I speak." These ancient cultures understood a fundamental truth: our spoken words have the power to shape reality itself.

When we speak with intention, we engage in an act of creation that ripples through our environment and relationships. Our words set the energy and tone of spaces we inhabit, shape how others perceive possibilities, and create emotional resonance that inspires action. Through careful communication, we can build bridges between people and transform abstract ideas into concrete plans. This creative power of speech has been recognized across cultures and throughout history.

A B R A C A D A B R A.

אברראכאדאכברא
אברראכאאדאאבר
אברראכאאדאאב
אברראכאאדא
אברראכאאד
אברראכא
אברראכ
אברא
אבר
אב
א

Creating your own personal mantra begins with deep reflection on what you truly wish to manifest, considering both personal growth and positive impact on others. Focus on one clear, powerful intention that resonates deeply with your authentic self. Shape this intention into words, using present tense to speak as if your desire is already manifesting. Example: *I AM ABUNDANT*. Keep your mantra concise but meaningful, incorporating active, creative language that feels personally significant.

The Quantum Field of Creation

When we unite three essential elements—crystalline clarity, emotional resonance, and unwavering certainty—we generate what mystics and quantum physicists alike recognize as an intention field. This field acts as both transmitter and receiver, broadcasting our precise intentions while attracting matching possibilities from the quantum realm. Our words, thoughts, and emotions serve as vibrational commands to this field, directly shaping the outcomes we experience. True mastery requires absolute precision in our speech. Rather than saying "I hope for change," we declare "Change is manifesting now," anchoring our intention in the present moment of creation.

In this elevated state of consciousness, we cease struggling against reality and step fully into our role as conscious co-creators. The universe naturally aligns itself with clear, coherent intentions. The quantum field responds not to wishful thinking but to absolute certainty and emotional alignment. Our thoughts, words, and feelings must resonate as one with our desired outcome, creating a focused force in the fabric of existence. When held with unwavering clarity, this intention field reshapes reality itself.

Human Design

Speaking your intentions into reality requires more than just words—it demands the power of your life force energy behind them. I'm a passionate advocate of Human Design, a fascinating system rooted in astrology and the I Ching, which I've used for years as a foundation to understand how a person's energy naturally operates. It's remarkably accurate, offering deep insight into how we are uniquely wired. I believe everyone should pull their free chart and explore their energetic blueprint—because understanding how you're designed changes everything.

Human Design reveals the way our energy moves through nine centers in the body, similar to chakras but with distinct qualities. For example,

Manifesting Generators have a natural superhighway of energy between their Sacral and Throat centers, particularly through the 34/20 channel, allowing them to effortlessly translate creative force into spoken word. However, even if this connection isn't defined in your chart, you can consciously cultivate it.

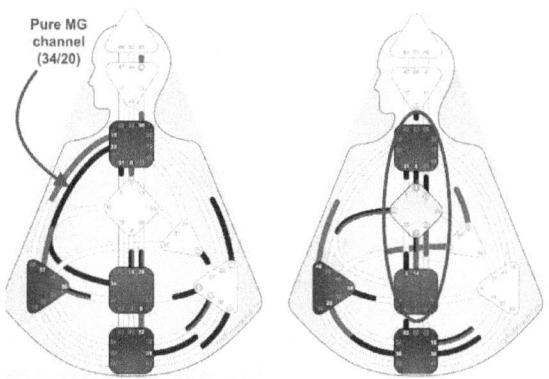

Pure MG
channel
(34/20)

Each type has its own special way of working with energy. Generators bring their powerful sacral response, Projectors their penetrating insight, Manifestors their independent initiative, and Reflectors their amplifying wisdom. Even if you don't have these centers naturally connected in your chart, you can intentionally activate this pathway. It's about understanding your unique design and then consciously working with it. Think of it like consciously drawing energy up from your creative center, your sacral space, and channeling it through to your throat when speaking your intentions. When we consciously bridge this connection, linking the raw creative energy of our sacral center to our throat center - our words become energized with life force. The key is working with your natural design while being intentional about channeling your creative energy through your voice.

Speaking Your Truth into Being

To become a Quantum Master Creator is to recognize the multidimensional nature of speech. When you speak your affirmation, your command, your mantra aloud, you're not just forming words—you're sending vibrations into the quantum field of possibility. Each word carries both sound and intention, creating ripples through multiple dimensions of reality. As you speak, feel the resonance in your body, the power in your voice, and the clarity of your intention merging into a single point of creation.

Practice speaking your mantra in different ways: whispered in meditation, declared with confidence, sung in moments of joy. Notice how each variation carries its own frequency and impact. Let your voice become an instrument of transformation, turning challenges into opportunities for deeper alignment. When you speak with this level of consciousness, you're not just communicating—you're participating in the sacred act of creation itself.

The true artistry of creation emerges when we maintain perfect balance between intention and surrender. While this may seem paradoxical, it is precisely in this space that manifestation occurs most powerfully. Our most potent intentions arise effortlessly from our connection to Source consciousness, carrying within them the perfect blueprint for manifestation. There is no need for force or control—these intentions emerge fully formed, already aligned with our highest potential, manifesting with natural ease and grace.

Just as ancient words held power to transform reality, your intentional speech can become a force for social change. Use your words to advocate for those who need support, challenge systemic inequities, and unite communities around shared values. Consider how your mantras can amplify marginalized voices, bridge divides, and inspire collective action.

Surrender

Imagine dropping a seed into fertile soil. You plant with clear intention, then provide perfect conditions, trust how it will naturally grow, and just allow perfect timing for it to happen. You don't dig up the seed daily to check progress. You don't force the sprout to emerge. You trust the intelligence within the seed.

$$\text{Surrender} = \text{Release} \times \text{Trust} \times \text{Allow} \times \text{Presence}$$

Where:
- ॐ **Release** = letting go of control
- ॐ **Trust** = faith in perfect unfolding
- ॐ **Allow** = acceptance of divine timing
- ॐ **Presence** = staying in the now

From the Quantum Master Creator's perspective, surrender represents the highest form of creation power. Rather than forcing reality to conform to our will, we enter a state of dynamic partnership with universal intelligence.

This isn't passive resignation but rather a masterful alignment with quantum field dynamics. Like expert quantum surfers, we read the waves of possibility and move in perfect harmony with them.

Surrender often seems counterintuitive in the context of conscious creation. We've been conditioned to make things happen, to force outcomes, to control results. Yet the quantum field operates through allowance, not force. Like trying to grip water tightly - the harder you squeeze, the more it slips away. True mastery lies in maintaining clear intention while releasing the need to control every detail of its manifestation.

ॐ *Release* - **The Art of Letting Go:** When we surrender the need to dictate exactly how our creations must manifest, we open ourselves to infinite possibilities. The quantum field often orchestrates far more elegant solutions than our limited minds can conceive. Masters understand that their role is to hold the clear frequency of what they're creating while allowing Universal intelligence to orchestrate the perfect path of manifestation.

ॐ *Trust* - **Faith in Perfect Unfolding:** Everything in nature has its perfect rhythm and timing. Just as a flower can't be forced to bloom before its time, our creations emerge according to divine timing. This trust in perfect unfolding allows us to remain in a state of peaceful expectancy rather than anxious forcing. The master knows that what appears as delay often serves a greater purpose in the perfect orchestration of events.

ॐ *Allow* - **Opening to Greater Possibilities:** When we release our grip on specific outcomes, we open ourselves to possibilities beyond our current imagination. The quantum field often has grander plans than we can envision from our limited perspective. By remaining open while maintaining clear intention, we allow our creations to evolve into their highest expression.

ॐ *Presence* - **The Power of Now:** Operating from a state of presence keeps us aligned with the quantum field's perfect orchestration. Like a master composer, the universe arranges countless elements into perfect harmony. What might appear as setbacks or delays often serve to align all elements necessary for optimal manifestation. The true time is NOW.

Through this conscious surrender, we align with the infinite intelligence that orchestrates galaxies, trusting it to guide our creations to their highest expression.

Integration into Your Life

Living as a Quantum Master Creator means bringing higher-dimensional awareness into your everyday life. Let me share how this looks in practice:

Imagine you're stuck in heavy traffic. Instead of getting frustrated, you use this as an opportunity to practice dimensional living. You might tune into the larger pattern - perhaps this delay is creating perfect timing for your next appointment or giving you the space needed to prepare mentally. I recently experienced this when a flight delay that initially seemed frustrating led to an amazing conversation with a fellow passenger who became a key collaborator.

Being a Quantum Creator isn't about controlling everything - it's about flowing with what emerges while maintaining your inner balance. For example, rather than pushing hard to make a project happen exactly as planned, you might notice subtle signs suggesting a different approach. One of my clients was set on launching her program in spring, but when she tuned into the quantum field, she sensed fall timing would align better. Trusting this insight, she used the extra months to refine her work, and her launch exceeded all expectations.

Here's how you can practice this in your daily life:
Instead of just making a to-do list each morning, take a moment to sense into your highest timeline. Ask yourself: *'What feels most aligned today?'* Sometimes this means following unexpected impulses - like taking a different route to work because it feels right, only to run into someone you needed to meet.

Practice maintaining coherent energy fields throughout your day. When you're in a challenging meeting, consciously hold a field of peace and clarity. I've watched room dynamics completely shift when even one person maintains this stable frequency.

Develop your field awareness by regularly checking in with the energy around you. Notice how different environments feel, how people affect space, and what your body is telling you. One of my students started doing this in grocery stores, letting her intuition guide her to the foods that would best support her energy.

Balance action with surrender. If you're working on a goal, take inspired action but stay open to how it manifests. Another client was manifesting a new home - she did the practical work of house hunting but also stayed open to unexpected possibilities. Her perfect home came through a random conversation at a coffee shop.

This way of living requires practice - it's like developing a new set of muscles. Start with small moments throughout your day. Notice the subtle signs, practice maintaining your center during minor challenges, and gradually build up to navigate bigger situations from this quantum awareness.

Remember, you don't need to manage every detail. Your role is to stay clear in your intention while remaining open to how the Universe orchestrates the details. Sometimes what looks like a detour is actually a direct path to what you're creating - just in a way your logical mind couldn't have planned.

Rewriting Your Quantum Story

Reality is shaped by the stories we tell ourselves. Often, we operate within limitations because we unconsciously repeat old narratives. As a Quantum Master Creator, you have the power to change the story and align with new possibilities.

- ॐ **Notice Limiting Patterns:** When a limiting belief arises, observe it without judgment. Simply recognize it as part of an old story.
- ॐ **Expand Your Perspective:** Ask yourself: What lies beyond this story? Shift your awareness to a higher perspective where new possibilities exist.
- ॐ **Choose a New Narrative:** Consciously create a new story that reflects your highest potential. Speak it, feel it, and embody it as your truth.

As you move through your day, remember that you are operating in multiple dimensions simultaneously. Your consciousness is not limited to your immediate surroundings. Allow your awareness to expand beyond what you can see and touch, tapping into the wisdom of higher dimensions.

- ॐ *Stay grounded in the present moment*, but let your consciousness explore beyond it.
- ॐ *Tune into parallel versions of yourself*—other timelines where you've already mastered what you're working on now—and integrate their wisdom.
- ॐ *Observe the quantum flow of your day*. Notice patterns, synchronicities, and subtle energetic shifts that point you toward your next step.

As you practice these principles consistently, you'll notice something extraordinary: manifestation becomes effortless. Your external world begins to shift in response to your inner coherence. Opportunities align. Synchronicities multiply. Reality bends to reflect your expanded state of being.

In this state of mastery:

ॐ Challenges become opportunities for deeper alignment.

ॐ Multiple dimensions inform your choices, offering new insights and pathways.

ॐ Your presence alone becomes a catalyst for transformation, expanding the field of possibility for others.

Always remember that you are a multidimensional being of infinite potential, temporarily focused on physical form. Every moment offers you a fresh opportunity to create a new, to choose a higher possibility, and to live in harmony with the quantum field.

▌Quantum Levels of Mastery

As we approach the culmination of our journey into Quantum Master Creation, let us turn our attention to the sacred process of growth and ascension itself. While we understand that our true nature is multidimensional, existing across countless planes of reality simultaneously, there is profound value in examining the specific stages of evolution we experience in our human form.

These stages form a magnificent spiral of growth, touching every aspect of our being—physical, emotional, and mental. Each level builds upon the last, creating an integrated foundation for accessing our full multidimensional potential. Through this process, we don't just transcend our limitations; we transform them into stepping stones toward higher consciousness.

At the core of this entire journey lies one fundamental truth: **Self-Love** is the master key that unlocks all higher initiations and levels. Without this essential foundation, even the most advanced spiritual practices remain incomplete and unproductive. To fully embody yourself as the powerful Quantum Master Creator, you must recognize and honor the divine essence of unconditional love that you truly are.

In the pages that follow, I will guide you through each initiation level, sharing the key points of each stage, drawn from my own journey, including the challenges I've faced and the solutions I've discovered. Most importantly, you will learn to recognize where you are on this path of evolution, understanding that each stage is perfect and necessary for your unique unfoldment.

As we explore these levels together, remember that this isn't about racing to the finish line. The process is both linear and multidimensional spiral, which means it goes up and down depending where you are in your state of consciousness. It's a living and breathing system. The Soul is in perpetual school of learning here. Sometimes it touches the next level, but only when fully embodied and anchored you progress forward. Each stage offers its own gifts, wisdom, and opportunities for deeper integration. Whether you are just beginning to awaken or are already experiencing advanced states of consciousness, these insights will help you navigate your journey with greater awareness and grace.

Awakening to Spirituality (Level 1)

This level marks the beginning of spiritual awareness. The individual starts to question materialistic values, exploring spiritual concepts and realizing the existence of the soul and higher dimensions. This level often feels like a "spiritual awakening," where one's interest shifts toward deeper life purposes.

- ॐ Growing interest in spirituality, meditation, or mindfulness practices.
- ॐ Questioning previously held beliefs, especially those centered around material success.
- ॐ Feeling drawn to explore spiritual texts or teachings, perhaps even sensing there is more to life than physical existence.

Challenges: Awakening can be disorienting or overwhelming.

Support Needed: Guidance from spiritual teachers, books, or communities can help.

Navigation: Allow yourself to question and explore without judgment

Recommended Actions:

- → Meditation: Begin with mindfulness or guided meditation to calm the mind and hyperactive ego critic and start connecting with your soul.
- → Study Spiritual Literature: Read introductory texts on spirituality, the soul, chakras, and universal laws.
- → Self-Reflection: Take time each day to contemplate what truly brings meaning to your life and what you feel is your purpose.

Deepening Soul Connection (Level 2)

At this level, individuals start to build a deeper relationship with their soul and Higher Self. There is a shift from curiosity to commitment, and you may begin daily spiritual practices to strengthen this connection. You are open to new ideas and perspectives. This level involves growing awareness and thirst for knowledge.

- ॐ A desire to connect more deeply with the Higher Self and explore inner guidance.
- ॐ Increasing interest in establishing a routine of spiritual practices such as meditation, journaling, or prayer.
- ॐ A sense of wanting to live in alignment with your inner values and purpose.

Challenges: Information overload and confusion can occur.

Support Needed: Discernment in choosing reliable sources and mentors is essential

Navigation: Stay open-minded. Be patient with yourself as you explore new concepts and ideas.

Recommended Actions:

- → Daily Spiritual Practice: Set a regular time for meditation, prayer, or journaling to deepen your connection with your Higher Self.
- → Inner Healing: Begin addressing emotional wounds by practicing self-forgiveness and compassion.
- → Seek Guidance: Consider joining a spiritual community or working with a mentor to receive support on your path.

Embracing Self-Love (Level 3)

At this level, individuals actively integrate their newfound spiritual knowledge into their daily lives. However, the key to progressing to the next level is fully embracing Self-Love. While moments of unity and deep connection with all life may occur, the true shift happens when one recognizes and accepts themselves as a divine being, aligning their ego (Free Will) with their Higher Self (Divine Will). This realization may be sparked through meditation, time in nature, or spontaneous insights.

This stage is pivotal in realizing one's role within a larger purpose. It involves releasing control of the ego and learning to surrender to the flow of life. This is where one allows personal will to harmonize with divine will. There is also an emphasis on purifying the physical body to prepare it to hold higher frequencies of light. As sensitivity to energy increases, individuals feel drawn to cleanse and care for their physical health more intentionally.

At this point, one becomes more aware of where the ego arises and begins the deeper work of Self-Love and Self-Acceptance, viewing the ego as a tool to be integrated rather than rejected. The third initiation is profoundly transformative, reinforcing the foundation of spiritual development. It heightens one's ability to perceive subtle energies, deepens the connection between physical and spiritual realms, and prepares the initiate for further progress in the realms of emotional and mental mastery.

Challenges: Resistance from the ego and resurfacing old habits. I often see my clients getting stuck trying to move beyond this level to the next one. They touch Self Love but have a hard time anchoring it due to traumas they carry in this lifetime or previous ones.

Support Needed: Regular spiritual practices like meditation, yoga, journaling can help to anchor self-love.

Navigation: Create regular meditation or breathwork practice. Learn to trust your intuition and your inner voice. Spend more time contemplating in nature especially in early morning hours gazing at the Sun and receiving light codes to anchor more light into the cellular memory. This will help to remember that you are quantum, you are that light of the Infinite Creator.

Recommended Actions:

→ Detoxification: Embrace a nourishing diet centered around whole foods, including fresh vegetables, fruits, and natural sources of protein. Minimize or eliminate processed foods and reduce exposure to environmental toxins.

→ Physical Activity: Engage in gentle movement practices that support energy flow, such as yoga, qigong, or daily walking. These activities help maintain physical health while promoting inner balance and grounding.

→ Chakra Balancing: Begin exploring the chakra system and practice techniques to clear energetic blockages. You can use crystals, essential oils, or sound healing tools like tuning forks and singing bowls to restore chakra alignment.

→ Self-Love Affirmations: Incorporate affirmations that reinforce self-love and acceptance, such as "I AM worthy of love and respect" or "I honor and embrace my divine self." Repeat these regularly looking in the mirror to nurture a strong foundation of self-acceptance and inner peace.

Alignment and Letting Go (Level 4)

This level is about bringing one's life into alignment with core spiritual values, often leading to changes in relationships, career, or lifestyle. As you have stepped into the unconditional love of yourself and accepted all aspects of your Divine spark, now it's time to let go. It requires releasing layers of reality and attachments that no longer serve the journey, especially materialistic aspects that feel misaligned with the soul's purpose. This stage also involves a process of releasing karmic patterns and completing emotional healing. Individuals work to let go of past traumas and emotional blockages, opening themselves to experience divine love more fully.

Emotional stability and self-compassion are essential as they learn to embrace their true nature with gentleness and acceptance. You might experience:

ॐ Old emotions and traumas surfacing for healing and release.

ॐ Increased self-awareness of emotional reactions, patterns, and triggers.

ॐ A desire to cultivate emotional balance, compassion, and inner peace.

Challenges: Fear of change and resistance from others.

Support Needed: Courage, trust, and self-care are crucial during this transition phase

Navigation: Practice mindfulness in daily activities. Seek balance between inner growth and outer responsibilities. Be gentle with yourself during this transition period as this is the hardest level. I often meet seekers on the spiritual path who go through different layers of this process with question: "Does this ever end?" Spiritual enlightenment is like unpeeling of the onion. Many can stay at this level their whole life and that's ok too. There is a lot to release!

Recommended Actions:

➔ *Shadow Work:* Engage in deep inner work to address and heal emotional wounds. Journaling, therapy, and meditation can help process grief and limiting beliefs.

➔ *Emotional Release:* Use techniques like emotional freedom tapping (EFT), Emotion Codes, and other techniques covered in chapter 4, also writing letters to express repressed emotions, or somatic therapy.

→ *Compassionate Self-Love:* Nurture yourself by practicing gratitude, affirmations, and creating supportive relationships. Self-love practices help to stabilize and harmonize the emotional body.

Consolidation: Mind and Ego Mastery (Level 5)

At this level, consciousness expands into the Atmic plane - a realm of pure, undifferentiated awareness. The Atmic plane represents a state where the artificial divisions between self and universe begin to fade, yet this expansion of awareness doesn't result in a loss of practical functioning in the world. Rather, it allows for a more complete expression of one's essential nature while remaining grounded in earthly existence. Here, the boundaries of individual identity dissolve as consciousness merges with the universal life force itself. One begins to experience the integration of all aspects of their being: the personality, soul, and Monad (the divine spark or highest spiritual essence) unify into a seamless whole, while maintaining their conscious presence and purpose on Earth.

The focus at this stage is mastery over thoughts, emotions, and actions. It involves purifying mental patterns and gaining mastery over the ego, allowing individuals to recognize and release egoic tendencies, attachments, and fears, creating space for divine truth to radiate through. The mind, now freed from limiting patterns, becomes a tool for spiritual clarity, supporting a life aligned with higher purpose and wisdom.

→ Becoming more aware of ego-based thoughts, fears, and judgments.

→ A desire to detach from material attachments and live with greater authenticity.

→ Increased mental clarity and the ability to observe thoughts without being influenced by them.

Challenges: Old patterns may still surface and desire to control the power. Sometimes, this phase can be a "Magician's trap" where old tricks of magic are being used to control power and others.

Support Needed: Continued daily practice, contemplation and patience are necessary

Recommended Actions:

→ *Ego Awareness:* Notice egoic patterns such as pride, control, or judgment, and consciously work on releasing them. Practicing humility and openness supports this process.

→ *Affirmations:* Use positive affirmations to reprogram negative thought patterns, such as "I am aligned with divine truth" or "I am calm and centered."

→ *Practice Detachment:* Focus on non-attachment to specific outcomes, achievements, or material possessions, reinforcing spiritual growth as the true measure of success.

Light Body Activation - Mastery (Level 6)

The light body, a higher-dimensional energetic body, begins to activate, allowing the individual to embody higher frequencies of light and love. The initiate feels more connected to divine energies and may experience heightened intuition and sensitivity.

ॐ Sensations of lightness, energy shifts, or tingling in the body.

ॐ Heightened sensitivity to energy and emotions of others.

ॐ Greater ease in experiencing states of unconditional love, compassion, and forgiveness.

One can only become a true Quantum Master when they are willing to play by their own rules in this reality. The person has truly stepped into mastery when their pure intention is to serve others. Their focus fully shifts from personal growth to contributing to the collective. This is a full merge with I AM PRESENCE Ascension experience while continuing to serve on Gaia/Mother Earth to help bring the New Earth reality.

Challenges: Balancing service with self-care.

Support Needed: Healthy boundaries and remembering to refill one's own cup are important.

Navigation: Living authentically, maintaining a high vibration, practicing unconditional love.

Recommended Actions:

→ *Energy Healing:* Support your light body activation with practices like Reiki, breathwork, or crystal healing.

→ *Light Visualizations:* During meditation, visualize yourself enveloped in white or golden light, allowing this energy to cleanse and raise your vibration.

→ *Physical Self-Care:* Take extra care of your body by getting adequate rest, staying hydrated, and incorporating relaxation practices to help integrate these higher energies.

Higher Self Integration (Level 7)

This level represents a deeper merging with the Higher Self, where the soul's essence increasingly influences everyday life and decisions. The individual's life becomes a reflection of their soul's purpose and divine guidance.

ॐ A strong sense of inner alignment and intuitive guidance directing choices.

ॐ Decreased attachment to personal will and increased trust in divine timing.

ॐ Feeling a sense of wholeness, unity, and purpose in life.

One who reaches this stage is now fully embodying their divine nature. They live in constant alignment with their Higher self and divine will. Psychic gifts and source language come fully online. The person is here to fulfill their divine purpose in helping others to reach this stage and beyond.

Challenges: Maintaining this state amidst worldly distractions and other non organic AI noise

Support Needed: Regular connection with the divine through contemplation, meditation, or other spiritual practices.

Navigation: Constant connection with the higher self, embodiment of liberation and divine love, expanding golden light quotient beyond 85 percent. Radiating light in everyday life as God/Goddess in this realm.

Recommended Actions:

→ Soul Alignment: Set intentions to align your thoughts, actions, and choices with your Higher Self's guidance. Notice how you feel guided from within rather than making decisions based solely on logic.

→ Divine Surrender: Practice surrendering personal goals and desires to divine will, trusting that your Higher Self knows the best path for your spiritual journey.

→ Journaling: Write down intuitive insights, dreams, or messages received from your Higher Self during meditation. Regularly reflect on this guidance to stay connected to your soul's purpose.

Quantum Leadership

As I have been writing this book, the focus has been on the individual Quantum Mastery and the Quantum levels we just covered—developing a relationship with energy, refining one's ability to shift timelines, and learning to navigate the unseen forces that influence life. However, there is a moment when this mastery must expand beyond the self. Thus, I felt it's necessary to mention the concept of Quantum Leadership.

A Quantum Master Creator is powerful, but a *Quantum Leader* brings this knowledge to a grander scale—guiding collective evolution, influencing communities, and shaping the trajectory of humanity. This is where personal sovereignty transforms into something greater: the ability to hold space for collective transformation and shift the energetic architecture of entire systems.

As you've journeyed through this book, you've been preparing for this expansion, building the foundation for your emergence also as a Quantum Leader.

Quantum Leadership is the ability to hold a field of coherence so powerful that it influences not just individuals, but entire communities and movements. It is leadership that transcends hierarchy, operating instead through resonance, frequency, and alignment with higher-order intelligence. It is about applying quantum principles—not just to personal manifestation, but to how we lead businesses, social systems, and even global consciousness shifts.

A Quantum Leader is someone who:

- ॐ Shapes reality not through force, but through energetic coherence
- ॐ Moves beyond personal manifestation into collective impact
- ॐ Sees beyond linear strategies and accesses higher-dimensional intelligence
- ॐ Understands that leadership is not about control, but about holding the field for transformation

Unlike conventional leadership, which is often based on structure, hierarchy, and linear thinking, Quantum Leadership operates beyond time, beyond limitations, and beyond traditional cause-and-effect. It is about leading from wholeness, from presence, from an intimate relationship with the quantum fabric of existence.

Becoming a Quantum Leader requires a shift from personal quantum creation to stewardship of collective energy. This means developing an acute awareness of how energy moves within groups, organizations, and even planetary consciousness. You are no longer just navigating your own reality—you are influencing timelines for others.

1. Holding the Field for Collective Shifts

When you master your own frequency, you naturally begin to influence those around you. A Quantum Leader is an anchor point for higher-order coherence.

In chaotic times, your stability becomes a gravitational center for others to align with. You've likely experienced this: when one person in a room holds strong, unwavering energy, it affects everyone else. This is not accidental—it is quantum entrainment at work.

This is why Quantum Leadership is felt, not just taught.

2. Moving from Personal Manifestation to Collective Impact

As a Quantum Creator, you learn to shape timelines for yourself. But as a Quantum Leader, you begin to affect the probability fields of entire communities.

This doesn't mean forcing your vision—it means holding space for aligned realities to emerge. Instead of asking, "What do I want to create for myself?" you begin asking, *"What reality am I holding for those I lead?"*

The Quantum Leader doesn't just build a business, movement, or initiative, they shape an energetic ecosystem that others step into and evolve within.

A client of mine, deeply attuned to quantum principles, wanted to create a conscious business. At first, she focused on her own success. But when she expanded her vision to include elevating the collective frequency of everyone she worked with, the business took on a life of its own. It became more than a company—it became an energetic vortex for transformation.

3. Leading Through Dimensional Awareness

Quantum Leadership requires moving beyond linear, strategy-driven leadership into multidimensional navigation. This means:

- ॐ Sensing the energetic currents before making decisions
- ॐ Aligning timing with quantum flow rather than rigid deadlines
- ॐ Understanding that unseen forces are just as influential as visible actions

Just like Quantum Master Creator, a Quantum Leader is always listening to the field. They don't force outcomes—they open pathways for higher possibilities to emerge.

I once planned a large-scale event but kept sensing an energetic misalignment. Logically, everything seemed fine. But rather than pushing forward, I tuned in deeper. I saw that if we waited just a few months, the right speakers and collaborations would naturally converge. By trusting the quantum field instead of forcing an outcome, the event became exponentially more powerful.

Integrating Quantum Leadership into Society

To truly lead at a quantum level, we must move beyond personal practice and integrate this wisdom into social systems, businesses, and collective movements.

Here's how Quantum Leadership can reshape the world:

- ॐ **In Business:** Organizations led by Quantum Leaders don't just focus on profit—they create resonance fields where employees, clients, and partners operate at higher frequencies. They attract synchronicity, innovation, and exponential growth.

- ॐ **In Community Building:** A Quantum Leader understands that a group's coherence determines its success. Instead of relying solely on rules and structures, they cultivate a shared energetic field where collaboration, trust, and alignment flourish.

- ॐ **In Social Evolution:** The greatest leaders of our time didn't just push ideas—they shifted consciousness. Quantum Leaders understand that real change isn't just about policy—it's about shifting the underlying energy of collective belief systems.

As we conclude this journey together, it's important to note that stepping into Quantum Leadership is not just about personal evolution—it is about planetary evolution.

Every great shift in history has been catalyzed by those who dared to operate beyond the ordinary. Those who understood that reality is not fixed, but fluid. Those who knew that true leadership is not about control—it is about holding a vision so powerfully that reality reorganizes around it.

▌Quantum Observer Exercise

The *Quantum Observer* exists in a state of pure awareness, beyond judgment and limitation. From this expanded consciousness, you witness reality unfolding across multiple dimensions without collapsing potential outcomes. This awareness allows you to see how your frequency directly influences creation.

Your mind operates at different frequencies, each shaping distinct patterns in the quantum field. Notice how your mental state shifts between:

- ॐ **Quantum Coherence**: characterized by crystalline clarity, timeless awareness, and seamless flow with universal intelligence
- ॐ **Linear consciousness**: marked by beta-wave activity, time-bound thinking, and separation-based perception

The key is not to judge these states but to observe them. Awareness alone begins shifting you into higher frequencies of manifestation.

Quantum Awareness Scan (5–10 Minutes)

Close your eyes and scan your present state:

- ॐ **Mental state** – Is your mind calm and expansive or agitated and constricted?
- ॐ **Emotional field** – What emotions are active in your system?
- ॐ **Energetic signature** – Are you vibrating at a high or dense frequency?
- ॐ **Timeline resonance** – What trajectory are your thoughts and actions aligning with?

Without judgment, simply **observe** which dimension of consciousness you are operating from. Are you ready to create a quantum shift?

Activating Your Quantum Shift (24- 48 Hours)

For the next day or two, embody the frequency of your highest self without seeking external validation.

- ॐ Reality will mirror your shift—synchronicities, effortless flow, and unexpected ease will confirm the transformation.
- ॐ Trust the process—the external world recalibrates in response to your new frequency.

From this elevated state, observe:

- ॐ What thoughts are passing through your consciousness?
- ॐ How is reality responding to your frequency?
- ॐ Are synchronicities appearing?
- ॐ What new timeline possibilities are emerging?
- ॐ Are you experiencing quantum coherence or points of collapse?

Your highest timeline is already available, the key is to match its frequency! Here's how:

1. Shift from Seeking to Embodying

- ॐ Instead of "trying to get there," feel into already being there.
- ॐ Ask: How does the highest version of me think, feel, and act today?
- ॐ Align to being it now rather than waiting for external proof.

2. Play with Synchronicity & Quantum Signs

- ॐ Notice what themes, numbers, and symbols are appearing—these are your next-step markers.
- ॐ Speak to reality: "Show me my highest alignment in an undeniable way."
- ॐ Follow the excitement breadcrumbs without overanalyzing.

3. Release the Old Frequency Locks

- ॐ Identify outdated beliefs, emotions, and habits that tether you to the past.
- ॐ Ask: What assumptions about reality am I ready to rewrite?
- ॐ Shift focus from "what's missing" to "what's expanding."

▎Building Your Quantum Foundation Daily

Your morning practice sets the energetic tone for the day. Align your frequency before engaging with the world.

1. Set an Intention for the Day

Choose an intention that resonates with your highest self. It could be a feeling you want to embody, a project you want to move forward, or simply a state of being, such as peace or joy. Ask yourself:

What timeline do I want to align with today?

2. Anchor in Supportive Emotions

Emotions act as the fuel for your quantum field. Take a few moments to anchor in feelings of **love**, **gratitude**, and **peace**. These frequencies stabilize your energy and expand your creative potential. Use the meditation in Chapter 5.

3. Heart-Mind Coherence

Synchronize your heart and mind through a short breathing practice.

Inhale for 4 counts, hold for 4, exhale for 4.

This creates coherence between your mental focus and your emotional state, amplifying your quantum resonance. Refer also to other Coherence exercises offered in the book and my website.

The 4Ds for Mastering Quantum Creation

Define it
Set your intention. Write the code for your reality.

Deploy it
Send your frequency. Push your code into the quantum field.

Debug it
Master your emotions. Optimize and realign your field.

Download it
Receive and embody. Pull your creation into reality

The 4Ds Framework for Mastering Quantum Creation:

This framework provides a clear, repeatable process you can weave into your daily practice to anchor your role as a conscious creator. By consistently defining your intention, deploying your frequency, debugging your emotional field, and downloading your manifestation, you establish a strong energetic architecture that keeps you attuned to your highest timeline. This daily alignment supports you in staying resilient, coherent, and fully receptive to the realities you are actively creating.

Activation of Quantum Code ▲ Mastery Embodied

This activation is designed to transmit the essence of the chapter as an energetic template—something you feel rather than analyze. By bypassing the thinking mind, it speaks directly to your body, energy field, and subconscious, allowing transformation to unfold on a deeper level.

◆ Begin Here: Set the Field

Find a quiet space. Light a candle if you feel called. Sit or lie comfortably with your spine aligned and your heart open. Close your eyes and take a few grounding breaths—in through your nose, out through your mouth. Let your body soften. Let your energy settle.

Bring your awareness to your heart space. Place your hands gently over your heart, or simply focus your attention there. Feel the warmth between your palms and chest. Let it grow.

When you are ready, speak the following words aloud or silently within:

"I now open to release all that is blocking my highest good.

I open to grace, to clarity, to healing.

I activate and understand all that I need to move forward on my path with ease and flow.

I open to remember who I truly am."

Breathe that in. Let it ripple through your entire being.

◆ Activate the Quantum Code

Repeat these sacred Source Language words below three times aloud, allowing the vibration to move through your body and field:

KA RA VI YA NA
SHU KA MA NI YA

Now read the following quantum transmission:

Within the stillness of the flame
Where soul and source are one, the same
No need to grasp, no need to strive
I simply be, and I arrive.

Through breath I shape, through thought I weave
No longer trapped in what I grieve
The field responds to who I am
A tuning fork, a silent command.

I walk as one who's shed the chase
No masks to wear, no roles to place
Mastery is not the climb—
It's rhythm, presence, sacred time.

The power lies in silent gaze

In steady hands and softened ways

I lead not loud, but through my glow

Aligned above, embodied below.

◇ ACTIVATION COMPLETE ◇

Sit in stillness. Allow the code to settle into your system. Feel the integration weaving into your cells, your field, your breath. Let the silence become your teacher.

♦ Ground & Center

Breathe deeply into your body. Imagine golden roots extending from the soles of your feet into the heart of the Earth. Feel the Earth holding you, anchoring you.

You are safe. You are protected. You are loved.

Begin to gently move your fingers and toes. Wiggle. Stretch. Return fully to your body.

Grounding Contemplation

After activating the Quantum code and grounding, stay rooted by taking time to notice what's shifting within. You might feel called to journal, draw, or simply sit in quiet awareness, allowing your inner wisdom to gently emerge. Use the following questions as gateways to deeper insight. There is no need to rush or force answers. Let them move through you like waves.

1. This is your opportunity to get crystal clear on your intentions. What are you looking to create in your reality? Write it down in appropriate boxes.
2. Physical Intention: What physical matter do you want to create? (i.e., a car, a house, an object, a project, or other manifestation that is denser in matter)
3. Emotional Intention: What emotions and feelings do you want to create? Who you are at the highest level (e.g. "I am ___")?
4. Spiritual Intention: What spiritual experiences (i.e., channelings, meditations, music, and other connections) you want to create?
5. How might your daily interactions change if you consistently viewed yourself and others as expressions of the same universal life force?
6. What is your main takeaway from this chapter/this book? What are you committing to doing or being based on what you learned?

After contemplating these questions, allow your inner awareness to settle. Feel the insights begin to integrate, forming clarity and connection.

Write freely in your journal, allowing the words to flow without censoring or judgment.

♦ Integration

You may notice subtle or profound shifts after this activation and contemplation. Honor this by giving yourself space to rest, reflect, and receive.

An audio version of this activation is available on my website if you'd like to revisit and deepen the transmission.

Conclusion

"Nothing lasts forever
No one lives forever
Keep that in mind, and love."

— **Tagore**

As these final pages came together, I received news that touched me deeply that one of my clients had transitioned from colon cancer. The irony isn't lost on me that during her Quantum Healing Hypnosis session a year prior, her Higher Self spoke with stark honesty: *"She needs to let that shit go!"*—a literal and metaphorical truth about survival on Earth. She became the third most beautiful soul I've lost to cancer in the last couple of years, and in the raw authenticity of grief, I've come to accept the impermanence of it all. They are my guardians now, teaching me about the deeper currents of creation that we can't always see.

The truth is both simple and challenging: while we can't control external chaos, our inner landscape is our responsibility. Yet even when disease manifests physically, I've learned to hold this truth with compassion. Every soul's journey unfolds exactly as needed, whether here or in other dimensions and realms.

We're not yet living fully in the fifth dimension, where creation and dissolution dance as one. Our current reality demands complete honesty with ourselves as we practice emotional alchemy. My own path has taught me that surrender isn't a one-time event, but a continuing spiral into deeper truth.

Just when I think I've surrendered fully, life presents another opportunity to let go even more, cultivating deeper gratitude for simply living and appreciating each moment. It's as if Source is constantly inviting us into greater authenticity: *"Are you ready to be even more real with yourself?"* and *"How much deeper can you surrender?"*

The key to quantum creation isn't in controlling outcomes but in showing up authentically, moment by moment. This includes embracing forgiveness, even when every fiber of our being resists. It means choosing the higher path, not because it's easy, but because it's true to our highest nature.

In a world fractured by division, I've discovered that true neutrality and sovereignty come from this place of radical authenticity—acknowledging all perspectives while remaining anchored in our own truth. This isn't a spiritual bypass; it's facing reality with open eyes and a big, open heart.

As my Soul Communication podcast completed its second season with over 40 episodes, I felt immense gratitude for the opportunity to create a platform where others could explore profound topics that might seem beyond conventional understanding. Hosting taught me that every question has value, and everyone deserves to be heard.

The experience of having the podcast also revealed how our soul's curious questions on the nature of reality also follow the law of magnetism, attracting the perfect guests at exactly the right time. When I found myself pondering season 3 and my connection to Sedona and Bell Rock, the Universe responded swiftly. Within a week, I connected with York Wang, a courageous 25-year-old who had transformed his pandemic depression through dedicated breathwork and emotional clearing.

His journey opened doors to remarkable connections, beginning with his Arcturian guide and leading to Shoshaina, his Essasani aspect dwelling on a ship above Bell Rock. It's a smaller ship than the one I have mentioned in chapter 3, that Bashar resides on, but equally potent in its purpose. His appearance on my show carried divine timing, validating my own experiences with Bell Rock as an ancient tree and interdimensional portal, and many such vortexes around the world, confirming my knowing about co-creating a retreat there in April 2025 with a beautiful team of channelers I recently met on the Galactic Cruise.

When York channeled Shoshaina, our conversation deepened my understanding of the hybrid children and the Essasani race, beautifully connecting with my own encounters with the children on the Bashar ship.

Through Shoshaina, I received a profound understanding of the Essasani - these remarkable 4th/5th dimensional beings who recognize humanity as their ancestral line. They've distilled the art of quantum creation into an elegantly simple formula for accessing joy and excitement:

Follow your excitement to the highest degree possible at any moment, at every moment. Always remain in a positive state regardless of what happens. Have no insistence or resistance towards what happens. As you do this, negative beliefs will come up. At that time, investigating and inquiring about those negative beliefs was creating that experience of reality. And replace it with beliefs that you do prefer. And lastly, repeat, do that all the time. The reason for this and the way it work mechanically is this, as you follow your excitement, you're raising your frequency.

Now, as you raise your frequency and you vibrate faster, that means structures within yourself that are not aligned with this faster vibration, the denser objects will then move up and rise to the surface. So, as it moves up and rises to the surface, you have two choices. One choice is to see what is coming up and then feel negative emotion towards it, and then limit yourself to that frequency and vibration.

And in that sense, you're lowering your frequency back to what it once was. Now, another option is looking at that and appreciating it for how it has served you in the past. When you do that and you let go of that negative belief, then you could rise faster as there's no longer a block of conflicting debris in your consciousness.

Now we're aware of both negative and positive to a greater degree. We simply choose to experience ourselves on the positive side.

This simple and beautiful wisdom mirrors everything I've shared about the quantum creation process throughout this book. When we follow our excitement without attachment, while staying true to ourselves, and taking inspired action, we align with the natural flow of creation. The Essasani collective demonstrate that mastery isn't about complexity - it's about the consistent practice of these fundamental truths.

As Quantum Master Creators, when we truly understand that we are made of the same conscious energy as Source, our relationship with creation transforms. Each thought becomes a creative act, sending ripples through the quantum field. The key lies not just in understanding this power, but in actively choosing to shift into higher versions of ourselves through conscious intention.

This journey of transformation requires:
- ॐ Recognizing old patterns and limitations
- ॐ Using the sacred pause between trigger and response
- ॐ Making conscious choices that align with your highest self
- ॐ Creating new neural pathways through consistent practice
- ॐ Operating at progressively higher frequencies

Each morning, before the world's noise crowds in, create sacred space for yourself. Begin by dropping into your Heart center, that quantum portal within. Let your breath become a bridge between your physical self and your higher aspects. As you breathe, feel yourself opening like a flower to the sun, ready to:

- ॐ Calibrate by centering in your Heart Space
- ॐ Connect to Higher Self
- ॐ Open to receive higher frequency transmissions
- ॐ Challenge old limiting beliefs
- ॐ Create new patterns of thought and behavior
- ॐ Speak your truth and creation out loud

The field responds to your practice in beautiful and often unexpected ways. Watch for synchronicities that affirm your inner guidance. Follow your YES—those crystal-clear downloads that strike like lightning bolts of understanding throughout the day. Gently ask yourself, "Is this in my highest good?" If the answer feels like a maybe, it's often best to ride the emotional waves until a true YES becomes clear. And it's perfectly okay if maybe ultimately becomes a NO. Your journey is about traveling from one crystal-clear YES to the next. Most importantly, honor those quiet moments of inner knowing - when something feels so true that it resonates in every cell of your being.

You are not fixed or limited by your past. Each moment offers an opportunity to make new choices and embody a higher version of yourself. Through awareness, courage, and dedication, you can break free from inherited thought patterns and create new, abundant and empowering ways of being.

Think of yourself as both a brilliant sun radiating conscious light and as an evolving being constantly becoming more. Your light carries creative abundance codes that shape reality, while your human experience provides the perfect classroom for growth and transformation.

This dual nature - Infinite Creator and Evolving Being - is your greatest gift.

The journey isn't about controlling reality but dancing with it - allowing your natural creative essence to flow while maintaining reverence for the larger divine design. For in the end, we are all faces of the One Consciousness, experiencing itself through infinite forms, eternally creating, evolving, and becoming more.

About the Author

Diana MaAra Divine (pronounced De-anna) is a Soul Guide, Multidimensional Channel, and Galactic Shaman, dedicated to the evolution of consciousness and unlocking humanity's multidimensional potential. As a Metaphysical Activator and Quantum Educator, she integrates an expansive array of quantum, shamanic, and psychological tools, offering highly personalized and transformative experiences for those seeking deeper spiritual awakening. She currently resides in New Jersey with her husband and children.

Founder of the Source Language Institute

Diana is the founder of the Source Language Institute (sourcelanguage.org), an organization devoted to teaching and activating the purest form of cosmic communication through Source Codes, also known as Light Language. Her self-paced Source Code Mastery course provides a structured pathway for individuals to awaken, embody, and express Light Language, enhancing their spiritual connection and energetic fluency.

One-on-One Healing & Transformational Sessions

For those seeking personalized healing and energetic recalibration, Diana offers:

ॐ Quantum Healing Hypnosis (QHHT) – A deep-dive journey into past lives, subconscious healing, and soul-level transformation.

ॐ Quantum Attunement & Crystalline Soul Healing – High-frequency energy work designed to harmonize the subtle bodies, activate dormant DNA, and realign individuals with their highest timeline.

For those ready to step into their true multidimensional nature, Diana provides wisdom, tools, and activations that empower individuals to navigate their ascension journey with clarity, confidence, and divine alignment.

Group Activations & Immersive Experiences

Diana also facilitates online and in-person workshops that catalyze profound energetic shifts, including:

ॐ Sound Healing Journeys – Utilizing frequency and vibration to clear energetic blockages and restore harmony.

ॐ Phoenix Rising Kundalini Activation – A powerful group experience designed to awaken and accelerate Kundalini energy, expanding consciousness and igniting transformation.

These workshops are regularly held in the New Jersey and New York areas, providing a sacred space for collective activation and inner expansion.

Soul Communication Podcast

Diana is also the host of Soul Communication, a podcast exploring multidimensional consciousness, energy work, and spiritual awakening. Available on major platforms including YouTube, Spotify, and Apple Music, her podcast serves as a gateway for seekers to access profound teachings, channeled messages, and deep conversations on the nature of reality and soul evolution.

https://youtube.com/@dianamdivine

Quantum Ancient Codes Oracle Deck

As a companion to the book, Diana has created the Quantum Ancient Codes Oracle Deck—a powerful tool for activation, reflection, and intuitive guidance. Each card is encoded with sacred frequencies, light language, and symbolic transmissions that mirror the teachings within *Mastering Quantum Creation*. Whether used for daily insight, ceremony, or to deepen chapter activations, these 44 cards serve as portals into your sovereign embodiment and intuitive mastery.

The deck is organized into four sacred paths:

ॐ Codes of Integrity – Anchor your divine truth through principles of alignment, sovereignty, and soul-authenticity.

ॐ Keys of Transformation – Unlock inner alchemy, transmute old patterns, and ignite powerful shifts in consciousness.

ॐ Pathways of Connection – Bridge the seen and unseen, deepening communion with your guides, ancestors, and galactic allies.

ॐ Portals of Creation – Activate your role as a conscious creator and birth new realities through sacred intention and multidimensional vision.

This is more than a deck—it's a **living transmission** and a multidimensional tool for awakening. Each card activates remembrance, alignment, and co-creation with your soul's highest timeline.

The journey with the deck can get even deeper—with an **interactive digital companion** included. This intuitive AI-powered experience helps you interpret your readings with clarity and beauty, offering insight, reflection, and real-time guidance from your Higher Self.

"The deck is amazing! The artwork is exquisite and even includes an AI feature that helps you understand your reading in a beautiful way."
— Will Rabil

The deck is available for purchase at Diana's website and her Etsy store

Glossary of Terms

5D Energy – A term referring to the energetic field beyond three-dimensional reality, often associated with higher consciousness, intention-based manifestation, and quantum healing.

Akashic Records – A metaphysical repository of all thoughts, events, and experiences, believed to exist in a higher-dimensional field.

Ayahuasca – A sacred plant medicine traditionally used by indigenous Amazonian cultures for spiritual awakening, deep healing, and expanded consciousness.

Aura – The electromagnetic energy field surrounding all living beings, often associated with spiritual, emotional, and physical health.

Aura Photography – A technique used to capture and visualize the energetic field of an individual, often employing biofeedback technology or specialized cameras.

Bashar (Essassani) – A multidimensional consciousness channeled by Darryl Anka, associated with the Essassani civilization, offering insights on quantum reality, human potential, and spiritual evolution.

Bioenergetics – The study of energy flow through living systems, including cellular functions, electromagnetic fields, and quantum biological interactions.

Biophoton Emission – The light naturally emitted by living organisms, thought to be a medium for cellular communication and quantum information transfer.

Biowell Measurement – A method of capturing and analyzing subtle energy emissions from biological systems to assess vitality and coherence.

Butterfly Effect – A concept in chaos theory that describes how small changes in initial conditions can lead to vastly different outcomes in a dynamic system, often applied to quantum mechanics and consciousness shifts.

Chakra – Energy centers within the body that regulate physical, emotional, and spiritual well-being.

Densities – A classification of consciousness evolution, where different densities represent various levels of awareness and spiritual progression.

Dimensions – Different levels of reality, often conceptualized as layers of consciousness and vibrational frequencies.

Dimensional Shifting – The concept of transitioning between vibrational states of reality, often linked to altered consciousness and quantum timelines.

Divine Union – The sacred merging of complementary energies, often associated with spiritual enlightenment and the harmonization of masculine and feminine aspects.

Entanglement of Quantum Entanglement – A phenomenon where two or more particles become interconnected, regardless of distance, such that the state of one affects the state of the other instantaneously.

Electrical Wars - A series of ancient interdimensional conflicts in which advanced plasma, scalar, and frequency-based technologies were misused to hijack stargates, distort timelines, and fragment Earth's original crystalline grid—leading to the fall of higher civilizations like Lemuria, Atlantis, and Tara, and derailing the evolutionary path of the First Root Race, who were seeded with a 12-strand DNA template to embody divine intelligence and anchor Gaia's 5D+ ascension.

Fifth Dimension (5D) Earth Template –Gaia's rebirth into her original Tara frequency. It is not a place but a vibrational shift—a collective return to a heart-based, multidimensional reality where co-creation, harmony, and higher consciousness thrive.

Fractal Consciousness – The idea that consciousness operates in self-similar, repeating patterns across multiple scales of existence.

Gaia – The living, conscious essence of Earth, a sentient being who holds the evolutionary blueprint for life and ascension.

Higher Self – The aspect of an individual's consciousness that exists beyond the physical self, often associated with divine wisdom and guidance.

Hologram – A three-dimensional projection of information, often used to describe the illusion of material reality.

Holographic Universe – The theory that the universe is a projection of higher-dimensional information, where every part contains the whole.

Hypercharging – The process of enhancing the energetic properties of objects, materials, or fields using quantum technologies or frequency infusion.

Infinite Creator – The supreme consciousness or divine source from which all creation emerges, often referenced in spiritual and metaphysical traditions.

Karma – The principle of cause and effect, where actions create energetic imprints that influence future experiences.

Kundalini Energy – A latent spiritual energy located at the base of the spine, which, when awakened, rises through the chakras leading to higher consciousness.

Light Body – A higher-dimensional energy field or structure associated with spiritual ascension, transformation, and expanded consciousness.

Light Language (Source Language) – A multidimensional form of communication believed to carry vibrational healing frequencies and divine information beyond linear words.

Mandela Effect – A phenomenon where a large number of people remember an event or fact differently from the commonly accepted history, often attributed to shifts in reality or alternate timelines.

Monad – The original divine spark or unit of consciousness from which all individual souls originate, often associated with unity and oneness.

Morphogenetic Fields – Proposed energetic blueprints that influence the development and organization of living structures and consciousness.

New Earth – A term used to describe an ascended reality or higher vibrational state of collective consciousness, often associated with spiritual awakening and planetary transformation.

Observer Effect – The principle that the act of measurement or observation affects the outcome of a quantum system.

Quantum – The fundamental unit of energy and matter that behaves according to the principles of quantum mechanics.

Quantum Biology – The application of quantum principles to biological processes, explaining phenomena such as enzyme activity, photosynthesis, and consciousness.

Quantum Calibration – The measurement and alignment of energy systems to optimize coherence, stability, and performance.

Quantum Coherence – A state in which quantum wave functions remain in phase, allowing for heightened connectivity and stability in energy systems.

Quantum Field – The foundational energy matrix that underlies all physical reality, where particles and waves exist in a state of potential until observed.

Quantum Healing – The practice of using quantum principles to facilitate healing, often involving energy fields, consciousness, and vibrational frequencies.

Quantum Infusion – The process of embedding quantum frequencies into objects, materials, or biological systems to enhance their energetic properties.

Quantum Manifestation – The intentional use of quantum principles, such as observation and entanglement, to influence reality and create desired outcomes.

Quantum Master – A being or individual who has attained mastery over quantum principles, utilizing them to shape reality, consciousness, and energy.

Quantum Master Creator – One who not only masters quantum principles but also applies them to create and influence reality on an advanced level

Quantum Superposition – The state where multiple possible realities coexist until an observation collapses them into one definite outcome.

Quantum Transmutation – The transformation of matter and energy at a quantum level, often associated with alchemy and consciousness shifts.

Quantum Tunneling – The ability of particles to pass through energy barriers that would be classically insurmountable.

Resonance – The synchronization of frequencies between two or more systems, leading to amplified effects.

Sacred Geometry – The study of geometric patterns and structures that are believed to represent fundamental principles of creation and quantum order.

Samadhi - A state of deep meditative absorption in which the practitioner experiences unity with the object of meditation, transcending ego and duality, often considered the highest state of spiritual enlightenment in Hindu, Buddhist, and yogic traditions.

Samsara - The cyclical cycle of birth, death, and rebirth, governed by karma, from which spiritual liberation (moksha or nirvana) is sought.

Scalar Waves - Non-linear, longitudinal waves theorized to carry information instantaneously without losing power over distance.

Soul – The eternal, non-physical essence of an individual, often regarded as the true self beyond physical incarnation.

Soul Contract – Soul contracts are sacred agreements your soul makes before incarnating—choosing relationships, lessons, challenges, and timelines that support your evolution.

Source – The original divine consciousness or energy from which all existence originates and remains connected.

Starseed Lineages – Starseeds are souls originating from other star systems and higher-dimensional civilizations who incarnated on Earth to assist in planetary ascension. Each lineage—such as Lyran, Pleiadian, Sirian, Orion, Arcturian, and Andromedan—carries distinct frequencies, soul missions, and energetic imprints encoded with gifts, wisdom, and lessons to help activate humanity's evolution.

Subtle Energy Fields – Non-physical, yet measurable, energetic layers that interact with the material world, including the aura and etheric body.

Superposition and Quantum Superposition – The ability of a quantum system to exist in multiple states simultaneously until measured.

Synchronicity – Meaningful coincidences that appear to be connected beyond cause and effect, often seen as signs from the universe or quantum alignment.

Tara – The original 5D+ blueprint of Earth—a higher-dimensional version of Gaia that existed before the fall into 3D density. It holds the pure crystalline codes of unity, love, and galactic connection.

Twin Flame – A deeply connected soul counterpart, often viewed as the other half of one's soul, embodying profound spiritual growth and transformation.

Universal Consciousness – The all-encompassing awareness that connects all living beings and matter in a single, unified field of intelligence.

Unified Field Theory – The theoretical framework that seeks to unify all fundamental forces and particles into a single, coherent model of reality.

Void – The infinite space of pure potentiality before creation, often seen as the backdrop for all existence.

Wave-Particle Duality – The concept that quantum entities can behave both as particles and as waves, depending on the method of observation.

Zero-Point Energy – The lowest possible energy that a quantum mechanical system may possess, theorized as the ever-present background energy of the vacuum. Zero Point Energy is the still, neutral core of creation—the silent source field where all possibilities exist before form, while the Quantum Field is the dynamic matrix of energy and potential that surrounds it, where consciousness shapes reality into being.

www.ingramcontent.com/pod-product-compliance
Lightning Source LLC
Chambersburg PA
CBHW061600120626
46550CB00004B/1553

* 9 7 9 8 9 9 2 7 3 2 0 0 9 *